THE OJIBWA WOMAN

RUTH LANDES

Introduction to the Bison Books Edition
by Sally Cole

UNIVERSITY OF NEBRASKA PRESS
LINCOLN AND LONDON

⊖ The paper in this book meets the minimum requirements of American National Standard for Information Sciences—Permanence of Paper for Printed Library Materials, ANSI Z39.48-1984.

First Bison Books printing: 1997
Most recent printing indicated by the last digit below:
10   9   8   7   6   5   4   3   2   1

Library of Congress Cataloging-in-Publication Data
Landes, Ruth, 1908–
The Ojibwa woman / by Ruth Landes.
p.   cm.
Originally published: New York: Columbia University Press, 1938.
Includes bibliographical references.
ISBN 0-8032-7969-8 (pa: alk. paper)
1. Ojibwa women.   2. Ojibwa Indians—Social life and customs.
I. Title.
E99.C6L324   1998
305.48'8973—dc21
97-24489   CIP

Originally published in 1938 by Columbia University Press, New York.

CONTENTS

INTRODUCTION

Sally Cole

Ruth Landes was a twenty-three-year-old doctoral student of anthropology studying under Franz Boas and Ruth Benedict at Columbia University when she arrived at Fort Frances, Ontario, on 6 July 1932 to begin fieldwork among the Boundary Waters Ojibwa at Manitou Rapids on the Minnesota-Ontario border. She had been directed to Manitou by Diamond Jenness, then director of the National Museums of Canada, Father John Cooper of the Catholic University in Washington, D.C., who had made a field research trip to the Rainy River in 1928, and A. Irving Hallowell of the University of Pennsylvania who, in the summer of 1932, was undertaking fieldwork among the Berens River Ojibwa of southern Manitoba. These scholars had all suggested that Mrs. Maggie Wilson, who lived at Manitou Rapids and had previously worked with Minnesota ethnomusicologist Francis Densmore in 1918, would facilitate Landes's ethnological research (Densmore 1929:4).[1]

The Indian agent in Fort Frances drove the young student to Manitou, introduced her to Mrs. Wilson, and made arrangements for Landes to board with the Indian Affairs Farm Instructor, William Hayes, and his wife, the one non-native family at Manitou. Landes spent July to September 1932 working intensively with Mrs. Wilson, paying her $1.00 a day, and hired Mrs. Wilson again briefly the following summer when she was conducting fieldwork in the nearby Chippewa communities of Red Lake and Ponemah in northern Minnesota. Landes returned for visits with Mrs. Wilson at Manitou in August 1935 and April 1936. In addition to the oral accounts that Ruth Landes recorded at Manitou, Mrs. Wilson mailed more than forty letters, transcribed by her daughter Janet, to Landes in New York. She was paid fifteen cents per double-sided page of a stenographer's pad. The letters are stories of women's lives and comprise the foundation of *The Ojibwa Woman*. The book is thus the product of collaboration between Ruth Landes and Maggie Wilson and biographical knowledge of both women's lives is a valuable aid to appreciating *Ojibwa Woman*.

Maggie Wilson's life spans important years of transition in Ojibwa society in the Rainy River District. She was born at the Little Forks Indian Reserve in 1879, six years after the Rainy River bands had signed Treaty 3 with the Canadian government, been settled on reserves, and brought under the administration of the Department of Indian Affairs in Ottawa. During her life Maggie witnessed the further erosion of Ojibwa political and economic autonomy as their lands were appropriated for Euro-Canadian settlement and as the seven bands were consolidated into one at Manitou Rapids.[2]

Maggie's paternal grandfather, Peter Spence, was a bilingual (English-speaking) Cree Anglican missionary teacher in the Rainy River District. Her maternal grandfather was a Scottish Hudson's Bay Company trader and her maternal grandmother was a woman whom Maggie Wilson describes as "a Cree halfbreed woman."[3] Her father, Ben, took a succession of seasonal wage jobs that included land surveying and working on the steamers plying the Rainy River between Fort Frances and Kenora. Her mother, Elizabeth, remained with her in-laws at Little Forks where she raised cows, pigs, and chickens, grew corn and potatoes, and established a local reputation as a midwife among both native and non-native women. Like Ojibwa families in the area, Maggie's parents and grandparents combined available wage work with an annual round of subsistence activities: gardening, fishing, and berrying at summer villages along the Rainy River; harvesting wild rice in the fall; hunting and trapping in the winter; and making maple sugar in the spring (cf. Ritzenhaler 1978; Vennum 1988). In 1895 or 1896 Maggie married Tom Wilson of the Hungry Hall band and moved west along the river to Hungry Hall. Tom Wilson died in 1911, leaving Maggie a widow with three small children. In 1914 she married John Wilson, the son of the chief of Manitou Rapids, and moved with her children to Manitou. Her daughter Janet was born in 1915 and her last child, also a daughter, was born in 1919 but died within her first year. In 1925, Mrs. Wilson adopted a three-month-old non-native boy who had been left one night in a basket at the door of her house. A seven-year-old boy when Ruth Landes was at Manitou, Gus Wilson (whom Maggie called Shaganash, meaning "white boy") was Mrs. Wilson's constant companion. Maggie died at Manitou Rapids in 1940.

Maggie Wilson was skilled in the Ojibwa women's crafts of porcupine quill embroidery, beadwork, and birchbark and deer- and moose-hide sewing and tanning. She was well-known for her knowledge of herbal medicine and midwifery and she was known as a powerful visionary with a keen intelligence and wide knowledge of Ojibwa custom and belief. For several years after moving to Manitou Rapids, Maggie had had a recurring dream in which supernatural thunderbirds taught her dance sequences, drum patterns, and more than eighty songs. They instructed her to teach these to the people of the community. For seven or eight years, in both fall and spring, Maggie had organized the dance that she called the Union Star Dance and which became a commercial attraction in the Fort Frances area. During these years, people also came to her for interpretations of their dreams. She discontinued the dance around 1928, in part because she had become lame in one leg but also because she said people had become jealous of her powers: "people became mean and jealous ... if anyone sickened or died, it was blamed on me" (in Landes 1968:212). By the time Ruth Landes met her, Mrs. Wilson lived a somewhat solitary life, surrounded by her family but disengaged from the social life of the community. Both she and her husband suffered from numerous health problems and Maggie supported them through sales of handicrafts to whites and through occasional work as an interpreter. Maggie's experiences as a visionary, and her bilingualism and biculturalism as a woman of Scots-Cree descent who had been raised and married in an Ojibwa cultural world, gave her "insider-outsider" status that made her a keen observer of Ojibwa life.[4] Her skills as a storyteller and her need for paid work were additional factors that encouraged Mrs. Wilson to work with the young anthropologist. In a letter to Ruth Benedict in October 1933, Ruth Landes wrote of Mrs. Wilson: "I consider her a gem and believe that we will have her with us till she gives up the ghost. I think that by now she is as good an ethnologist as any of us. I gave her some instruction this summer, which she snapped up. She gets the real point of what we want."[5]

Ruth Landes also brought particular experiences and motivations to the collaboration. The daughter of eastern European Jewish immigrants, Landes was born in 1908 in New York City and raised in a secular, labor Zionist household. Her father, Joseph Schlossberg, a tailor and self-taught man who had no more than a few years of formal schooling, was cofounder of the Amalgamated Garment Workers' Union and worked for the AGWU throughout his life. Her mother, Anna Grossman, had received a high school education before emigrating to America, where she met her future husband and became a homemaker. Ruth Schlossberg received her bachelor of science degree from New York University in 1928 and her master of social work from the New York School of Social Work the following year. Her master's thesis was a study of African American storefront churches in Harlem (Landes 1967). During her Harlem research, and through her parents' friend, anthropologist Alexander Goldenweiser, she had been introduced to Franz Boas and anthropology and she entered the graduate program at Columbia in 1931. In 1929, she had married a medical student, Victor Landes, whom she had known through her family's holidays at the Jewish summer colony at Tamiment. Two years later, however, Landes and her husband had separated, unable to reconcile her scholarly ambitions and his expectations that she would confine herself to the domestic roles of a middle-class wife (Landes 1970). Attracted by the ideals of the so-called New Woman, Ruth Landes had imagined a companionate marriage and a more egalitarian relationship. Questions about men's and women's roles and alternative models of marriage and gender relations, although not the subject of her dissertation research, were clearly important to Landes at the time as she sought to integrate personal and professional goals—a challenge that would elude her throughout her life and affect her work and place in the history of anthropology.[6]

Ruth Landes went to Manitou Rapids to collect data for an ethnological study of Ojibwa culture. Her doctoral dissertation, published in 1937 as *Ojibwa Sociology*, is a classical description of political organization, kinship, marriage, and property. Her training under Ruth Benedict had also directed Landes to pay attention to psychology and religion and to the knowledge of extraordinary individuals, especially shamans and visionaries, and these data Landes later published as *Ojibwa Religion and the Midéwiwin* (1968). It was Maggie Wilson, however, who directed Landes to the possibilities that gender offered as a theoretical domain for the illumination of Ojibwa culture. *Ojibwa Woman*, first published in 1938, is an important early contribution to the anthropology of gender, specifically for three central components of its analytical framework. First, the method of data collection and presentation relies on the recording of life stories. Second, the analysis gives centrality to the domains of marriage and work ("occupations") as the keys to understanding women's place in society. Third, gender is theorized as both a sociological and a cultural phenomenon.

Ruth Landes was interested in the individual. She collected stories of individual lives in order to illustrate how individuals negotiate with formal rules and cultural ideals from the standpoints of their particular circumstances and in order to reconstruct meaningful lives. Her analysis of marriage and kinship in *Ojibwa Woman* is a far remove from the formalist kinship charts of some of her contemporaries and her use of life stories is directed to illustrating how individuals construct lives in spite of cultural rules, not how they live within parameters set by those rules.[7] Landes understood culture to be located in the interstices between formalist rules and individual behavior. For Landes, individual actions—moments in life stories—represent negotiations and contestations of cultural rules that emerge from the particular circumstances of individual lives and that will necessarily produce contradiction and conflict. Patterns can be described but individual lives find meaning only in particularized contexts. In the foreword to *Ojibwa Woman*, Landes writes: "The Ojibwa material shows that the social norms institutionalized in even a simple nomadic culture do not provide for all of the population, nor for the entire range of tribal activities" (xix). Cultural analysis for Landes is the elaboration of moments of engagement between individual lives and the constraints of society, environment, and history—hence the importance of Maggie's life stories as analytical tools for Landes.

As a grandmother situated in a culture that prescribed storytelling for women, Mrs. Wilson told the anthropologist stories of women's lives in part to educate the younger woman and in part to provide testimony of Ojibwa women's experience in the late nineteenth and early twentieth centuries. The remarkable achievement of their collaboration is that Mrs. Wilson spoke to Ruth Landes across the cultural differences between them, as an older woman to a younger one who was having trouble in marriage and who was seeking to develop her own skills as an autonomous woman.

The majority of the more than 100 stories Mrs. Wilson told to Landes have a similar plot: they recount how women struggle and overcome hardship through resourcefulness and reliance on skills and knowledge learned from other women. They describe women whose autonomy and skills enable them to survive starvation, abandonment, abuse, and loss. The stories often highlight women's responses to predicaments such as a husband's laziness, adultery, desertion, or abuse. They remind women that they have choices and responsibility in the construction of their lives. For example, we learn in the stories that some widows choose to remarry and preserve the conventional gendered division of labor whereas others choose not to remarry and employ "masculine" skills in order to maintain their independence (83–84). We are told of women who leave polygynous marriages and others who choose to stay because they value the company of another woman (71). Maggie's stories are cautionary tales told by older women to enjoin younger ones to develop practical skills and personal autonomy to survive challenges that may arise in their marriages and in the wider conditions of their lives (cf. Cole 1995a; Cruikshank 1990). The paradoxical cumulative message of Maggie's stories is that, although autonomy is the key to women's survival, the accomplishment in their telling is the creation of a sense of community for women in a culture within which masculine roles are idealized and whose apotheosis is the male shaman. Ojibwa women, like Maggie Wilson, tell stories of their own and other women's lives in order to create a cultural space for women's experience. The stories may be understood as "narrative resources" (Passerini 1989:191) deployed by women rather than as historical or biographical accounts of specific women's lives or as a generalized portrait of marriage and gender relations in Ojibwa society. The stories and the events they recount may be understood as metaphors of experience. The historical "truth" of events in the stories is not the primary concern of the narrator.[8]

Ojibwa Woman is written in five parts: "Youth," "Marriage," "Occupations," "Abnormalities," and "Life Histories." More than half of the discussion in the book is devoted to descriptions of women's experiences of marriage and work. The ethnographic data illustrate the diversity of ways in which women (and, to a lesser extent, men) experience the institution of marriage and transgress static definitions of women's and men's occupational roles.

In the chapter entitled "Occupations," Landes uses excerpts from Maggie Wilson's stories to illustrate how Ojibwa women both fulfill and negotiate the culturally constructed division of labor according to which men hunt and procure raw materials and women process raw materials and manufacture clothing, shelter, and utilitarian objects. The stories of Sun Woman (138–39), Half Sky (154), and Kath (161–62), for example, are of women who not only excelled at "feminine" tasks but who were also well-known as hunters and trappers, athletes, or shamans and healers—skills the Ojibwa defined as "masculine." Stories like those of Thunder Cloud (163) and Gaybay (169) reveal that most women at some point in their lives will be required to take up "masculine" occupations. The stories urge all women to develop occupational versatility and flexibility regarding their gender identities. Gaybay, for example, as a girl had learned to hunt with her mother after her father died. Later, married and widowed several times herself, Gaybay "during the married intervals functioned like a conventional woman inasmuch as she never hunted, trapped or fished, but confined herself to the sedentary activities connected with the wigwam and to assisting her husband on the hunt when so requested. But during the periods of widowhood, which were far longer than those of marriage, she found no difficulty in adjusting to the occupational life of a man" (169). According to Landes:

> even the most conservative women usually find it necessary to take up some prescriptively masculine work at one time or another. The cultural view of the normal woman remains unchallenged and finds expression in the training that is usual for young girls. Those women whose behaviour is exceptional [women shamans, for example] are not judged with reference to the conventional standard but with reference to their individual fortunes only. The conduct of the ideal woman, therefore, and the behaviour of any individual woman may be quite at variance. (135)

In Landes's view, individualism was the strongest Ojibwa cultural ideal.

In the chapter entitled "Marriage," Maggie's stories illustrate how, although the lifelong cooperative economic partnership was the cultural ideal, in practice both men and women might have several marriage partners over the course of their lives. Both men and women were expected to desire romantic and sexual fulfillment in a marriage and to terminate marriages when these were not present. Although some gift-giving might take place in the case of first marriages, marriage was not an exchange of property and was formalized simply by a man "sleeping through the dawn" in a woman's home. According to Landes: "marriages are from the start private, independent affairs, and are usually contracted with equal good-will by both parties" and, "Marriage is theoretically the union of two people who like each other deeply, and in practise this is borne out. Divorce is supposed to be a natural consequence of indifference, or of offense, and this also is normally the case" (56, 119–20). Thus, according to Landes, Ojibwa men and women had similar rights, expectations, and responsibilities within marriage.

Finally, the analysis of gender in *Ojibwa Woman* is both sociological and cultural. Landes delineates what men and women do *and* the cultural constructions of gender in Ojibwa society. She describes how gender constructs do not directly reflect gender relations, men's and women's activities, or men's and women's contributions. Rather, contradiction, contestation, and conflict characterize local gender practice. After cataloging examples of women who excel in so-called male domains or who unproblematically take up masculine occupations when required at various points in the life cycle, Landes nonetheless concludes that there is a cultural bias in favor of men— that the cultural ideal is the male who excels at so-called masculine pursuits, most notably shamanism. This conclusion led second-wave feminist scholars to describe *Ojibwa Woman* as "flawed and male-centred" (Green 1980) or like Eleanor Leacock (1978) to interpret the book as "downgrading . . . women . . . [in] unexamined and ethnocentric phraseology."[9] While some of the phrasing that Landes uses may be problematic for late-twentieth-century readers, dated language should be disentangled from her theoretical analysis, which remains important for scholars of gender. Leacock's critique stems in greater part from fundamental differences in their theoretical approaches, in particular the interpretation of the meaning of the higher status symbolically awarded masculine roles in Ojibwa society and the role of history in gender analysis.

Ruth Landes was clearly aware that Ojibwa society in the 1930s had undergone and was undergoing radical change. She makes abundant reference to wage labor, forced relocation, increasing intrusiveness of Indian agents in domestic life, and so on. But she (like her Boasian contemporaries) does not attempt to analyze how these social and economic changes impact gender relations. Feminist scholars in anthropology in the 1970s and 1980s, however, were primarily interested in questions surrounding women's status and the origin of gender asymmetry (Moore 1988). Leacock, for whom gender relations are rooted in the relations of production, maintained that the emergence of inegalitarianism in Ojibwa gender relations is a product of recent history, of colonization and of engagement in the fur trade (Etienne and Leacock 1980; Leacock 1978). For Leacock, the transformation from an egalitarian foraging society to an inegalitarian society based on commodity relations is at the root of the emergence of the male dominance described in *Ojibwa Woman*. Landes, however, was concerned less with the origin of gender hierarchy than with illuminating the diversity of ways men and women negotiate their relations—what she calls "the moot problem of men and women" (1938a:v). Gender relations, in Landes's view, necessarily require individual strategies for both accommodating differences and contesting hegemonies whether societies are pre- or post-contact, whether in equilibrium or in flux. This is because the relations between men and women especially within marriage are the relations that also often define rights of access (to resources, position, privilege) and status in the wider society. It is within relations of intimacy that men and women negotiate these broader relations and initiate strategies to better position themselves socially and economically. It is also in the context of strategizing and negotiating that gender becomes symbolically loaded. For Landes, contestation and contradiction are necessary components of gender practice in human societies and Maggie Wilson's stories highlight the skills and values that one society teaches women they need in order to negotiate gender and survive as individuals. Maggie's stories teach Ojibwa women to uphold the ideals of romance, sexual fulfillment, respect, personal autonomy, responsibility, resourcefulness, flexibility, struggle, and survival.

In *The Ojibwa Woman*, Mrs. Wilson's teachings are made available to all women across histories and cultures.

NOTES

1. Funding from the Social Sciences and Humanities Research Council of Canada enabled research in the Ruth Fulton Benedict Papers (RFB Papers) at Vassar College and the Ruth Schlossberg Landes Papers (RSL Papers) in the National Anthropological Archives at the Smithsonian Institution as well as interviews with descendants of Maggie Wilson in Manitou Rapids and Thunder Bay, Ontario. Maggie Wilson's letters to Landes are catalogued in the RSL Papers. Research was undertaken as part of a larger study of the life and work of Ruth Landes.

2. See Waisberg and Holzkamm (1993) for further discussion of the relocation of the Rainy River bands and the impact of Canadian government policies on the Ojibwa economy.

3. Autobiographical data on Mrs Wilson's life are found in Story 119, Box 38, RSL Papers, in a letter to Landes that begins "Dear Ruth, This is the story of my mother, Mrs Bunyan." See also Cole 1995a.

4. Biculturality distinguished other well-known native ethnologists such as George Hunt, who worked with Franz Boas, and William Berens, who worked with A. Irving Hallowell (Brown 1989; Cannizo 1983).

5. RFB Papers, 12 Oct. 1933.

6. See Cole (1995b) for discussion of Landes's later career. On the "New Woman," see Freedman (1983).

7. Landes's use of life history data thus contrasts with that of her contemporaries. Where Landes shows individuals who contest, negotiate, and struggle against cultural norms and ideals, the conventional approach at the time was to record life stories of individuals who exemplified cultural rules (see, for example, Reichard, *Dezba, Woman of the Desert*, 1939; and Underhill, *Autobiography of a Papago Woman*, 1936). Landes's approach is closer to Marjorie Shostak's in *Nisa: The Life and Words of a !Kung Woman*, published almost half a century later.

8. Ruth Landes did not consistently use pseudonyms in *Ojibwa Woman* because her intent was not to report on the lives and actions of specific individuals. Rather, like Maggie Wilson, Landes intended the stories to serve as metaphors of experience, to illustrate values that individuals try to uphold as they meet challenges in life. Maggie Wilson and Ruth Landes understood women's storytelling as women's community-building (cf. Cruikshank 1990). In this edition, however, an attempt has been made to replace names with pseudonyms to protect the identities of individuals in cases where their actions are described as having harmed others.

9. By contrast, Herbert Alexander in his 1975 review of the second edition of *The Ojibwa Woman* in *American Anthropologist* charged that the book represented "an idiosyncratic female viewpoint."

REFERENCES CITED

Alexander, Herbert
   1975   Review of *The Ojibwa Woman*. *American Anthropologist* 77: 110–11.
Brown, Jennifer S. H.
   1989   "A Place in Your Mind for Them All": Chief William Berens. In *Being and Becoming Indian: Biographical Studies of North American Frontiers,* James A Clifton, ed. pp. 204–25. Chicago: Dorsey Press.
Cannizzo, Jeanne
   1983   George Hunt and the Invention of Kwakiutl Culture. *Canadian Review of Sociology and Anthropology* 20(1): 44–58.
Cole, Sally
   1995a   Women's Stories and Boasian Texts: The Ojibwa Ethnography of Ruth Landes and Maggie Wilson. *Anthropologica* 37: 3–25.
   1995b   Ruth Landes and the Early Ethnography of Race and Gender. In *Women Writing Culture,* Ruth Behar and Deborah Gordon, eds. pp. 166–85. Berkeley: University of California Press
Cruikshank, Julie, in collaboration with Angela Sidney, Kitty Smith, and Annie Ned
   1990   *Life Lived Like a Story: Life Stories of Three Yukon Native Elders.* Lincoln: University of Nebraska Press; Vancouver: University of British Columbia Press.

Densmore, Frances
　1929　*Chippewa Customs*. Washington: Bureau of American
　　　　Ethnology Bulletin 86.
Etienne, M., and E. Leacock, eds.
　1980　*Women and Colonization: Anthropological Perspectives*. New
　　　　York: Praeger.
Freedman, Estelle B.
　1983　The New Woman: Changing Views of Women in the 1920s. In
　　　　Decades of Discontent: The Women's Movement 1920–1940, Lois
　　　　Scharf and Joan M. Jensen, eds. pp. 21–42. Westport, Conn.:
　　　　Greenwood Press.
Green, Rayna
　1980　Review Essay: Native American Women. *Signs* 6: 248–67.
Landes, Ruth
　1937a　*Ojibwa Sociology*. New York: Columbia University Press.
　1937b　The Ojibwa in Canada. In *Cooperation and Competition among
　　　　Primitive Peoples*, Margaret Mead, ed. pp. 87–127. New York:
　　　　McGraw Hill.
　1937c　The Personality of the Ojibwa. *Culture and Personality* 6: 51–60.
　1938a　*The Ojibwa Woman*. New York: Columbia University Press.
　1938b　The Abnormal Among the Ojibwa. *Journal of Abnormal and
　　　　Social Psychology* 33: 14–33.
　1967　Negro Jews in Harlem. *Jewish Journal of Sociology* 9(2): 175–89.
　1968　*Ojibwa Religion and the Midéwiwin*. Madison: University of
　　　　Wisconsin Press.
　1970　A Woman Anthropologist in Brazil. In *Women in the Field*, Peggy
　　　　Golde, ed. p. 119–42. Chicago: Aldine.
Leacock, Eleanor
　1978　Women's Status in Egalitarian Society: Some Implications for
　　　　Social Evolution. *Current Anthropology* 19(2): 247–76.
Moore, Henrietta
　1988　*Feminism and Anthropology*. Minneapolis: University of
　　　　Minnesota Press.
Passerini, Luisa
　1989　Women's Personal Narratives: Myths, Experiences, and
　　　　Emotions. In *Interpreting Women's Lives: Feminist Theory and
　　　　Personal Narratives*, Joy Webster Barbre, et al., eds. pp. 189–
　　　　97. The Personal Narratives Group. Bloomington: Indiana
　　　　University Press.
Reichard, Gladys
　1939　*Dezba, Woman of the Desert*. New York: J. J. Augustin.
Ritzenhaler, Robert E.
　1978　Southwestern Chippewa. In *Handbook of North American
　　　　Indians*, Williak C. Sturtevant, ed. vol. 15, *Northeast*, Bruce
　　　　Trigger, ed. pp. 743–59. Washington, D.C.: Smithsonian
　　　　Institution.

Shostak, Marjorie
    1981 *Nisa: The Life and Words of a !Kung Woman*. New York: Vintage
          Books.
Underhill, Ruth
    1936 *Autobiography of a Papago Woman*. Memoirs of the American
          Anthropological Association, no. 46.
Vennum, Thomas
    1988 *Wild Rice and the Ojibway People*. St. Paul: Minnesota Historical
          Society Press.
Waisberg, Leo G., and Tim E. Holzkamm
    1993 "A Tendency to Discourage Them from Cultivating": Ojibwa
          Agriculture and Indian Affairs Administration in Northwestern
          Ontario. *Ethnohistory* 40(2): 175–211.

FOREWORD.

THE OJIBWA WOMAN is an ethnological field study of social behavior in a society characterized by very different cultural forms from those which obtain in our own society. Practically all studies of behavior in psychological literature are carried out within our own culture and show behavior conditioned by cultural forms of Western civilization. The present study was designed to investigate, against the whole background of an alien culture, the moot problem of men and women. It shows how basically the social institutions characteristic of this different group are involved in the resultant type of behavior observed among Ojibwa men and women.

The study is the result of seven months' work in the field, financed by Columbia University, with close observation of village and tribal life, and a large collection of life histories of women as told by a native woman. It is felt that only detailed studies of individual cultures, to put beside the detailed studies in our own culture, will give the data for a valid comparative human psychology.

The Ojibwa material shows that the social norms institutionalized in even a simple nomadic culture do not provide for all of the population, nor for the entire range of the tribal activities. Among the Ojibwa only the male half of the population and its activities fall under the traditonal regulations, while the female half is left to spontaneous and confused behavior. As the training of women is left largely to the hands of fortune, there is a wide range of developments in their personalities and careers. Some rival the most successful men in ambitions and in honors received, but do not pursue these in systematic male fashion; others excel in both male and female pursuits; still others are reduced to an incompetence that continues until death.

The material leads us to the following conclusions concerning the organization of Ojibwa life:

1. In a region where game is often scarce, trapping is the chief economic activity of the Ojibwa, and the small, autonomous and often hostile households are obliged to scatter over great distances for six to nine months of the year. This way of life affects the form of marriage and brothers and sisters arrange the marriages of their children, who are called cross-cousins. Even where the cross-

cousin marriage is now proscribed under Christian influence, the full terminology and associated behavior still obtain except that marriage is not allowed. Thus, both terminologically and in behavior the cross-cousin is potential spouse; mother's brother is potential father in-law; and sister's daughter (man speaking) is daughter-in-law, etc. Mother's brother and father's sister are respected just as are the parents-in-law, the cross-cousins flirt just as do sweethearts, etc.

2. From the first days of life, males are trained to shoulder economic responsibilities. They are unremittingly taught initiative, individuality and fortitude in the hunt, and also in war parties, sex adventures, and supernatural pursuits. Few men deviate from these standards, so rigid is the discipline and so drastic the penalty of starvation. No such prescriptions, however, affect females. They are taught chiefly to be the recipients of male favors, economic and sexual, and are supposed to be ignored by men. But this very lack of positive formulations actually offers some the opportunities of the male world. For a man may take his daughter as a hunting companion, if she is the only or favorite or most gifted child; a man may so train his wife; a widow may be pressed by economic or temperamental needs to take up male work. Consequently there are great variations in behavior among the women, and also variable behavior in different periods of one woman's life.

3. The men's sex life is dominated by ideals of personal freedom and of romance. This results in frequent violations of all the conventions of courtship, marriage, and family responsibility. Divorce is easy and often whimsical. Many women act as men do in this field as in others, and the result is a brittleness of marriage that is not counteracted by social and economic obligations found among other tribes. Tradition sanctions polygyny, but these women veto tradition by deserting a polygynous husband.

PART I.

YOUTH.

The Ojibwa of western Ontario live in well watered woodlands. Through the fall, winter, and early spring, while the snow is frozen deep upon the ground, men hunt big game and trap animals for fur. The scarcity of game compels the men to hunt individually over wide distances. Vicissitudes of the hunt, like dearth of animals and snow, are always dread likelihoods, harboring the threat of starvation; and this threat causes the hunters, each with a small family, to scatter still more widely. Scattering in the hope that the greater area por hunter will net greater results in game, each family withdraws into complete isolation. While he thus minimizes competition, the hunter runs the risk that a few weeks without game will wipe out his family by death from starvation. At all times, but especially during the winter, life is an unending struggle to satisfy the elementary wants. The need for food drives hunters insistently. Technological and religious thought are focussed upon the hunt, intent upon improving weapons, luring game, controlling the weather, placating the supernaturals, maintaining the health of the hunter.

Late in March and in April when the snow is thawing, the individual families go to their respective privately owned maple groves, where the same economic and household structure obtains as during the winter hunt. This is a remarkable perseverance of the winter habits, for nothing in the nature of the sugar industry requires them. Individual families neighbor one another at fairly close quarters, and commonly two families live in one tent for the season. But each family, even when two families occupy one tent, works for itself as though isolated. Late in May, when the snow is all off the ground, a number of families come still closer together, forming a neighborhood, or village about some body of water suitable for drinking, fishing, bathing, and near berry patches. Still the individualistic economic and household structure of the winter persists. The neighborliness and numbers of the village permit some social activities such as religious and secular dances and war parties, that are not possible at other seasons. The village breaks up in August, each family going individually to the rice beds and maintaining here, too, its independent economic and household structure. In September and October individual families leave for the duck-hunting; by November the winter hunting has begun and will continue through the following March.

The child is reared in the small economic household which consists usually and ideally of his parents and siblings. Often his grandparents live in the household. Frequently the ideal composition is disturbed by the death or desertion of one or both parents, or by other causes. Then the child lives with other guardians than his parents, perhaps with his own father and a step-mother, or with adoptive parents, or with the grandparents. In any case, the child's world is the small household, which for half the year is shut off from other households.

Economic pressure outlaws inefficient and non-contributing members of the household, and makes it imperative that the child become mature as quickly as possible. From the first, all the adult values are presented to the child. The very bugaboos that harass children are the ones that harass adults.

After a few months of infancy the baby is addressed and reasoned with as though he were an adult. This does not mean that fondling and solicitude are withdrawn, although discussion is often rife as to the desirable limits of fondling. A father says, "You must not kiss your children when they cry, or you will never be able to leave them for the hunt. How then could you live, and how would they learn to do without you?" The nature of the case is explained to the children, even to the infant, and it is further explained that each person must busy himself with his duties if the household is to prosper. The baby is then laid aside and told not to stir, a somewhat older sister is told to keep an eye on it, another is sent for water, a third for wood, a fourth to examine the rabbit traps.

At some short time after a child's birth, a naming feast is given it by its parents. A few people are invited who are known to possess the supernatural power of naming. At the feast, each of these individuals calls upon his supernatural patron, requesting that the child be endowed with vigor, with a variety of gifts proper to its sex, such as hunting or fertility powers, and that all the difficulties of its life be eased by the kindliness of the supernaturals. The parents rejoice that now fewer of the powers of the universe are hostile to the infant, and the baby is given symbolic tokens by the intercessors. One gives a tiny cane, signifying that the infant protégé will live to old age; another gives a tiny gun signifying that the baby will become a mighty hunter; another gives a queer-shaped stone having mystic force. At the same time, each intercessor gives the child a name, a cryptic phrase which is charged with meaning to the giver because it recalls some circumstance of the vision vouchsafed him by a supernatural patron; and to the recipient in later years it will be a constant assurance of some supernatural's concern for him.

This feast starts a child's education. The name-tokens are hung over the baby's cradle, to dangle before his face so that he may play with them. As he plays, or as the tokens are drawn to his attention, someone tells him about them, how they came, what responsibilities they place upon the child as well as what assurance and what hopes they hold for the parents. As the infant grows older and learns to move about, they are hung over his sleeping-place and occasionally referred to. But as the child grows older the emphasis is shifted, especially for a boy. He is urged not to rest content with the bare receiving of a protective name, but to seek blessings, visions granting "power", directly from the supernaturals. The child of four or five years is besieged by his parents, particularly by his mother and grandmother: "Go without food for this meal, that you may learn what to do with your life." The child often objects to the fast, stamps and cries, or runs around to snatch some food for himself. But he does not successfully evade the ritual, and one of his parents will catch him to smear charcoal about his eyes in token of his approach to the supernatural. Then the child goes to play with his brothers and sisters, forgetting about his fast and not understanding its purpose. If it is summer, the child plays also with the children of other families of the village, some of whom are also charcoal-smeared and fasting, supposedly for a revelation of "power". It is uncommon for children to eat outside of their own lodges, but should some children be offered food, the hostess always excepts the charcoaled one. By evening the faster returns home from his play and is rewarded with an especially good meal.

From this time until puberty there is never a break in the parents' insistence upon "dreaming for power". The insistence is decidedly more pronounced for boys than for girls. Always, "it is more important for a man to have dreams than for a woman". The parents anxiously watch the child's demeanor for some outward sign of the "dream experience", for it is tabued to inquire of another if and what he has dreamed. If a child wakes in the morning without appetite, his parents are full of hope. It means that, although perhaps without the child's own knowledge, he has been visited by a supernatural, a *manido*. The parents arrange a schedule of fasting, graduated to the child's age and strength and to their own fanaticism.

A child of eight years may fast for two meals a day every other
day for long weeks through the winter. His father greets him on
those mornings with the words: "Which will you eat? Bread or
charcoal?" If he answers "bread" he is cuffed severely and the
question is repeated. The answer then is always "charcoal". The
punishment of children is to a considerable extent corrective, and
therefore employs "fasting for a vision" as a technique. A naughty
child, usually one who has been disobedient to mother or father,
is sent to bed hungry with the admonition, "Go, and think of what
to do with your life".

By the early adolescent years, children are expected to handle
this important matter themselves, just as they are expected to
be self-reliant in other concerns of life. However, a ceremonial
fast is arranged for them at puberty, again typically with more
attention to the boys than to the girls. Every few years the parents
of the village decide that their pubescent boys should be sent out
on an isolated and prolonged fast for visions. Each family talks
to its boys, urges upon them the significance of this trial, teaches
them how to work up a vision, and how to recognize and reject
an "evil" vision. The boy is reminded that the vision will picture
the future, promising to him success in the hunt, in war, in curing,
and in other fields; and it will advise him as to precise ways of
winning success; but he must concentrate upon the vision so it
will become as real as life to him for then he will understand it
better, it will visit him often, and he will acquire greater "powers"
from it. So the boys are sent out to a neighboring island or to an
isolated spot in the woods, without food or drink and each with
a worn blanket to lie on. Some boys lie on the rough ground,
others on rocks, some build themselves a "nest" in a tree. The fast
lasts four to ten days. Every morning the parents, especially the
mother, visit the boy to encourage him in this difficult and vital
task and to see that all is proper, that he has not injured himself,
that he has not strayed, that he is not ill, that he has not played
or talked with the others scattered about. The boys return as early
as they choose if they have "dreamed". Some boys who have not
dreamed cannot endure the hunger after several days and cry to
return; some swoon. The parents bring them back, but the boys
are sent out during the next village fast if they are still "empty"
or "powerless". Occasionally boys remain out eight or ten days,
when they "die" and are taken to the sky-land of the supernaturals.
They have generally secured important visions, but when they
return from the "death" they are very ill from starvation and the
parents must take prolonged care of them. Such children often

have an aptitude for visions, seeing them readily either spontaneously or by fast. The household is informed tacitly about the success of the vision-seeker when he is noticed going through some arbitrary behavior as tabuing certain foods, preparing a sweat tent, offering sacrifices, collecting, or making strange objects as mementos. Then his parents remind him throughout the following months to concentrate upon his dream, to identify himself with it so thoroughly that he "can pretty nearly talk to his *manido*".

The girl goes through her ceremonial fast at the time of her first menstruation. But no party of adults is convened to discuss it, even when it occurs during the months of village life, and the girl is put through no training preparatory to it. Her vision pursuit is neglected in the face of a greater portent, the blood discharge. The discharge is a token of the maleficent "power" that invades every woman during her years of fertility, a "power" which comes to a high point at the time of catamenia, and to its highest point when "the woman is new". The girl of first menses is a menace to herself as well as to others. Her proximity blights all young and living things. She is hurried by her mother or grandmother out of the family lodge into a tiny isolated one built for her in the forest. She is dressed poorly, soot is smeared about her eyes, her gaze is downwards and she must not look at any living thing. She is supplied with a body scratcher that she may not poison herself by the touch of her own fingers. She may not eat fresh food, only a little of old food such as old bannock bread, dry fish and dry meat; otherwise the young growing animals, fish, and vegetation will be blighted. Indeed, "she lives poorly", and is supposed to sit quietly and meditate during the period of the flow. None should approach her but women who are past the menopause, and girls in a condition similar to hers. Often she is supplied with materials for moccasins, beadwork and routine mending. If she walks about she must strew leaves as a warning to men, pregnant women, and babies. Unquestionably her puberty ceremony has a different import from that of the boy's. His is a hopeful striving for broader horizons, hers is a conscientious withdrawal of her malignant self. While obsessed and saddened with this terror of herself, she is supposed to seek a vision. That many girls do not secure any at this time is not surprising for they are offered many and not unpleasant distractions. To begin with, this new view of themselves is startling. They see their brothers and fathers in a new light; also, derivatively, the weapons, clothing, and other objects belonging to males. They experiment with the ideas of strewing leaves in warning, and of shrinking away from the path of a man. Instead of brooding upon

the supernatural, at least to the extent determined by a hungry
stomach, "new" women visit one another in their isolated lodges.
They discuss their newly acquired sexual eligibility, and their
general coming into adult importance. Older women visit them
and discuss their new state with them and teach them sewing skills
so that they will be desired in marriage. Besides, if the isolation
occurs in spring or summer when the country can be traveled
easily and people live all about, parties of young men will crash
through the barrier of tabu: Roaming in the forest, the young men
spy a menstrual lodge and make for it in defiance of all dogma.
The girl cries out, covers her eyes to defend the men against her
lethal gaze, and thrusts out her arm against the anticipated rape.

After the discharge has ceased, the girl washes, is dressed in new
clothes, and goes through seasonal ceremonies during the coming
year in which she sacrifices to the food life of the season and to the
spirit of evil womanhood. She thus secures sufficient absolution
from her maleficence to be allowed to eat fresh foods without injury
to their mystic principle and without injury to the men and young
people who come in contact with these foods and with her. These are
simple ceremonies conducted, like the menstrual ceremony, by the
older women of the household, usually the mother and grandmother
and during the summer neighboring old women of the village are invited. With these ceremonies the girl secures her adult title of being
eligible for marriage. The boy's ceremony does not make him eligible
for marriage, however. He must first prove himself economically.

The fast is not considered to be the sole condition of a power-
giving vision. It is considered to be merely a very effective technique
in wresting this gift from the supernaturals, for by wearing the
faster out, it provokes the "pity" of the supernaturals. In Ojibwa
idiom, to "pity" another is to adopt him and care for him as a
parent or grandparent cares for a child. Consequently the pitying
supernatural is bound to the protegé by the firmest loyalties that
exist in Ojibwa. When the mortal parents die, a visionary can
always rely upon his spiritual guardians. As a result of incessant
suggestions to children that they seek visions, spontaneous visions
are fairly common—spontaneous inasmuch as they are not deliberately pursued by a person fasting but are unpremeditated
personal realizations. In retrospect, such occurrences are always
attributed to some stress situation which compelled the pity of the
supernatural in the same way that a fast does. In a child's life these
stress situations are orphanhood, neglect by parents, jealousy of a
step-mother, resentment of a step-father, starvation. Girls and
women are more conspicuous for getting visions in this informal

way than are boys and men. This is intelligible from the fact that girls are less persistently urged to fast for a "dream", and therefore are susceptible to spontaneous visitations; whereas boys are all conditioned to the more deliberate technique. The child's stress vision often takes a simple wish-fulfillment form. For example, nine-year old Sky Woman, whose father frightened and often beat her, ran away to escape him, and one day wandered so far into the bush that she was lost. She fell asleep and when she woke did not realize that she had been gone four days. "All that time she dreamed that she was in a place where there were a lot of people, and she was very happy and had nice things to eat... Here she was blessed so she could *nanandawi i we* (an important curing technique)..."

Another girl, Part-Sky-Woman, deeply mourned her father's death and was unreconciled to life without him. Through a vision which came to her she not only escaped from her unbearable grief, but was given courage to make a wholesome adjustment to her new life. "One time when she was crying she heard someone speaking to her, saying, 'Do not cry any more as your days are to be long upon this island [idiom for "world"], and I will give you something here with which you will have fun. See this...' and she looked to see the shadow of a large cloud pass before her. 'This I will give you. Your body will be just like this cloud, and sickness will not kill you.' She did not see anyone near her but the voice she heard sounded from above her. So she stopped crying and wondered what it was all about. It was the shadow of this cloud which had pity on her. And that was her dream. So then she made up her mind that she would not cry so much... She commenced fishing again doing just as she used to see her father do..."

Another vision is direct in its wish-fulfillment. Earth-Woman, badly treated by a step-mother, one day dreamed that her deceased mother appeared to her, promised to care for her, and announced that she would soon take the father away from his wicked second wife. Earth-Woman told this to her father; he later had the same revelation and shortly after, he was "pushed into the fire" by his ghostly first wife and burned to death. Just before her father's death, Earth-Woman had had another vision. One day her step-mother had driven her away from the camp. "She went back into the bush crying. She climbed up a tree and started to cry. After she had sat there for a long time she heard someone yell and she looked around. She knew it was not a human person [from the quality of the screech, which is stereotyped]. She thought, 'Let it kill me, whatever it is', and when she looked up she saw a *ba. gȧk*, mystic skeleton [sometimes seership powers come

from this, the soul of neglected children who have died of starvation]
and it was yelling hard. She listened and she understood it to say,
'Grandchild, don't cry'. [In the original, the Indian term appears in
an especially endearing and familiar form, an abbreviation of the full
form of the kinship term.] Soon we will laugh. Indeed you will
laugh hard [in revenge upon the step-mother]'. She did not understand what the skeleton meant by saying that. So she came down
from the tree and walked home."

The spontaneous vision often gives evidence of certain natural
bents that cannot be so readily inferred from the vision encouraged
by fast. In repeated cases, the spontaneous vision was experienced
by women and girls who showed decided talents in other fields.
Sky-Woman, the first girl visionary cited above, was noted for
her life-long mastery of nearly all the techniques allowed by the
culture. She took up all the skills regardless of whether or not
they were prescriptively male or female. She "dreamed" several
times in her life. She liked to live alone, and did not marry until
late in life; after her widowhood she continued to live alone and
"think". She was undoubtedly an intelligent, resourceful person,
sensitive to all the influences about her, eager to speculate about
them. In a world whose every idiom of thought and expression is
cast in "vision" terms, she had to be a visionary. One wonders
how far she would have gone had she been a man, with the high-
pressure encouragement that is given men in youth and the rewards
accorded them in maturity. As it was, she was considered "queer"
for living "like a man". The second girl visionary was also distinguished for her abilities, though due to her father's influence
she specialized more in male activities than in those conventionally
female. In later years she became the Nurmi of the entire region,
defeating men and women, Indian and White, in a variety of foot-
races, obstacle races, and endurance races. She was supreme for
more than twelve years until she had to withdraw because of the
jealousies of Indian competitors. Unlike the first girl, she was a
person of gay and explosive temperament, who formed strong and
sociable attachments. The third girl visionary was a docile person,
with a strong need of affection, and strongly drawn to warm,
protective relationships. She loved to be kind to people and to
have them kind to her. Her hate of her step-mother was rather
terror at seeing her father's affection withdrawn from her; so she
struck back rather pitifully in the two vision experiences reported.
She loved music, and in later experiences had sound visions. She
ultimately became a Christian because she enjoyed being in a
"brotherhood", and she enjoyed singing.

In each of the three cases mentioned, excessive loneliness was an important factor which encouraged spontaneous dreaming. Ojibwa households are always isolated, and for most of the year one lodge is separated by miles of forest from the rest of the world. A lone neglected child is consequently in a desperate way. The social set-up would seem to urge a spontaneous dream, natural inclinations determining the content. The first girl, an only child, was left alone when her parents fled the house in their quarrels. The second visionary was the favorite daughter of a man who made her his closest companion, and whose death left her in chaotic bewilderment and loneliness from which she escaped by dreaming. The third girl was an only child, given exclusive and loving care until the father's remarriage. After this she was brusquely shut out, not only by the father and step-mother, but from the care and companionship of a little sister born of the second marriage. Her parents and the baby would leave her for long hours. Then she began to "dream".

Intelligence, strong feelings, and docility are all qualities hospitable to the Ojibwa spontaneous vision experience. Specific artistic interests promote or are understood to be spontaneous vision experiences, although the instances I know are the experiences only of adults. Women "dream" beadwork patterns, songs, decorations for a dress, complicated dance patterns; men dream traditional tales, or tales about culture heroes, or have visions of the architecture of the after-world.

It is evident that a "dream" is any vivid imaginative activity: it may occur at any age in either sex; at any time of the day, night, or season; with the visionary dozing, sleeping, or wide-awake; on a full stomach or fasting; sought for or unsolicited. The dream is remembered for the duration of life; in many cases it recurs inasmuch as the incidents develop or the characters reappear in different settings. The characters or guardian spirits of the dream are often called up at will when the visionary needs to discuss urgent matters with them and this sober and deliberate speculative thought is also called a vision. Stereotypes of character, phrase, and incident appear in every dream. These are identical with the stereotypes of the traditional tales, myths, and religious ritual. The stereotypes are common material; their particular combination in an individual's dream is esoteric and must not be casually and directly divulged on pain of forfeiting the "power" of the dream. Parents warn children not to discuss their dreams, and halt them if they should thoughtlessly do so. However people generally have a fair understanding of their acquaintances' powers because the exercise of

2

any power, as in curing, requires that the experience be mumbled
over in preliminary invocation and certification. Also it is required
that warriors in training openly discuss their visions with their
chief and fellow-warriors (who may include an occasional woman).
Again, people privately discuss their dreams with their spouses.
In this way dream material spreads through the community,
providing gossip, speculation, and the visions of coming generations.
This dream material strikes a child forcibly when he lives in a
household whose members have "powers" of curing, the hunt,
war, etc. For he spends three-quarters of the year in an isolated
world peopled only by his lodge-mates; these are his mentors
and companions who talk in his presence as though he were an
adult, and set him adult standards. So when the older generation
is accomplished, and has visionary powers, there is constant sugges-
tion on all levels for a child to experiment in acquiring the same
powers. I have reported elsewhere genealogies which testify to
this (See *Ojibwa Sociology:* Property).

Just as boys are carefully coached to secure power by a special
technique of fasting, so they are carefully coached in special economic
and honorific pursuits. Just as girls pick up power by the way, adopting suggestions which fall about their ears but which they are not
pressed to adopt, so they may pick up the economic and honorific pursuits of the men. Traditionally, however, there is a cleavage between
the pursuits of men and those of women. Men occupy themselves
outside of the home: they hunt, trap, fish, hold religious performances,
and engage in war. Women are supposed to stay at home and
convert the fruits of hunting and fishing into edibles and clothing,
they make the lodge furnishings, do bead-work and porcupine-
quill work, make twine, fish-nets and bark matting, pick berries,
cure sugar and rice with the help of the men, collect medicinal
herbs, cook, mend, and bear children. Whenever men fulfill their
duties creditably, they are lauded. In company they tell endless
stories about their adventures, for their duties are always "adventures"; they hold stag feasts of religious importance after a successful hunt. Even the mythology occupies itself with the pursuits
and rewards of men. The important visions, which men have been
driven all their youth to pursue, bestow power for the masculine
occupations. A successful hunter can parade this fact in ways
licensed by his visions: songs that he sings publicly, amulets that
are conspicuous and worn in public, charms that he can sell. He
has also sumptuary privileges, such as polygyny. Women's work
on the contrary "is spoken of neither for good nor for evil"-at
least in a gathering of men. Conventionally it is not judged in

any way, it is simply not given any thought. Privately, a man
may be proud of his wife's handiwork in tanning or bead-weaving;
in an unguarded moment he may even explain that these excellences
had led him to walk many miles to claim the woman as his wife.
The women themselves live in a world of values all their own, a world
closed to the men. Mother and daughters discuss the merits of
their work just as men do the merits of theirs, and when the village
quarter of the year comes about, the various families visit, and
wider groups of women discuss their own interests. But these
discussions and boasts are not formal, as the men's are; they belong
to the level of gossip.

From the earliest years children are trained in terms of these
sexually differentiated backgrounds. The birth name-feast has
started the education. If the child is a boy, many of the name-
tokens will be symbolic of the manly professions. The growing boy
is told by his lodge-mates about his toy bow and arrow or gun,
what the instrument does, how it is made, the honor it brings, the
supernatural sanctions behind his personal use of it. His "namesake",
the name-giver who gave him the name-token or directed its making,
visits him ceremonially and talks to him further along the same
lines. The child is brought for a return visit during the summer
when people are near together. The little boy is among the company
of men that meet sociably over a ritual bear feast and discuss
their hunting exploits. His father may call his little "trapper"
to him so that he will be in the center of the talk. At the same
time his sister is outside the room with the other women, looking
on and listening from a distance. In the winter privacy of the
lodge, the father tells long stories of men's deeds in the hunt, war,
and supernatural medicine. The women and girls listen to applaud,
the boy listens to learn. As the child grows older his father makes
him a sturdy but small bow of ash, and arrows too, and deer-bone
arrow-heads. These can kill birds such as partridges, and can
badly injure small animals at close range. The boy practises with
it, and the day he lands his first bird he is acclaimed extravagantly
by his parents. He is honored even if he strikes a bird by accident.
One day in spring three-year old Leonard threw a stick at a little
bird; then his father ran out, calling "Oh, my boy has killed a bird!"
Leonard was surprised. His parents prepared the bird ritually,
bought fruits, biscuits, whiskey, sausage for a feast, and traveled
to a neighboring village of relatives to call them together for a
ritual feast. Men were invited who had supernatural powers and
hunting deeds to their credit. They told of their hunting deeds,
even to such length that the little boy fell asleep, then bestowed

2*

their wishes for like success upon him. The same celebration was made by the parents each time he killed a larger and more significant animal or fish: sturgeon, goose, beaver, moose, bear. Each time the father said over the boy, "We wish to show our gratitude to the *manido.* We are proud that our boy killed the bird (or animal). May our boy have a long life and be blessed with hunting powers!" Mother, sisters, and other female relatives sit at this feast, listening to the stories and prayers, sharing the same sentiments of pride. But nothing of the sort is ever done for them. The girl's first tanning job or piece of beadwork goes unheralded. It is so little heeded conventionally that she continues to make moccasins even in the polluted atmosphere of the menstrual lodge. "They never think about a girl except when they want to sleep with her", a woman said casually.

The boy's further hunting career is as assiduously coached by his parents as is his visionary career. When he is very young, his mother teaches him to make simple twine traps for snaring rabbits. Later his father teaches him to make traps and dead-falls for beaver, fisher, bear, and fox. He also teaches him hunting, the tricks of scent, of light, of sound decoys, the details of moving silently through dense woods with branches reaching out and dry leaves and twigs underfoot; he teaches him to orient himself by the light and shadow and movements of the leaves, by the growth of moss on the north side of a tree; he teaches him marksmanship, employing the living targets of the animals they seek. A boy's independence as a hunter comes quite early, by increasing degrees. At nine years Albert had killed enough furs of good quality to sell to the Hudson's Bay Company. By twelve years he had his own hunting and trapping grounds, and cooked for himself. Every few days he returned to his parents' home, bringing furs and hides for his mother and sisters to cure. He sought his father, brother, and brother-in-law for a ritual hunting feast in honor of a bear he had slain (but was not yet strong enough to move alone). His family was proud of him. His sisters' conventional respect for him was sharpened by the fact that he was not only economically independent, in male terms, but that he was also socially independent for he lived as a "stranger" in his own trapping lodge. He needed only a wife to be fully a man—at twelve! The more usual age for such maturity is fifteen to seventeen years.

At the same time that the boy learns to hunt and trap, he is taught to fish. The difficult fishing is in the winter, when two methods are used. The easier method is to spread fishnets in the lake water under the ice. This the boy learns in company with his sisters, when the children are taken to assist their mother or father. The other mode, learned by a boy when he accompanies his father or older brother, can be followed only by an adult male, and would be the only one pursued by a hunter isolated as Albert was. This is fishing by spear and torchlight (now also lantern light), squatting over a hole in the ice under a blanket or tiny wigwam. The boy's success in fishing is signaled by the same religious and honorific feasts as success in hunting. He is honored, which means concomitantly envied, as the beloved of the supernaturals, and for the energy and initiative which his success presupposes.

He becomes known in his village, and the inter-village visiting carries his fame elsewhere. This means that shortly he will be approached by a war-leader for enlistment in a war-party. Now he will use his training to seek new visions and powers, or he will turn to old ones that will help him on the war-path. His hunter's training will carry him noiselessly and unseen through the woods to the enemy's camp; it has taught him to observe signs such as tracks, ashes, new scents; it has taught him also to follow his independent judgments on the war-path as though he were alone. Before their departure, warriors are honored in song and dance by the girls, women, little children, and old men; when they return victorious, they are honored even more furiously. A boy's life is marked by constant and increasingly intense public recognition.

A girl's education lies in very different channels from that of a boy. At their birth-name feasts, baby girls are given generally "protective" names, and if they are ill, names which have a curative effect. I have discovered no names or name tokens of the vocational character commonly given to boys. If a boy is named "Crashing Thunder", the cryptic phrase has a dynamic meaning because of his sex. It is likely to mean that the namer was blessed by the Thunderbird, who is associated with the sound of thunder and who confers powers of war and strength. None of the Ojibwa could imagine that a girl would be given that name, or any name with such active, masculinely honorific content. Maggie "dreamed" about the gleaming body and wings of a Thunderbird: "It shone so you could hardly look at it". So she named her infant daughter, "the Shining of the Thunderbird", but the name meant no more than that; it held no vocational promise. The baby was not given a name-token. One man named his daughter "Little Tug" because he had seen in a vision a boat sailing on the sea, and he gave her a toy boat as a name-token. Here too the name and the name-token carried no vocational promise; but the child was considered, analogously with her more significantly named brother, Crashing

Thunder, to be protected by the name and the token. The latter was hung over her cradle or over her bed to play with. She was told stories about it, and how it came to her father in a vision. This was her introduction to the vision pursuit, a much more casual introduction than is given to boys. A girl's name and token and intercessor are never employed so pointedly in her education as are the boy's in his.

At the time that the boy is being feasted for having killed his first little bird, the girl simply trots around playfully after her mother and grandmother. A few years later, however, she is useful on errands, carrying small loads of wood and water. In her parents' absence she can be trusted to mind her baby brother or sister, with her grandmother around to mind them both. At this time her grandmother tells her stories: fabulous ones about the culture hero Nenebush and the wicked supernatural like *windigo;* stories about relatives whom the child sees only occasionally during the summer months; stories about everyday matters such as searching for a vision, and about the sib *do.dem* or eponym, and relationship obligations. Her little brother also listens if he is not busy with his traps. The grandparents are store-houses of knowledge which they impart gladly to their adult children and to the grandchildren alike. The grandparents and small grandchildren are thrown very much together, for the grandparents no longer carry on sustained active work and the grandchildren are still too young to take it on; they treat one another with the camaraderie of equals. All this is particularly true of the girls, for they always remain about the lodge, while the boys are gradually removed for outdoor fasting, trapping, hunting and war.

Boys and girls of eight aid the mother at setting the fishnets. The boys, however, do less and less of it as the years progress, while the girls do more and more until in time they are able to handle their own nets. In time the girl hauls in and preserves her own fish, makes her own nets, prepares the sturgeon bladders as she has been taught by her mother and grandmother. The two older women come to recognize their child and pupil as a reliable fellow worker, but there is no public recognition of the fact, and no vision stereotypes celebrate a woman's industrial abilities, as they do a man's hunting abilities.

Through these early years the girl has been taught to "think a lot" of her brother. If she is older than he, her respect for him has a motherly tinge for she has cared for him in his babyhood; indeed if the mother is dead, the boy often calls his elder sister "mother". If she is younger than he, her respect for him has an aura of hero-worship, for she knows him as a member of the company of hunters who accomplish great deeds. The girl is supposed to hasten to attend to her brother's comforts. In return, the boy is trained to feel that he must be his sister's economic provider and guardian. Even after marriage, he brings her some of his meat and furs, and she mends for him and makes him moccasins and beadwork. A woman's sexual honor is peculiarly her brother's concern; if she disgraces herself by illegitimacy or wantonness, he is so shamed that he leaves the locality for a strange one where he is unknown. The sexually determined attitudes of loving respectful service on the one hand, and of economic resourcefulness, bounty and guardianship on the other, are supposed to be transferred later to the marital relationship; they also enter into the relationship between adult unmarried daughter and father, between mother and adult unmarried son, though never so sharply as between sister and brother.

When the adolescent boy is successful as trapper, hunter and fisher, he brings his spoils to the family lodge as his father does. His sister is told by the mother that he has brought them for her to convert into food and clothing, just as the father's spoils are converted by the mother. The brother, or the father in his turn, comes home weary after an absence of one or many days on the cold snowy trails, throws some game into the lodge and indicates where the rest remains outside. The women prepare food and drink for the hunter, remove his clothes and mend them and give him tobacco. Then they go for the remainder of his game, fish and furs. He smokes and tells them about his adventures. Perhaps he has killed a bear. Great event! For "a bear is just like a human being, and must be honored like a guest from foreign parts"; then the spirit master of the bears will clothe the skeleton of this one with new meat and fur and send it again to the lodge. The bear is honored with a ritual feast conducted by the men of the lodge and neighborhood, and by having its bleached skull adorned with bright paint and ribbons from the Hudson's Bay factor. It is the women who make these preparations; the sister paints the skull for her brother, the wife paints it for her husband; likewise each woman prepares the food for the feast celebrating the enterprise of her brother or husband. After this the hunters leave the lodge again, each to return to his individual trapping trails; the grandmother, mother, daughter and young children remain together working at the meat, furs and hides left by each of the men. Each woman works at the materials left by her particular male partner. Mother works at father's materials, drying

the meat, tanning, cutting and sewing the hides which will go
into food and clothing for herself, father and the young children.
The older daughter works in the same way at her brother's materials, which will be used as food and clothing for herself and for
him, and of which some will often go to the domestic economy of
the parents. Her work is supervised by her mother and grandmother. They teach her the varying techniques of tanning: that
smoke of a certain volume and density from the burning of a particular bark effects a light yellow color or a deep tan color; that the
soaking of the hide for varying lengths of time in different natural
oils, like the oil of fatty brains, also affects the color, flexibility
and thickness of the hide; that certain parts of the hide are too thin
and worn for decorative or tough use, and consequently need not
be carefully tanned, etc. Even the scraping of the hide is an art
and must be supervised. The same supervision attends the drying
and freezing of meat and fish, and the cooking of dried flesh as
against the cooking of fresh meat. The cooking of blood, bones,
brains and the digestive glands all have their lore. The large organs
of large animals are set aside for special curing and later use as
food receptacles; these processes must also be carefully taught.
The days are very busy and pleasant, enlivened by stories told
largely by the grandmother and mother about the work at hand:
how Nenebush masqueraded as a woman and floundered about
trying to do woman's work, in handicrafts and procreation; how
Mrs. Blue-Sky's tanning is so poor that last summer she had to
take her hides to Maggie for redoing; how Mrs. Kokran's mother
turned windigo and wanted to eat everybody around her raw, for
beavers; how a girl was kidnapped by the Little Crane men last
summer while she was out alone in the bush tanning; how K's
father trained her to hunt and trap like a man, and her grandmother
taught her to tan, sew and cook like a woman; how G's first wife
drove away his second wife, and the latter tried to steal him back
by making him beautifully tanned and bead-embroidered moccasins; how S's wife takes his meat and hides, but makes them up for
G whose baby she is carrying in her belly; how C dreamed of a
new style for tailoring moccasins; how the legendary Evil Woman
went out to catch a porcupine so that she might embroider her hide
dress with its quills, but her foolishness was so great that she took
Nenebush for a porcupine, and let him rape her while she cried,
"How nice!" and finally she stood stripped while Nenebush danced
in front of her and made off with her dress.

When one woman has finished her individual chores, she helps
the others; or if one woman's work involves certain difficulties,

the others aid her. Each woman calls indiscriminately upon the children for assistance. Still each woman is thought of as carrying her responsibilities individually; this is impressed upon the girl by giving her her brother's spoils, although her mother, grandmother, and even little sister and brother aid her.

Some days have passed and the men return to the lodge again, individually or in pairs. The women attend to the comforts of father and brother, listen to the stories, execute the routine ritual sacrifices and feasts. Then they go out for the new spoils. They mend the garments of the men, and show them the progress upon the hides and meats of the last trip. This time the men may take their furs to the Hudson's Bay factor. Upon their return they show the results of their trade: ammunition, weapons, traps and tobacco for themselves; yard print, ribbons and beads for the women and children; candy, fruit, whiskey for all.

In spite of the economic and sentimental exchange between brother and sister, there are no intimate contacts. "They never speak to one another, as though they are shy". The shyness commences when the boy's voice first changes and he begins to leave the lodge for long periods on the trails, and "when the girl receives her first menstrual sign" and is taught to avoid her brother and his important possessions for his own safety. Sex references to them or between them are tabued. This "shyness" is initiated by the one who first shows signs of pubescence, whether boy or girl; it is only moderated by the elder one when he or she is out of the lodge, married, and the parent of several children. Then they visit in the summer and "talk together again", but never freely.

The girl's avoidance of her brother is one instance, and the most emphatic instance, of the conventional avoidance existing between a person and all the relatives forbidden in marriage. The avoidance is lessened, however, towards certain relatives of the ascending generations; notably for a woman it is the father, his brother, and the grandfather. The lessened avoidance means that the relatives are permitted to remain alone together for long stretches of time, that they may talk together more or less freely, but they are not supposed to make sexual allusions. This is the one relationship which permits of a certain disinterested companionship between the sexes.

These lesser avoidance relatives conventionally acquaint the girl with some aspects of a man's lonely trapping and hunting life. A man takes his daughter with him when he goes duck-hunting. She goes to paddle his canoe while he sights, to cook his meals, to put up the temporary lodge if they stay over night, to clean

the birds during idle hours, to be company. Desirable as her assistance is, it goes uncelebrated; the importance of the trip lies with
the man. If the girl is orphaned, she assists her grandfather or her
father's brother in the same way, depending upon the lodge that
houses her. After her marriage, she renders the same services to
her husband, leaving her household temporarily in the care of the
aged parents or of the older daughter.

The hours that a girl spends with some man of the household
are relatively few. Naturally, her closest associations are with
the women of her lodge: with her mother, her grandmother, her
sisters, sometimes with an aunt. In company these women work
at their individual unpublished tasks. These chores take long
hours and some never end through the isolated five months of
winter; they continue during the remainder of the year as well,
but with many interruptions due to the sociability of the spring
and summer. While the women work, they talk. They talk a
great deal, but never with idle hands. Men on the contrary can
talk only when they are idle, from the nature of their work. In
the absence of the men, the women form a closed world where
each woman is distinctive, where women's work is valued explicitly,
and where women's values are pursued. It is completely dissociated
from the world of men where women's work is conventionally
ignored and where no individual woman is distinctive. In the
relaxed smoking hours after the hunt and at the feasts, men talk
about the "important" things within their experience: about
adventures of the hunt and war, quarrels of shamans, metaphysics
of the *mide* rite. The women listen and say little. In their continuous
busy hours, while the men are gone from the lodge, women talk
about *their* important experiences: the number and peculiarities
of their husbands, the number of their children, the reasons for a
case of adultery, the objections to plural marriage, the queerness
of some women who war, hunt, and practise seership like men,
the merits of individual women as tanners, beadworkers, or midwives,
the merits of individual pieces of work in regard to technique or
ingenuity of pattern, sexual aberrations such as illegitimacy, abor-
tion, incest, or suspected homosexuality, the private motives behind
interesting actions.

From living in the same lodge with the older women, listening
to their talk, assisting them, trying to imitate them, the girl learns
the duties and also the opportunities of her sex. She develops
incentives in the women's world that in limited ways parallel the
incentives of men in their world. Thus, excellence of handiwork
excites the informal attention of women as widely as the boy's

talent in hunting excites the attention of men. Other women —
relatives, village neighbors, visiting women from distant villages —
come for instruction and to place orders; the achievements of a
gifted woman set the standards for a region. Maggie is known for
miles about as competent and original in her beadwork: she lays
down the beads on velvet or on hide with equal neatness and
firmness, her color combinations are startling but pleasing, her
designs are graceful and she employs both floral and geometric
patterns, she works rapidly and unerringly although she never
traces a pattern. Years ago her bartered beadwork could be found
in scattered families for fifty miles about. An equally gifted worker,
noted for her silk embroideries, lives about seventy miles northwest.

Excellence of handiwork finds also a negative recognition in the
form of jealousies felt by other women, usually by women engaged
in the same handiwork. Those less skilled feel ashamed, believing
that another's success is a pointed reflection upon their own adequacy.
Sometimes they strike out at the insulting situation, using malicious
gossip or "bad medicine". Successful women feel that they should
be envied; although they go through the gestures of resenting
jealousy, they look to the jealous manifestations for reassurance
of their importance. Maggie said that she alone in the village was
without friends or visitors because the women "hated" her for her
skill in beadwork and tanning. They did, especially when the
white tourists discovered her. Maggie pretended to some distress
over the hostility of her neighbors, but she took pains to remind
me that it existed. Girls are urged to do work of such quality that
it will excite admiration and envy. In other competitive spheres,
such as in women's athletic games, the envy of rivals may even
result in violent fights where hair is pulled, faces scratched, bodies
slashed with knives, and shamanistic revenge pursued. A basic
jealousy of this order finds its extreme expression among shamanistic men, who unremittingly duel to the death over long years.

A second incentive in women's work is marriage. Men learn
about gifted workers from eavesdropping upon the chatter of their
own women folk, and seek them in marriage. So the hunter Dubiday
heard about such a "smart" girl at Yellow Girls' Village, walked
miles to make her acquaintance, and married her. A third incentive
is the association of female activities with visions. These are
spontaneous visions which occur generally in maturity. They are
products of an already active interest in some work, in contrast
to men's early visions which are insistently coached and which
precede the development of special interests. The women's visions
sanction irregularities and any conspicuous innovations. Thus

Maggie envisioned the beadwork possibilities of brilliant autumn foliage, and executed them. Women also have spontaneous visions in connection with midwifery, songs, dress patterns. To their reputation for skill is added the prestige accorded any visionary.

The cleavage between the world of women and that of men is bridged by many unconventional girls and women. These become occupationally hermaphroditic as it were, for they practise specialties and share the viewpoints of both men and women. Men never take up women's work, as is frequently done among the Plains Indians. Unlike the Plains invert or berdache, however, the unconventional women among the Ojibwa who follow men's occupations are not recognized as having deserted the status proper to their sex. This subject is discussed further in part 3.

Games are very important in the social life. They are important in a child's life, for they plunge the child immediately into the values of the adult world. They are important in the adult's life, for they provide one of the few opportunities for large-scale joint activities.

The child's organized play commences on the day of birth. Those about the mother notice the first non-human living form that comes around the bedstead at the time the baby is born, and pounce on it calling it the "little sweetheart" or "little spouse" or "little lover" of the infant. Just as one baby girl's navel cord was being cut, a mouse ran past. "So we joked the baby, and said she had a visitor who had come to flirt and sleep with her." Another baby, a boy, was "married" to a grasshopper! Through babyhood the relatives joke the child in this way, and the little companions echo the joke. Children learn a good deal about relationship terms and obligations, and about marital life in this way. The child is told to view all young mice or all young grasshoppers or all young birds of the particular species as potential spouses, cross- cousins,[1] brothers-in-law and sisters-in-law, and is taught to behave towards all members of this class in a conventional manner of flirtatiousness and broad joking. Older animals of the species are the father-in-law, mother-in-law, cross-uncles,[2] and cross-aunts,[3] and the behavior appropriate to these relationships is grave respect that deepens into conventional avoidance of the parent-in-law of opposite sex.

---

[1] One's cross-cousin is the child of one's father's sister, or of one's mother's brother.
[2] Mother's brother.
[3] Father's sister.

Children "play house" endlessly until the age of puberty, with careful attention to unexpected ramifications. During the winter, children necessarily play only with members of the household, that is, with siblings and frequently with the grandparents. At the spring sugar-making they have some opportunity to play with children of other lodges, since often two families lodge together, and also there are neighboring lodges within visiting distance. In the summer a number of lodges draw still closer together into one neighborhood or village, and then children from a number of lodges play together. Before puberty children "play house" together regardless of age or sex, and unsupervised by adults. In the summer they go off in bands to shoot birds with bow and arrow. The boys usually get the "game" and return with it to the girls. The group then breaks up into "couples" and "households". Each boy takes a "spouse", supposedly careful not to violate the marriage regulations of kin and sib, and the couple takes "children", usually younger siblings of the boy or girl. Each girl cooks for her "husband and children" over an individual fire, but the fires are near together, and the whole scence precisely parallels the adult village. After the meal, the couples "spoon". They practise the verbal and physical ribaldries that are conventional to the relationship of "prospective spouse", having been taught these directly by parents and grandparents and also having learned by observation of others in the same "prospective spouse" relationship. They visit one another. They return to their fire or to the bush to simulate retirement to the marital or the courting bed. There they indulge in a good deal of sexual experimentation. Intercourse is forbidden before marriage, especially for a girl, but it does take place "as long as nobody knows". Intercourse seems to have two origins among the children. One is mimetic: they like to imitate the movements heard in the parental lodge. Another is simple curiosity aroused by the explicit sexual jesting between cross-cousins, jesting which makes stereotyped reference to the genitals, and by the lewd incidents in the Nenebush myth cycle which the older men tell constantly.

"Playing house" includes all of life's incidents. The girls attend one another as midwives, and practise the complicated art of brewing herbs, administering massage, and preparing special diets. They send their "children" out on vision quests, and put them through the routine vocational training. The boys play at being shamans and enact the fierce feuds of that class, cursing their enemies with winter starvation and *windigo* insanities, attacking one another with "knives" when meeting at the spring migrations, gloating

over "deaths" they have supernaturally caused in the enemy
family. Actually, the shaman play is forbidden because the real
shamans resent mockery and punish the children sorely if they
are discovered. It is also forbidden to simulate death and to conduct
"funerals" because this is taking the supernaturals in vain; nevertheless they play "shaman" and "death". War is played as it is
among white children, with the added features of preparing the
scalp, dancing with it, singing victory songs. Girls are kidnapped,
as they are in real life. They like to "play store", and they run up
debts in strict realistic fashion, and loll around drunk. A few girls
sit on a bench opposite a few boys, all playing to be sodden drunk
like their parents; they pretend to try to sit upright, and then topple
over. They screech with laughter. In actual life, drunkenness
licenses incest, but the children do not seem to include this.

"Playing house" includes playing the systematic games of the
adults, with the exception that children do not play for stakes,
while adults always do. Certain games are played more regularly
by children than they are by adults, and others played more
regularly by adults than by children. Thus, children of all ages
and sexes race their tops, whipping them along with sticks. They
also race "snow sticks", by throwing long smooth sticks of ash
with both arms along the hard snow. Generally the sexes separate
when playing these games, as they separate also among the adults;
sometimes, however, a team of girls challenges a team of boys. Men
accompany their games of chance with an unceasing, unchanging
beating of the tom-tom; but women and children do not do this.

Girls and women play exactly the same games as the men, with
the exception that squaw (corruption of the Algonkian particle
meaning "female") hockey is substituted among the women for
men's lacrosse. The games are generally played by people of the
same sex, although in the summer women of the village occasionally play the men of the village. In the summer too, the team
of one village challenges the team of another; this arrangement
is confined largely to the men. Within the village, other alignments
are possible, such as a group of young men opposed to a group of
older men, or the lodges from one end of the village opposed to
lodges at the other end. The winter isolation necessitates other
alignments of lodge-mates: thus the grandparents play opposite
the children.

Athletic games offer women the same recognition as men, the
only sphere in which this is allowed. In racing, the standard of
accomplishment is the same for both sexes. Little girls race their
brothers in the winter; many a boy says, "My sister beats me in

the foot-race". Girls have visions empowering them to be runners, just as do boys. Women runners and hockey players are cheered by men, and very successful ones are sought by other women for instruction or blessing. Like men, they receive the negative face of acclaim. Defeated rivals, generally women, may knife them, sicken them with "bad medicine", and sometimes fall in abject fear before them. The successful woman develops a complementary attitude, a sneering sadism. She cannot carry this attitude far in any other relationship; but in this one sphere her behavior precisely duplicates that allowed to successful men in all relationships. It is sometimes difficult to say what specific factor disturbs the defeated rival: perhaps "shamed" resentment of the other's superiority, or of the other's right to the large stakes, as evidenced by protests: "She makes (earns) too much with her medicine".

The case of Part-Sky-Woman clearly illustrates the position of a successful runner. In her youth she was blessed by a cloud in a spontaneous vision and was told that her body would be as light, as swift, and as strong as his. Years ago the Hudson's Bay factor at Fort Frances, Ontario, used to arrange two holidays in the summer time, when the women competed at squaw hockey and at foot-races. Part-Sky-Woman liked to participate in the holiday games because of the sociability in the reassembling of many lodges after the winter isolation. She also looked forward to the large prizes offered: yards of dress goods and of differently colored ribbons, shawls, shoes, hats, cotton thread, sometimes even silk goods. She felt confident of her success in the games because she "talked" regularly with her guardian cloud and was thus reassured that she would not tire nor become ill. "She was one of many who were lined up for the race. The course was a half-mile and back again, and she won and was given the prize. Every summer she would win, on each of the holidays. For nine years she was the one woman always taking the prize in the foot-races and in squaw hockey. She beat the best squaw hockey players; the women used to quarrel as to which side she would play on. She always went on the young girls' side. Moreover the women used to come to her with bundles of stuff to ask her what kind of medicine she used for running. She used to tell them that she did not use any medicine at all. [She meant that she did not use material aids, such as charms, but used only her dreams.] Some of the girls and women never looked at her, they were so jealous of her and hated her. But the Hudson's Bay people thought an awful lot of her. So for nine years she took three prizes a year for racing. The tenth summer she could not come to the celebration. The Hudson's Bay factor

waited for her, but the race had to go on without her. An Ojibwa
woman from the States, named Bird-Woman, won the race. But
that was when Part-Sky-Woman was not there. And Part-Sky-
Woman came to the next celebration, two days in advance, with
her mother and sisters. Her next younger sister was already married,
but she was not. The Indians did not want her to come because
they knew she would be the one to take the prizes again. As soon
as the Hudson's Bay man heard she had arrived, he came over and
got her and asked her why she had not been there the previous
year, and she said she could not come. So he took her into the
store and made her pick out the dress goods she wished to win.
She chose a black silk which was very dear. When the day came,
there were four women to compete in the race: the ones that had
come first and second the previous year, one new runner, and
herself. She used to fix her moccasins with 'medicine', and also
smoke them so that no bad medicine would affect her legs while
she was running. They started off. The woman who had won the
previous year was right at her heels all the time, and after they
had turned back the woman was even with her. Part-Sky-Woman
could hear that Bird-Woman was out of breath, and the woman
said, 'I guess you will beat me', and Part-Sky-Woman answered,
'I don't know. I do not care to win this race.' After the woman had
sprinted ahead of her, she said (muttering to her guardian cloud),
'Now is the time to help me out, you that told me I would have
fun. It would be shameful if I got beat.' She was speaking to the
shadow of the clouds, and right away she felt her body light as
a feather, and, as if she were running on air, she passed the woman.
She was way ahead of the woman and won the race. So again she
took the first prize; there was a second prize but it was not so good
as the first. Then they got ready for the squaw hockey game. Many
girls and women wanted to play against her, only a few were on her
side. Many people put up stakes for the winners. So they started
to play. One of the girls, the one that came second on the foot-race
of the previous year when Part-Sky-Woman was not there, was a
good player. She was the best player from her part of the country,
and claimed to be a good runner too, but she could not do anything
this time. When Part-Sky-Woman got the balls, she ran, and this
girl was right behind her, but Part-Sky-Woman made a goal anyway.
So they won that game and divided up the prizes. They were
talking and laughing and this same girl (the defeated one) came up
to her and asked her threateningly what she was laughing at. Part-
Sky-Woman said nothing, and the girl said, 'Oh, you're laughing
at me because you beat me!' and then hit her on the face with a

crooked knife. Part-Sky-Woman did not move or do anything.
The blood was streaming down her face; she was cut on her cheek.
Then the girls took her to their tent, washed her cut and put some
medicine on her. Many of the women had it in for her and tried to
do her wrong all the time, but she did not care. Her face healed
right away. While they were staying there, the Hudson's Bay
factor came and asked her if she would go to Kenora to race a
white woman who was the champion runner, and she said she was
willing to go." She traveled with the factor, his wife, and her
sister to the big town of Kenora—then Rat Portage. It was a
July 4th celebration, and people were gathered from many parts.
Bets were put up for the White and the Indian woman. "So when
two o'clock came they were on the road. They were to run half
a mile and back again. She had on two long skirts and her beaded
moccasins. The white woman wore shorts and no stockings. She
was not a bit scared, though there were many people watching
them. A gun was fired and then they were shooed to go. The white
woman was a fast runner and was ahead of her from the first. She
did not mind her. She ran steadily along and when they turned
back she ran ahead of her. Just when this white woman wanted
to pass her she spoke to the shadow of the cloud again. Right
away she thought she was running on air again, and as she was
coming close to the line where they were to stop she could see the
Hudson's Bay man waving his hat and yelling for her, saying
ámbe! (hurry up! come on!). Then she ran with all her might and
beat this woman by a big margin and broke her record as champion
runner. So fifteen dollars were given to her as a prize. Men and
women were in the next race. They were to go just a little way,
and there was only one prize of five dollars. Her boss (the Hudson's
Bay man stood in the position of one who hired her for work) told
her to run again, and she won again. So that was twenty dollars
she had now. And she was to get another five on the bets. That
was to finish her racing. All at once the boss came running to her
and asked her if she would race a man who was betting fifty dollars
that he could beat her. She said she would. So she stood on the
road again, ready to race a man. Everybody said she could not
beat this man, but she was not a bit frightened. The man was
dressed only in shorts. So off they went again. The man was very
slow. But she did not mind him; she ran as fast as possible, for
they had to run a longer distance. Well, she beat him; and so that
was fifty dollars more that she had won." She married an Ojibwa
man who saw her race in Kenora and admired her. She did not
race for some years afterwards because she was bearing children.

3

Then "she got sick on her face, sickened by the bad medicine sent
her by a jealous shaman. The Indian doctors treated her. When
her little girl was four years old she got strong again, and she was
mad. She made up her mind that she would race the women again
and play squaw hockey (to spite those she had defeated in the games
and who had tried to cripple her shamanistically). She talked
through her nose, as this was where they had made her sick. Whenever she ran, and whenever she played squaw hockey, she always
won. And she would say, to make the jealous women mad (the
defeated rivals), 'It's all right if I have to talk through my nose
because of what the old Indians did to me. Only if they break
my legs will I not be able to run any more.' And she always tried
hard to beat everyone. At last the women were afraid of her; they
thought she was *manido*. They never raced her again."

The venomous resentment that attends women's athletic games
is matched by the fury and brutality of men's lacrosse. The games
of chance and skill are much quieter among women than among
men, although there is no lessening of the intense concentration. It
is customary to surround these games with an atmosphere of
gaiety, to head off the attention of the opposing players. The
players who are "up", laugh, joke, sing, dance even when seated
on the ground, make all kinds of contortions of the face, body,
arms and legs. Unmarried girls spend a great deal of time in the
summer visiting and playing these games. The equipment for the
games is individually owned and only one set of equipment is
needed for a large number of players. There are only a few sets
in the village, and as the games are very popular, there are frequent
gatherings of nearly the entire village about some set. Children
bunch around, volunteer claquers and accountants of the scores.
Powers from visions attend these games, as they do athletic games,
for ability at games of chance is highly valued. Among the men
the games can continue in the summer for days and nights unending,
with excitement at a maddened pitch, the stakes rising to enormous
proportions, steel flying, the players reeking of alcohol. The
women's games last for only a few hours at a time. One reason
for this is that women do not possess enough property for extensive
gambling; another is that the household routine forbids long
absences; another is a general feeling that moderation is proper to
women.

Iron-Woman was notably skilled at these games of chance and
skill, and defeated even the best men players. She had been taught
by her "medicine" father and by her grandfather. As the only
child in the lodge she had been much fondled and adopted completely

into the circle of adult interests. In the winter, when her grand-father was cozy and inactive behind the wigwam fire, he would talk about his exploits at the moccasin game, and demonstrate his ability to deceive the opposite guessing side and to outguess the other side when it tried to deceive him with some sleight of hand. Through the winters the family repeatedly ran the gamut of all games. And in the summer time Iron-Woman showed the results of her winter's practise, being so consistently successful a player, so untiring and ingenious, that the villagers said her par-ents must have provided her with a notoriously "bad medicine". "One day the women (during the village season) planned to chall-enge the men to a moccasin game. So at one end of the Indian village they started to play. The men were on one side, and the women on the other. She was the one that was hiding the little balls which they use at the moccasin game, and her cousin was the one that was singing for her, and no one could discover where she put this certain little ball. So her side won that game, and every time she played she won. She was a good moccasin player. She played every kind of game, such as the dice game (played with wild plumstones, carved, each carving differently evaluated, and the combinations of the throws differently evaluated), bone game (thrusting a bone point into certain holes punched into a trailer of deer-hide, played with one hand; each turn of the play is a matter of skill and has a fixed value), and snake-stick game (a variant of the dice game). And she was also a good runner, and a good hockey player, and a good hunter, because her parents had taught her, and had some kind of bad medicine for her to use. She did nothing else but these things when she was young, and was always the best."

Individual differences in ability are clearly recognized by the people, and include such careful distinctions as that of small ability hitched to great ambition, or that of potentially great ability confined by small ambition. Maggie, who was noted for superiority at crafts and for general sociability, just could not get interested in games of chance and skill. She did not care about the fairly involved native scheme of tallying, nor about the gamble of winning and losing. She often attented the women's games, but less and less as a performer. She came with some beadwork at which she worked automatically while engaged in the stereotyped gay and swift banter and in the always fascinating gossip with its piecing together and disentangling of motives. As her daughter, Shining-of-the-Thunderbird, grew to girlhood, Maggie retired even more to the gossip fringe of the women's games, while her daughter

3*

moved nearer to the performing nucleus of the games until one day
Shining-Thunderbird was acclaimed as a talented player. Maggie
was very proud of her daughter's ability, and wondered at the
ease with which she handled the difficult tallying, but this never
stirred her out of her own disinterest.

There are certain conspicuous differences between the atmosphere
surrounding game playing in the winter lodge and that of the
playing in summer. In the winter, household relatives always
play in a light-hearted, good-humored spirit, seeking success for
the purpose of bantering the discomfited one. In the village, where
persons of different households play together, the atmosphere is
charged with challenge. This is true even when the closest relatives,
belonging to different households, play together. Defeat is generally
taken as a jeering judgment that must be revenged or stricken
out at the first opportunity. If it cannot be offset by subsequent
triumph at the game itself, the insult will be settled in a fight.
Endless tales are told of successful men who have had knives
drawn on them. These respond with some deadly magic, or with
the sublime unconcern of one who knows that his "power" is great
enough to warrant resentment. Shaboyez was a noted hunter,
warrior, and shaman. He and his family visited an Ojibwa village
one summer. "After a couple of days, some men invited Shaboyez
to a moccasin game. (This is a Cree name. He was of mixed
Ojibwa-Cree origin, as many of these Ojibwa are, living among the
Ojibwa and married to one of their women as well as to a Cree
woman.) So he said he would play. The moccasin game started,
and of course Shaboyez was a good player, and his side was winning
a lot of blankets and clothes of all kinds. Later he beat them at the
hand game (played on the same principles as the moccasin game
but using the hand as a hiding place, instead of the moccasin),
at lacrosse, and at other games. While he was winning again at
the moccasin game, one of the men got mad at him and stabbed
him on the chest with a long knife, and the blood gushed. So the
men took him home, and the two women (his wives) brought him
home to their own village. He never got over the stab on his chest.
After some years he sickened to death. He knew that he was
going to die... He said goodbye to everybody he knew, and he
said, 'I have no hard feelings against the man who stabbed me...' "

Magical battling between shamans is a not uncommon result of
the enmities that arise from the gaming of the villagers. It may
arise, too, from the quarrels that frequently punctuate the "playing
house" of village children. In the latter case, the parents of the
children take up arms for the children, and inaugurate a feud

between the respective households. In any case of shamanistic combat, all the members of the principal's household are enlisted. Most households are affected by such combat at one time or another, and the entire region is always vitally interested in the outcome. Most mishaps are considered the casualties of combat between shamans. If a child or an adult falls ill, or if an accident befalls some member of the household, it is attributed to a shamanistic thrust at the family. If game is scarce in winter, a vengeful shaman is held responsible. When the households depart from the village for the winter sites, each child and adult is on the lookout for signs of "bad medicine": the hoot of a night-owl, the howling of a dog, the midnight drifting of a "ball of fire" (marsh gas), horrible dreams of the *windigo*, a voracious appetite. As winter progresses, the household anticipates shortage of game, and usually such anticipations are realized. "The animals become afraid of them and go away. They stumble clumsily through the woods, and after a time they see the spirit of Poverty." All members of the family fear that starvation may come upon them; and when it does, they know that they will become *windigo*, crazy, desirous of eating their lodge-mates cannibalistically under the delusion that they are eating luscious beavers. The victims seek to retaliate shamanistically, with the intention to kill, even if the victims are close relatives, though of another household. Thus Thunder-Woman gloated when she heard that her father had died, killed shamanistically by her in defense of her husband.

Feuds go on magically in the winter, and reach a climax when the combatants meet in person in spring on the way to the village. "Deceased's" husband met his winter-long opponent at the crossing of a creek. The opponent saw him first and immediately fired upon him. The two men killed each other while their wives and children stood on opposite banks and watched. The deaths "began with their children fighting over their play; next the two women took it up, and one of them sent starvation to the other's winter lodge; and then the two men finished."

Shamanistic combat is dreaded by ordinary people, and disliked even by the shamans themselves because of the suffering it brings to members of the household. Consequently people are taught from earliest childhood to behave most carefully towards shamans so as to avoid trouble. Children are forbidden the most casual laugh in the vicinity of a shaman for fear that the shaman will suspect mockery and let loose his armaments. Over and over children are told, "You must not even smile at the medicine man. Keep your eyes down and your face straight." One summer a shaman went

around muttering, "I'll get him! I'll get him!" Every mother of
a young son trembled, for at a recent dance the young men had mocked
the old man, plying him with whiskey until he lost control of his
natural functions and defecated in the dance hall, and then they
had laughed in his face. He did "get" somebody, a boy whom he
caused to be paralyzed for months. Girls learn to avoid a medicine
man, for should one catch his fancy, she cannot avoid marriage
with him unless she is willing to brave the consequences of insulting
him: horrible deaths to herself and to her family. Girls see their
companions snatched by a medicine man as by a monster, and see
them shrink away, shamed by their fate and forlorn over the black
future. Because of his power, a shaman can even violate girls,
unresisted.

Fears figure prominently in the background of life. Men are
taught to fear shamans, but girls and women are taught to fear
almost every other man as well. For example, girls were often
kidnapped by strange men during the summer months, both in
peace time and in war. The girls were made to fear not simply
the abduction, but also the likelihood of rape. The rumored
charms of a girl sometimes excited the lust of one or of a few men
in distant parts, and a kidnapping resulted. Such was the fate
of one girl, caught while she was alone in the bush working on leather.
"She looked up and saw a man crawling towards her. She jumped
up and looked the other way, and saw another one crawling. And
also the other way was another one. They were circling around her.
She had no place to run to, and the men grabbed her and gagged
her so that she could not yell. They tied her up and ran away with
her. She did not know who these men were." They carried her to
a canoe, and went over many portages with her. They carried her
always tied up. "She used to cry an awful lot. She never ate
anything although there were good things given to her. She did
not eat because she was very lonely and worried. She was afraid
that they would tackle her. But only one of them used to bother her,
and he would also laugh at her, and shove her around when he saw
her crying." Finally one of the kidnappers effected her escape...
Young married women were also abducted. Cree-Woman was
in the bush, cutting away the bark of cedars in order to make a
mat; "just as she was getting ready to leave, some men grabbed her
and tied a rag over her face and ran away with her." They took
her to an unknown land, called the Land of the Little Crane Men,
a general term for unknown, distant, and therefore much feared
regions. A compatriot of the abductors let her escape. Thenceforth
she never ceased to warn all women against being alone in the

woods. The fear of kidnapping is so strong that it also obsesses the men; they are forever after young girls, begging them to be careful in the woods. Every summer a scare arises among the people, that "the little men" have have seen peering on girls from behind trees. The scare is by way of being mythologized, for the "little men", or the "little Crane men", seem to be neurotic figments about whom imaginary abduction tales are spun. Other stories describe an ogre's abduction of a princess, or a manido's abduction of a fair girl. War attacks are colored by the abduction-rape fear. In a Sioux attack, the Ojibwa's first concern was for the menstruating girls isolated in the woods. Several tales currently told about Sioux raids sound precisely like the kidnapping stories. In them the Sioux creep up on an attractive Ojibwa or Cree girl and kidnap her, torture her, at least mentally, and are preparing to rape her when she escapes because of the repentance of one of the party. In one story the mental agonies of the victim's father are described as he imagined "the Sioux going along making fun of his daughter."

Girls also fear rape by men of the household. Numerous tales are told about a man's attacks upon his step-daughter. Less often, there are stories of a man's attacks upon his daughter-in-law, and occasionally those of a man's rape of his daughter, or of his daughter's daughter. Rape from other relatives is rare because they live in separate and often isolated households; such instances as were reported had occurred during drunkenness. One such story concerned Brother-In-Law and his sister: befogged with drink, he was trying to discover the genitals of his sister, herself in a drunken sleep.

A step-father's rape can occur in a conventional fashion. Privileged as he is to request his step-daughter's assistance on the duck-hunt or on the trapping trails, a man has the girl alone and at his mercy. One step-father protests to the horrified girl, "That's what everybody does when they go out hunting for ducks!" The girl usually manages to flee, and raises an alarm at the camp. Her mother undertakes to punish the incestuous one, and greets him at the lodge door with an axe. The axe is never used but a hearty fight between man and wife ensues. Sometimes mother and daughter leave for good, or for varying lengths of time, sometimes only the daughter leaves. Great Buffalo Woman did not leave after her step-father's first attempt, so he pursued her subsequently in the lodge itself, adopting the "bundling" procedure of young lovers. Thereupon she and her mother left.

Tempera was a medicine man who used another method for rape, a variant of one that is fairly common in the improper sexual approaches of shamans. His adolescent step-daughter was ill, and he treated her with his special curing method. After a time he commenced giving the girl "some medicine to make her sleep. Then he would play over her, until at last the girl knew she was going to have a baby, only she did not know who its father was." After the baby was born, the man married his stepdaughter, making her a co-wife to her own mother. The mother accepted this status, horrified and shamed, but anxious to care for her duped daughter. Shortly thereafter the girl became violent, "crazy from shame and worry", and died. The step-father conducted the girl's funeral services. "After everything was over, they went home, and his wife took the axe to cut his head off. But some men grabbed her before she hit him. She was so mad. She said, 'You killed my daughter!' Then she got ready and returned to her (family's) home, taking the boy with her"... The more common shamanistic approach to incest and rape, which **Tempera** used at another time, is to announce to the victim a message from the *manidos* that a young man will come to court her at night; and then the shaman pretender is received by the girl.

Step-daughters are approached even when they are no longer girls, but are already middle-aged divorced women or widows who have returned temporarily to the parental lodge. Their greater sophistication, however, enables them to handle the situation without panic. **Kath** was a woman who had left several husbands and had returned to her mother's home. After she had lived there a year, "her step-father commenced going after her at night. He used to go out (of the lodge) and pretend to come in again. Later he would sneak in and lie down by her, but she thought it was someone else. Then she began to hit him and send him away. She could tell by his actions in the daytime that he was trying to get her. One time she got a stick that was burned because she wanted to find out who it was that came and bothered her in the night. So that night she lay down with the burned stick. Again that night he came along, went out and pretended to come in, and a little while after he came and lay down beside her. So she took the stick and hit him across the back. The next morning she knew it was her stepfather that was bothering her because his shirt was marked with the charred coal of the stick. So she told her mother, and then she went away and stayed with another old woman."

Not all step-fathers care to violate the daughters of the wife. Some have a tender and disinterested love that withstands all temptation. But this is so uncommon that they are suspected nevertheless. **Rabbit** married when her illegitimate daughter was an infant. The child was dearly loved by her step-father, and was his hunting companion through childhood and girlhood. But when the girl reached adolescence, her mother became wildly, and groundlessly, jealous of her "because her step-father was so good to her. When the man went to Kenora to get some stuff, the girl always ran down and helped him carry the stuff up. And she would cook whatever he brought for she was a smart girl. Her mother never had to do any work. And that was why her mother got jealous of her (because in fulfilling her womanly tasks, the girl was behaving as a wife). But they did not know, or even think that of each other. She just thought of him as of a father, and he the same. So one time when he was doing some hard job and his wife was helping him, he said to her, 'Call the girl to come and help me. You are not strong enough.' And she got very mad and said to him, 'Oh, so you're ready to turn me down for her!' But the old man did not say anything. He thought she was joking. So the girl came and helped him. And the old woman never spoke to them." The mother's resentment grew to the point where she forbade the girl any association at all with the step-father, and did not allow her even to wash his clothes. The girl gradually understood her mother's suspicions, and as the mother saw that, she became more violent and beat her daughter. Once the girl fled for a short period, and when she returned "she was not the same towards her step-father... (Nevertheless) whenever the old man brought any goods for his step-daughter, his wife would take it away from her and say, 'You should get married yourself; then your own husband will bring you something to wear.'" The mother's jealousy never abated, and the girl endured it quietly until one day the mother gashed and bruised her in a fight; then the girl left to live with her grandmother. When the step-father learned the reason for the girl's departure, he too deserted his wife.

Fathers are not symbolic of incest and rape, as step-fathers are, but they are guilty occasionally. One widower, Sweet, lived alone with an adolescent daughter and eventually violated her. When she announced the fact to the village, the man was greeted with most insulting scorn, his relatives repudiated him as a "dog", and until the end of his life he was ostracized by the Indians... Grandfathers are also likely to err, as was the case with Farrin. He and his wife lived with their widowed daughter and her young daughter. The girl dutifully accompanied her grandfather on his hunting trips. "At last he camped out and wouldn't come home at night. He used to have some excuse... it was too windy, or it was too late for him to come home. And he kept on like that until at last the girl was to become a mother. Her mother knew that she was to have a baby, and she got angry and kept on asking who the father was, but the girl wouldn't even speak to her mother (because she was ashamed). So when the baby was born the old woman said she would kill the baby if the girl refused to tell who the father was. And while she was talking and just about to kill the baby, the old man came in and grabbed the baby. Then they all knew that it was his baby. So the girl took the old man away from her own grandmother, and she had five children with the old man. This girl's own grandmother became her co-wife, and her own mother became her niece." The grandfather was not scorned, as a father would have been in his place. Apparently this was not considered to be a primary incest, such as incest with the father or father-in-law; and the origin in rape was overshadowed by the succeeding marriage.

Attack by a father-in-law arouses tremendous protest, just as attack by a father does. Inasmuch as a father-in-law is an avoidance relative, he must manufacture situations that permit him to approach his daughter-in-law; he does this by falsely claiming a visionary sanction. He therefore offends the people on two counts: contempt of the kinship formulation, and contempt of the religious formulation. Crow held séances with his widowed young daughter-in-law in which he mediumistically declared that "his dead son would come at night to kiss his little boy," not yet conceived. Crow advised his daughter-in-law that her deceased husband would visit her, and that she was not to make any light. A man did visit her, dressed in the beaded burial suit of the deceased. The woman's suspicions were aroused, but as her father-in-law had forbidden her to make any light, she was prevented from fully grasping the situation until she discovered herself pregnant. Then she called her father-in-law to account, and screamed the news about the village. She and her mother-in-law fell upon the culprit, nearly killed him, and then moved away from him. Another man named Marten tried to secure a girl towards whom he bore the responsibilities of a father-in-law. She was Little Maid, the virgin sister of his actual daughter-in-law. He was a fire-handler (a diviner who employs tricks with fire), terribly feared, and accustomed to having his sensual and other whims satisfied. At one of his ceremonies, when announcing the designs of his guardian spirits, he said, "'Eh, the *manido*s want me to sleep with Little Maid,' and he slung the fire around and put it in his mouth. His daughter-in-law heard him. She ran to where he was sitting, kicked him on the chin, and gave him an awful beating because she didn't want him to ruin her young sister. And after she got through beating him she went away with Little Maid for good."

Girls stand in terror not only of the step-father but also of the step-mother. The step-father is feared for his lust, but the step-mother is feared for her cruelty. The daughter, identifying herself with her mother, fears and hates the woman who has usurped her mother's place, and the step-mother often gives her good cause. Pona was a child when her widowed father remarried. She "felt very badly when she knew her father was married again. When her father saw her crying he said to her, 'Do not cry,' and she said, 'I am sorry to see another woman already taking my mother's place.' And he answered her, 'Don't cry, she will be a mother to you, and I will tell her to be good to you.' So she stopped crying. But soon after she learned that her step-mother was awfully mean. She no longer got the best of what her father brought. She was not even allowed to eat with the others. Her step-mother always gave her the worst of everything, and when her father was away hunting, her step-mother gave her nothing to eat. She would tell her to cook for herself, and always scolded her and slapped her. When her father returned, her step-mother would tell him all kinds of lies to get her into trouble, and so her father sometimes scolded her for nothing. Whenever he went to the Hudson's Bay Company, he came back with lots of calico, and of it her step-mother always got the most and the best. Pona always got the poorest and dullest colored print, and barely enough for a dress. This went on for a couple of years. Her father never made a fuss over her now. She felt very bad, and missed her mother's love and her father's love." The tale goes on with numerous incidents to the same point. Pona grieved and grieved for her dead mother. The exasperated step-mother told her husband that his daughter was jealous of her, that the daughter herself wanted to marry her father. Soon after the father died in an accident. The step-mother moved away and left the girl deserted on an island, with the parting shot, "You can stay right here and marry your dead father. That's the reason you were always mad at me. And your darned mother can take care of you. I don't want to be bothered with you any more."

Great Buffalo Woman had a similar relationship with her mother's co-wife, that is, with her categorical step-mother. (The relationship term is identical for mother's sister, mother's co-wife, and father's second wife taken after the death of the first.) The co-wife had been the first wife, and in the usual way resented her husband's taking another wife. The daughter of the new wife was made to suffer from this resentment. The step-mother gave her unceasing chores of mending moccasins, chopping wood, and drawing water, and scolded her continually. At the time of first menstruation, she had the child put out of the house for two months because she was "dirty". When the family traveled by canoe, the "dirty" step-daughter was forbidden to enter the canoe, but had to walk barefooted alongside. The step-mother became most difficult when the step-father took his new wife hunting with him. Finally the girl balked, and pleaded with her mother to leave the man and his wife. After that the step-mother commenced to be kinder. But a new fear arose. The girl had always been uncomfortable with her step-father; now that she had matured, he sought her as a hunting companion and attacked her. Eventually she was forced to leave.

Even grown women are hostile to a step-mother. The adult step-daughters of Mizino "wouldn't own her for a mother at all, and were mean to her. At last they went away from their father's home." Edna Bombay, on the other hand, is devoted to her young step-mother; the gossips consider the relationship remarkable enough for comment.

An occasional variant of this step-daughter relationship is found among boys. In these cases the step-father is considered cruel, and the step-mother is occasionally lustful enough to marry her step-son.

A girl's fears of her closest relatives, those in whose household she lives, are characteristic of a general mistrust of the near relatives. This does not mean that those outside the household, those who assemble in the summer time, are met with any more confidence; but rather that the outer world in general is unimportant, casual, and is not thought of attentively, either for good or for evil. For example, the shamans most dreaded are the blood relatives and house-mates, for they deliberately exercise a power which according to Ojibwa dogma endangers the lives of those closest to them. "About six months or a year after bad medicine is sent out, it returns to the one that owns it because that is where it belongs, and it kills people in the family." When people observe that repeated deaths occur in a shaman's family, they "know" he is using bad medicine. Consequently undisguised deep rifts arise among relatives. Brother openly accuses brother. "Red Sand said to his brother, Whitefish, 'You must be doing bad medicine... that's why your children and grandchildren are dying. Why don't you quit and let your children live?' And Whitefish didn't answer a word." Daughter openly accuses father, as did the daughter of Whitefish when her son died from the recoil of his grandfather's sorcery. She swore to get her revenge, so she had her father jailed on a charge of drunkenness. And at Kenora, the daughter of Warrior denounced her father publicly as the cause of her children's deaths. "Finally the bad medicine got *him*, and he got crazy and died. And his family felt easier." There is no social procedure for controlling sorcerers. They must be done away with completely, and that only by magic combat. Consequently the female shaman Pelican Woman felt quite content that she had magically caused the death of her father, because he had used his sorcery to sicken her husband. Other stories besides Pelican Woman's point to a general suspicion that shamans like to injure their sons-in-law. Women feel uneasy about their very husbands, if the husbands are medicine men and become annoyed with them; a deserting woman is always badly punished by her shaman husband. One much feared medicine man named Big Falcon was poisoned and killed with the connivance of his own daughter; then he and his possessions were burned. Men like to blame sterility upon their wives; they justify the accusation by saying that the wife, although perhaps without her own knowledge, has had evil visions that wedded her to an evil supernatural and made her a dreadful sorceress.

The continuous fear of starvation is often personalized into a fear of certain relatives or house-mates. This is because starvation makes some people *windigo*, that is, so disoriented that they imagine the people about them to be beavers, and desire to eat them to satisfy their tremendous hunger. Thus Eminent, a noted and feared medicine man, spent the winter on his trapping grounds with his three wives and twelve children. Starvation struck them, sent by an unsuccessful lover of the youngest wife. The day came when the people lay about stuporous. One of the wives warned her children to keep away from their father; she feared that he was becoming *windigo*. He himself feared to become *windigo*, since he had lost his "power". Even a nursing baby rouses fear in time of starvation; so a starving baby in this family was killed by an older sister because she "knew he was to become a little *windigo*. His eyes were blazing and his teeth rattling. He was eating his fingers up, and biting off the heads of his dead mother's breasts." ...When Ayash found his grandparents dead of starvation, and their adoptive granddaughter gone, he immediately surmised that they had turned *windigo* and eaten their granddaughter.

The conventional attitudes of relatives should be the opposite of distrustful. Relatives are supposed to be "kind" to one another, and the kindest of all should be the lodge-mates. A couple is supposed to contract marriage because they love each other; they are supposed to have children because they love them; and in some districts because a brother esteems his sister, and she him, they are supposed to arrange marriage between their respective offspring, who are cross-cousins to one another. The kinship terminology consistently reflects the supposed existence of cross-cousin marriage. Where the marriage of cross-cousins exists, as in southeast Manitoba, it is considered ideal because the closely-related couple founds the new household with a headstart on "kindness". Of such a marriage it is said approvingly, "She (he) is married to her (his) very own relative." However, other classes of relatives are forbidden to marry.

This view of cross-cousins as preferred prospective spouses is institutionalized in a distinctive etiquette which the cross-cousins observe. Any persons employing this etiquette announce themselves thereby as eligible lovers and spouses,[1] and may proceed to actual love-making or marriage when the wish arises. This etiquette obtains all through the lives of the cross-cousins, except for a pair that becomes formally betrothed. The cross-cousin courting etiquette exists even in such districts as southwest Ontario, where the actual marriage is now forbidden; and in this region the set behavior never alters, as it does in Manitoba, because the actual betrothal is not supposed to occur. Unrelated people who are eligible in marriage behave to one another as though they are cross-cousins, but some of the zest is lacking. The relationship is felt to be a very exciting one, for it consists in attracting the recip-rocal's personal attention. The cousins do this in a striking way: they try to embarrass one another, just skirting the fine edge of insult. The Ojibwa are generally very sensitive to insult, scenting it in the most obscure connections, and punishing it with sorcery. Cross-cousins therefore are playing with explosives; the poison is extracted by the conventions of the relationship, but an attention-getting barb remains. They joke and prod very rudely, from their viewpoint as well as from ours. They use sexual phrases that are explicit and detailed. The point is to do all this in public where outsiders can see, hear, and laugh in ridicule. The situation would be intolerable under any other circumstances, and it is often difficult to bear in the presence of an avoidance relative, as the sibling of opposite sex. Cross-cousins of the same sex emulate the joking freedom of those of the opposite sex. This behavior contrasts with that of siblings and parallel cousins[2] of the same sex who in

---

[1] The kinship term "cross-cousin of opposite sex" is also the term for "sweetheart" or "lover".

[2] Parallel cousins are related through siblings of the same sex.

public always try to protect one another's dignity. Thus male or female cross-cousins of the same sex jokingly wave one another off in public with, "Go, turn your buttocks to the sun. Stay there four days and get seasoned." Or, "Go, you who exhibit yourself." Siblings and parallel cousins of the same sex do this privately if they are very friendly; indeed any relatives of the same sex do this privately if they are friendly enough, but never in public. Siblings-in-law joke like cross-cousins; and in Manitoba they often are actual cross-cousins.

From the day of birth the child has been taught these forms, from the moment it was "betrothed" to its insect or other ridiculous non-human "sweetheart". Shortly after birth it probably enters into another mock betrothal, one which is arranged by two friends whose children have been born on approximately the same date. Later on, the child is goaded to the conventional contentious behavior when his parent tries to tease him by bragging about his "sweetheart" or cross-cousin. The cross-cousin or other sweetheart is treated the same way, for his parent, also, teases him by rallying to the support of the other. A man said, "When father would get me mad with teasing, my aunt (father's sister, parent of the cross-cousin) would praise me up." That is, the parents of the cross-cousin (with whom are classed the parents of any "sweetheart") act reassuringly and "respectfully" to their niece or nephew. In Manitoba the "respect" aunt and uncle often become eventually the mother-in-law and father-in-law, in which case the respect becomes so heavily stressed that it develops into avoidance. In Ontario, the respect relationship with the mother and father of the actual cross-cousin continues unchanged for there these relatives are not supposed to become one's parents-in-law; and the avoidance is confined to the actual (unrelated) parents-in-law.

The courting season is the spring and especially the summer, when people live near one another, meet at sociables, and can travel around easily. The first condition of courting is to know the genealogies of everyone in the neighborhood, so as to delimit courting possibilities. A person's acquaintances fall into groups of (1) those he (she) cannot marry; (2) those he can marry; and (3) the Ontario classification of the cross-cousins whom he cannot marry but with whom "sweetheart" etiquette is enjoined. Ojibwa villages are small and the families closely inbred, both within a village and between the villages of a region. Usually, therefore, most persons are related in more ways than one, and often in ways that prescribe opposite behavior with respect to marriage and "sweetheart" prerogatives. The relationship that should be observed is the one that is closest, and when other relationships exist they should be ignored. But between collateral relatives who are not connected in the first degree, the formal injunction is often ignored in favor of a personal preference for a relationship that is more distant but more congenial. Thus Nathan Whitefeather, after his marriage, chose to regard his classificatory "mother's sister" (mother's parallel cousin) as his "sister-in-law" because she was classificatory "sister" (parallel cousin) to his wife; by stressing the latter relationship he could be her sweetheart, as he could not in the former relationship. In the same way Leonard Wilson chose to ignore his classificatory "brother" ties with a certain young girl in favor of his even more distant cross-cousin ties with her. So private inclinations are frequently as important as the formal rules, and are often consulted in providing oneself with a greater number of sweethearts.

The second condition of courting is its objective. There are two very different motives behind the meetings of prospective spouses or "sweethearts", and the choice of one or the other motive seriously affects the nature of courtship. One objective of courtship is immediate marriage; the other is dalliance. The motivation underlying the first is the confinement of women's sexual activities, the motivation of the second is the licensing of men's sexual activities. The standards of the first require that a girl be kept in a state of prim maidenhood until her marriage night. The behavior of all marriageable girls is measured against this standard, and gross deviations from it are severely denounced. No such standard exists for boys and men. Some parents or other guardians train their daughters to live up to the standard of female conduct, and exercise a careful surveillance over the girl's private life. Usually it is the daughter of some arrogant shaman, or the ward of some cranky grandmother who is given the elegant prim finish. Especially after she has become a "new woman", the girl is carefully watched to see that she is not free in her cross-cousin contacts. Along with the inculcation of fears of kidnapping and rape go the admonitions, "Don't let a man get near you! ... Don't do anything that will make men talk (lewdly) about you! ... Be careful! Men know all about these things and they can make a fool of you!" The men referred to are of course the ones belonging to other lodges, for the men in the girl's own home are forbidden in marriage and conventionally are never identified with sex. So while the men outside the lodge can easily be thought of as monsters, those inside the lodge are theoretically a different order of estimable humanity. The brother is still worthy of confidence and love. The girl is kept largely in the company of her mother, sisters, and grandmother, doing her work, and attending dances in their company. If she stays too long in the bush, she is followed to see that she is not attending a rendezvous. At night she is kept in the family lodge, while her brother absents himself and courts as he wills. All night a fire burns brightly to deter the casual suitor who might think of visiting or lying with the girl. The grandmother sleeps with a poker, awakening at intervals to stir up the flame; the father is prepared to drag out a venturesome suitor by the legs. The girl must not be passed around from the hands of one lewd man to another; she is to be reserved for one man only, the one who will be sought in betrothal by her parents, who will be the father of her children and the supporter of her household. The girl is not to be friendly with a "sweetheart" even in the most casual way, for the symbol of her virginity is not the intact hymen, but the inability of any man to talk about her. The parents seek a son-in-law whose economic qualifications are known in detail; however the betrothal is usually contingent upon the daughter's consent. The period of betrothal is the only courtship allowed the girl. A man courting this girl does so under bond of immediate marriage; the girl's reputation is such that all men know they will be admitted to her side only under this bond. The courtship is brief, lasting only a few days, and is supervised by the elders. The girl "talks" with the boy; that is, the pair exchange a few quiet words that are not at all "joking" or suggestive in the unbetrothed cross-cousin style. After some talks, the boy creeps to the girl's side one night, lies there innocently, and slips out before dawn. Soon the girl's parents advise her to detain the young man, so one night he sleeps with her past the dawn. Courtship and legal youth are over, the girl and boy are married. Sometimes a girl talks with a young man of her own choice before her parents have made any marriage arrangements. People pass remarks about this which reach the ears of the parents. The parents will not have neighbors say of their unbetrothed daughter, "She talks with a man," and so they chaperone her even more strictly until her suitor is investigated and marriage arrangements made.

A girl's courtship is sometimes conducted more colorfully by her father, but with no less emphasis on primness. Licensed by a "dream", her father announces that he is taking his daughter with him on a war-party he is organizing, and that after the campaign he will present her in marriage to the boldest warrior of the party. A man does this only when his daughter is desirable in person and reputation, using her popularity to further his own ambition of raising a large command, since he knows that more warriors will flock to him in hope of love than in hope of mere glory. In this way Josie's father once secured the large following of forty men. Despite the fact that women are discouraged from warfare, the Amazonian girl and bride are honored, and are given the male title of "brave". Such women are recognized as unusually spirited, and some, like Josie, even have war dreams of their own. No sexual intimacies are allowed on the war-path, but after the victory the successful warrior-suitor immediately becomes a bridegroom.

Dalliance, however, is the common purpose of courtship, certainly from the man's point of view. A woman is to be had for the taking, and the flirtation with her is indulged in without thought of responsibility. In summer, boys and men (chiefly unmarried men) go around in parties to the different villages on a "woman hunt". They like to find new people with whom to engage in cross-cousin flirting, and they want new sensuous experiences. Young men rove about in search of courting adventures, and bring into play the same tactical and imaginative attitude with which they search for enemy scalps or wily game. They compose love songs to which young couples dance; girls compose romantic ballads which they sing at their work and which continue among the women down the generations.

Most girls have become habituated to dalliance through the "playing house" experiences of childhood. Loverlike irregularities were quite a matter of course during that playtime, engaged in in a prankish spirit, like the proper use of the cross-cousin etiquette. In childhood, before physical adolescence, a single standard of sex behavior obtains, except for the detail that the boy, like the man, is supposed to be the active courter. Childhood's single standard, with promiscuous love practised between boys and girls, exists not only because of the absence of adult supervision, but also because of the general attitude in the community regarding love and sex. These are considered very enjoyable, socially and sensuously. The culture-hero myths contain a great number of incidents that express this taste, and often incidents are told by men in friendly small talk; the incidents are told broadly and humorously, and sound as though inspired by the intercourse of cross-cousins. Other legendary and semi-historical tales, and even gossipy tales are concerned with sexual and romantic relations. Through the winter months older women often tell their life histories and devote a great amount of time and interest to elaborating their past affairs with lovers and husbands.

Suddenly at the time of first menstruation, the girl is brought up short on the matter of sex standards. While she is quarantined outside the neighborhood and introduced to the status of womanhood, she is told to forget all her past freedom, and to be guided instead by a standard of primness and timidity. At best, her childhood habits and the unrestrained desires of the men must clash with this ideal. But in most cases, the double standard is ignored, and childhood habits continue. The very menstrual quarantine is violated by "woman hunters". And when the child emerges suddenly as a "new woman", she attracts the attention not only of boys but also of seasoned men. Cross-cousin banter takes on a new significance. "Sweetheart" dances become less rough-house and more amorous. Courting irregularities, at least in the more innocent stages, are as certainly a condition of sociability among adults as they are among children. Community gossips, however, begin to judge the adolescent girl by the double standard. They whisper about flirtations at dances, and in the bush. Since all of a girl's early training licenses carefree love-making, it is not surprising that many present "younger generation" problems.

The role of the household relatives is now very important in the life of a girl. If she is watched sharply she may avoid intercourse and pregnancy before marriage. But often the relatives are lax in their supervision. They do not care to saddle themselves with the systematic duties of chaperonage and general discipline. The girl, therefore, drifts or is forced in to delinquencies. The boy or boys with whom she has markedly "talked cross-cousin" and who have been allowed to catch at her breasts and hips in public try to see her alone at night. The girl's bed is usually at the outer edge of the lodge-space, flanking her mother's or grandmother's. The boy comes to this side of the lodge, lifts the lower layer of the bark wall, noiselessly creeps in between the supporting side-poles to the sleeping girl, and lies down beside her. Often the tryst has been prearranged, but frequently not. If the girl does not know who the visitor is or does not want him, she can drive him away by striking him or by crying aloud to her parents. But it is always wise, girls are taught, to think twice before driving a suitor away lest he be "shamed" and retaliate by sending bad medicine. No girl should risk having it said that "she acted as though men weren't good enough for her," therefore she generally receives her night visitor. A girl usually confines herself to one boy, however. If a boy has not been sent away the night of his first visit, he has the right to return at his pleasure. The couple is quiet, so as to remain undetected by the other inmates of the lodge. If the couple are a "new" woman and a "new" man, they are children enough to consider the secret night companionship largely as great fun.

4*

They know they are doing a categorical wrong, but the wrong is still considered a prank. However a critical time for the girl approaches. Signs of pregnancy appear, arresting people's attention, starting a flow of malicious lewd talk, causing the girl's mother to nag and threaten punishment if the father's identity is withheld. The girl tells her lover of her condition. If the two like one another, they privately arrange their marriage before the child is born. But often the girl cannot solve her difficulty. The boy may be reluctant; or the girl may have had several lovers, none of whom feels responsible. Instead, each may brag about his conquest, and discuss the details of her anatomy and responses. Harried, the girl now begins to appreciate the ideal womanly conduct, the advantages of which no one had sufficiently impressed upon her.

Household relatives who themselves violate the moral standards, bring a girl into the category of delinquent in other ways than by merely ignoring her. Here belong the tales of incestuous rape, sometimes by the father or grandfather, but far more commonly by the step-father. Although such incest brands a man, the girl's reputation is more seriously damaged; she usually leaves home and may even be forced to leave the community.

There are instances of a girl's becoming a flagrant delinquent in spite of a proper home atmosphere. All-Over-Grass was such a girl, and her behavior was discussed for two generations. Orphaned in childhood by the death of her parents, both her father's two sisters and her mother's mother wished to rear her. The grandmother secured her, cared greatly for her, and determined to bring her up as an ideal young woman. So "her grandma was very strict with her, didn't want her to go with any man at all, and at night would always tie up the door so that no one could come in." But in the summer time, All-Over-Grass joined other young people, attended their dances, and "talked cross-cousin". Finally a courtship commenced. The young man expected the usual intimacies, and she too desired them. But the grandmother was bothersome, for at the slightest unexpected noise she would blow up the fire. The young man disliked this intensely, not only because it testified to the old lady's hostility, but also because he could not remain exposed by the light unless he was willing to remain as a son-in-law, and he did not care to marry. So with the girl's connivance "he fired up some gunpowder and tied it in a little rag which he tied onto a stick and shoved it into the fireplace of the old woman's tent. Then he made a noise at the door, and the old woman jumped out of bed and started to blow the fire so there would be light, and the gunpowder got on fire and exploded in her face. She was

frightened. She never did that again." Now that the old lady
was intimidated, the couple courted freely but discreetly. "The
man sneaked in and slept with this girl, but he did not marry her.
The girl used to tell him to come in from the back of the tent, and
she would lift the birchbark up for him to come in. She went
with him for a long time and at last she had a child." Her two
aunts who had previously desired to raise her, now disowned her.
The girl killed the baby when it was three months old. A year
later she gave birth to another illegitimate child. She became
sullen and silent over the censure of her grandmother and aunts.
She killed this baby too; she hated it. Her aunts said, "This serves
the old woman right. She wouldn't let *us* bring up the girl." The
grandmother became tender to All-Over-Grass and took her away
from the region. All-Over-Grass ceased her irregularities; after
some years she married a white man, "turned out to be a lady,
and forgot about her past life. But people always used to tell
about her."

Some girls are more crafty than All-Over-Grass. Thus Thunder
Woman, who was carefully guarded, did not care to challenge her
parents by inviting her lover to her sleeping place. Instead, she
met him quietly in the bush. She followed him, still without
informing her mother, when he went to a distant village. Her
persistence ultimately won him as a husband, but the entire procedure
was considered highly irregular. Thunder Woman's shamanistic
father was infuriated by the shame of it, and determined to kill the
man who had "stolen" his daughter. He worked himself into a
resentment which eventually concentrated upon his son-in-law.
First he tried to kill his son-in-law by stabbing him with a knife.
When he was prevented from doing this and released from the
strait-jacket in which some of his relatives bound him, he levelled
his full battery of bad medicine upon his son-in-law and nearly
killed him. His wife then said to Thunder Woman, "'I do not
want to stay with him any more. If you want me, I will go along
with you.' And so she got ready and left with her daughter and
son-in-law."

The girl is usually held responsible for her predicament, except
in cases of rape. Had she not been interested in "dirty" matters,
there would be no problems. She should have kept her eyes down,
her tongue quiet, and her hands busy with work. "But she was
busy with other things," they say, "... always after the men!" The
neighborhood's reaction expends itself in this quasi-punitive gossip.

The girl's family is embarrassed by the gossip, ashamed of being
discussed slightingly, even in those cases where the misconduct

has been due to neglect or to the lust of some member of the household. When an illegitimate child results, the sin assumes practical as well as social significance. The family feels that it has been "fooled ... insulted" by the guilty man who escaped with his "fun". The economic responsibility for an illegitimate child is a vital handicap in a region where starvation is always an imminent possibility and where every helpless person is a liability. It is easy to understand the strong feeling that each child should be the care of its own parents, of the people that "made" it. Not only does the girl's brother share the general resentment at having to care for the child, but in addition he is shamed at having to be reminded by the child's very existence of his sister's sexual nature, a realization which is strictly tabu. Traditionally the brother leaves the locality where his disgraced sister lives, and tries to obliterate her memory. The father, too, grieves from shame. The mother, however, unlike the men, faces the issue squarely and tries to remedy the situation by providing for the baby. The mother can talk freely with her daughter since she is not bound by inter-sex tabus or cautions. She implores her daughter to name the father of the baby, and if she learns it, she seeks to make the man marry her daughter. If no father can be provided, the grandmother kills the infant, or she rears it in her own household.

Delinquent girls themselves react in different ways to the situation. Some are sufficiently influenced by gossip and the mother's attitude to care about making the correct marital adjustment; others follow personal inclinations without regard to the conventions. Shining-of-the-Thunderbird is a gentle, sweet-tempered person, willing to follow another's lead. These qualities, rather than any boldness, led her into a flirtation. Her lover never spoke about marriage, so she never thought of it. At thirteen years she bore an illegitimate child. Maggie, her mother, demanded the name of the father, and approached the young man through his guardian, his grandmother, for as a prospective mother-in-law, she could not talk to him directly. She told him that she expected him to marry her daughter, the mother of his child. He came to the house in the night and married the girl by sleeping with her through the dawn of the next day... All-Over-Grass, on the other hand, refused to name her baby's father. No one knew whether she did not care to marry her lover or whether she resented his unwillingness to marry her... Sun Woman's daughter had a different history. Sun Woman herself had been remarkable for her general solitariness and avoidance of men; her husband was a quiet, conservative man. Her daughter however developed into a "fast" woman. At fifteen

she had an illegitimate baby. She could not name the baby's
father because she had slept with several boys and men, so she
did not marry. The baby died. The girl's excitable and passionate
traits became pronounced. She drank, even in company with her
brothers (avoidance relatives). She also fought with her brothers.
She became known as a wanton. Her parents were aghast at her,
but could not control her.

Lovers always exchange gifts, the man generally giving the more
substantial ones because he has greater means. Sometimes, perhaps
under white influence, this develops into a system of mild prosti-
tution among delinquent girls. This is the case with Falcon, who
had early borne an illegitimate child. She is a vigorous young woman,
whose flaring nostrils and gleaming eyes make a curiously intense
impression. She has a barrel-chested body which she swings along
in seaman's style, and she prides herself on her ability at all masculine work. Her energies demand also a sexual outlet. She always
said she would never marry and be restricted to one man. One lover
at a time is usually not enough for her; she has several, and since
each lover pays her, she is kept in silk dresses and hair waves. Gossip
does not trouble her. Her independent attitude is due in part to
the fact that she is known to possess bad medicine taught her by
her feared shamanistic father. Through fear of her sorcery, the
very gossips who denounce her come to her parties and witness the
irregularities.

Little Berry had an illegitimate child when she was fourteen.
She named her lover, slept with him one night in token of marriage,
and soon left him. Her parents took care of her baby. She moved
from one lover's arms to another's; the unions were too short-
lived to be called marriages. She had no abilities, and no interests
other than sociability, drinking, and love-making. After six years
of nymphomaniacal indulgence, she married.

Christina Big's behavior was unusual. She is a handsome,
excitable, rather stupid girl. She was attached to her mother, a
conservative strong character; and torn between her mother's
admonitions, and her desire to follow the pace of the young people
with whom she associated in the village. At one time she left her
home, to live with Falcon. Then, like Falcon, she took a lover, a
white man. Falcon advised her to go out with others too. She
became pregnant, but did not realize it until quite late in term
when her body became distorted. The shame unsettled her. She
cried and cried. What would her mother and sisters say? They
knew she was not "like that". She was further unnerved by the
fact that she could not marry, because her regular lover had left

her when, in a bravado coached by Falcon, she had refused to give up her other suitors. She delivered her son in hiding, then brought him home to her mother. This was eleven years ago. Ever since, she has cared for him passionately. Just as intensely, she has come to hate Falcon and all men, and has remained celibate. Recently she has been taken into an evangelical sect.

The behavior of Daisy Greatfisher   was also unusual. She is a remarkably good-looking girl, in the ideal Indian fashion, and courted by several men. When she was about fifteen she bore an illegitimate child. Daisy privately named the father to her mother. But her lover, Sanford, prevailed upon his sweetheart and her mother not to insist upon a marriage, because he was already a married man and did not wish to compromise his job in the Government service by divorcing his wife and confessing his illegal responsibilities to another. Daisy continued to live with her widowed mother and reared her child alone. Daisy's mother was an evil old shamaness who alternately denounced Sanford and defended her daughter, but who learned to put up with the situation. Daisy and Sanford liked each other so well that they were faithful to each other and continued their affair. Another illegitimate child was born and reared. Daisy would never consider another man as lover or husband. At one time Sanford tried to disguise the relation by having Daisy go through a mock marriage with another man, Harry. Daisy and Harry simply lived in the same lodge together, while the affair with Sanford continued. After two years Harry "deserted", and the affair with Sanford persisted.

A man who is named by a girl as father of her child and who is approached with a reminder of his obligations, usually acknowledges his responsibility if he knows himself to be the child's father and the girl's sole lover. As people usually marry "for love" only when they marry without coercion, any reluctance on the part of a lover is probably due to the fact that he no longer cares for the girl and is already courting another. In cases of incestuous fatherhood, usually the woman as well as the man is ashamed to acknowledge the relationship. Thus both Farrin and his granddaughter were ashamed to confess their baby's paternity. Even brazen Sweet had the good grace to be ashamed of his connection with his young daughter's illegitimate child. When girls have relations with several men over a short period of time, the men usually take the girl lightly, and no one feels responsible for the child. No one is likely to be approached with a view to marriage. The paternity of such a child is a matter for ribaldry. At one gathering of gay fellows, men lay bets on the paternity, and

one man tried to shout the others down with the assertion, *"I'm
the fellow! I* know! Because *I* was doing the work that time!"

Drunken orgies are times of extreme sex license, and young girls
may participate. Women at such times almost invariably throw
up their skirts or strip themselves and invite any man in the
vicinity, or all the men. Incest tabus are forgotten, and women
if ignored even try to force the men. Men do not undress but
creep around looking for women, usually women tabued to them,
scrupulously avoiding their own wives. During one orgy a man
walked around dropping his clothes in anticipation; first he took
his mother, then his mother's sister who lay on the other side of
their joint husband. Elsewhere a man was investigating his
sleeping sister, while his drunken wife sang lustily alongside...
Mary lived very satisfactorily with her husband and daughters.
Her husband was often gone for long periods, and at these times
Mary indulged in drunkenness and general license. Her daughters
grew up in this atmosphere, and after they had matured she made
them participate. Mother and daughters shared the same men,
and in company... Many girls are reared by mothers who are
pleasant enough normally, but who under the influence of drink
forget all standards in favor of "throwing up their skirts at a pair
of pants." Drunken fathers cohabit with any passer-by, forgetful
that children are looking on. Parents always give their children
"moon" when there is general drinking; the "moon" leaves some
people stuporous, especially young unaccustomed people. Girls and
women found drunk in the road are dragged in to the bush where
boys or men have a "picnic" with them.

Young men traditionally are the ones who organize social dances
for the village; they do this also for the adopted "white" dances,
although the older Indians refuse to attend them. "White" dances
and the new native dances based on white dance forms allow
unprecedented courting liberties, and are therefore very popular.
In the native dances each person dances alone, and usually the sexes
are segregated. The new dances require that a man and a woman
dance together, arms wrapped around each other. In this close
position, bolder courting couples press or catch at one another.
No "respect" relatives take part in these dances; they are called
"sweetheart" or "cross-cousin" dances, and even many young men
are still shy of the public liberties encouraged by these dances.

The courting interest invades even the supernatural sphere. Thus
Hole-In-the-Sky has from one of his visions the blessings of two
gracious female *manidos* who promised him success in love, as well
as a duogynous marriage. Again, an occasional man has a vision

sanctioning a sacred dance (called the "Snake Dance") where selected guests of both sexes meet, turn out the lights, strip naked, and, in the dark, walk rubbing against one another to the beat of a drum. While walking and drinking (peyote infusion?), as well as afterwards, each guest receives wonderful visions, often colored, that promise a "good life". The most common supernatural aid to courting consists of a number of love-magic prescriptions. This is considered "bad medicine" because it is irresistible and because it is monopolized by shamans who are personally too unattractive to conduct a courtship on their own merits.

The Ojibwa double standard, like others of their cultural traits, seems to be an adoption from the neighboring Dakota of the Plains. But the Ojibwa handle their borrowed trait clumsily, in contrast to the Dakota who employ the scheme intricately to satisfy a variety of honorific ends. Among the Ojibwa the double standard serves chiefly to produce a general social disorganization. The double standard seems to be unknown to the simpler northern Algonkian congeners of the Ojibwa, among whom pre-marital liberties also prevail.

PART II.

MARRIAGE.

Tribal youth or immaturity closes with marriage, no matter how early marriage occurs, nor under what circumstances. It is said, "She is no longer young, she is a married woman." The adult status that ensues upon marriage is significant because it imposes full economic obligations upon the pair. The economic responsibilities of marriage are not novel, but simply an accentuation of those which have been assumed progressively throughout youth. The outward sign of the new status is an independent domicile for the pair; from this point of view, marriage is an economic incorporation.

Public recognition of economic independence carries a train of corollaries respecting the individual's freedom and initiative. Youth, which to the newly married closed just yesterday, was the time of regimentation, when life was a ceaseless round of learning lessons under the authority of parents and, to a slighter extent all older people. Children had to be trained repeatedly, insistently, often against their will, to seek the supernatural, to fast, to respect private property, to perfect economic techniques, to play their parts in the required economic individualism, to accomodate to the confinements, opportunities, and responsibilities of their sex, to practise the courtesies of relationship. With marriage, all institutional discipline ceases. Within the limits of his horizon, of the cultural habits established in youth, the married person is free to follow his own inclinations. This new freedom is a direct result of economic self-sufficiency; a married person having relinquished claims upon a household not his own, is simultaneously released from any institutional authority over him.

It is not unexpected to find a certain lag on the part of many parents in respecting the erstwhile youth's independence. The parent still likes to correct the child, though now the latter may toss off the criticism with impunity. Certain slight institutional arrangements, which are not widely observed, sanction this parental lag. They empower the parent, if he is so minded, to arrange the marriage of his child; and, having done so, to advise in the domestic affairs of the young couple during the early years. Parents do not commonly make these arrangements. The custom is perhaps most common among those Ojibwa who prefer the cross-cousin form of marriage, when a brother and sister agree to propose the marriage to their respective children. Older couples who are friendly to one another also like to arrange marriage between their children, but ordinarily do not press the issue against the inclinations of the children. Sometimes parents are acquainted with a young person who has such desirable traits that they try to secure him or her as a son- or daughter-in-law. It is immaterial whether the parents of the girl or of the boy broach marriage to the parents of the other. If the girl's parents take the initiative, it is often, though not always, the two mothers who make the arrangements; and if the boy's parents take the initiative, it is often the two fathers who discuss the matter. If the boy's father broaches the subject, he may do so with or without the previous consent of his son. He comes with some gift offerings to the girl's father, for men always preface weighty requests with gifts. The latter accepts the gifts tentatively, until such time as he has discussed the proposal with his wife, son and daughter. If the family agree to the proposed marriage, he keeps the gifts (which include a miscellany of gun, or canoe, coat, shirt, etc.). Usually the agreement means that the boy, and girl personally are willing to marry. Each child then goes to the father or to both parents of the other, and says, "I am willing to marry your son (daughter)." The consummation of marriage follows after a short time and usually takes place in the girl's home. If difficulties arise between a couple married in this ceremonial way, the parents have the right to try to remedy them since they were originally responsible for the marriage. This is, however a ceremonial rather than a personal intercession on the part of the parents. They "have no right to interfere" in marriages for which they are not primarily responsible.

Gifts are not always brought by the girl's parents when it is they who broach marriage. This may be symbolic of the fact that women conventionally do not own much property, but rather passively accept what their men bring them. A girl's parents try to become friendly with the parents of the young man they desire for their daughter; they bring small respectful presents of tobacco and food, pass the time of day, render small services. These small acts are conspicuous and well understood, for ordinarily they are done only by relatives who are personally fond of one another. "At last, then, between them they would make plans for their children to get married, and then they would tell them, and then of course the two would get married." The parents contribute to the housekeeping of the young couple, "They give them a canoe, or something for roofing, a gun or a net, just to start their children off."

As a variant on this theme, the giving of presents is employed to placate the parents in those cases where a marriage has been arranged without parental endorsement. Such an announcement may be made by a suitor even after a girl is advanced in pregnancy. The young man states his intentions to the girl's father by presenting him with valuable gifts, after the couple (or even the man alone) has decided upon the marriage. Sometimes no further announcement is necessary: "He gives the girl's father a gun, blanket, coat, and lots of grub. And of course the old man knows by that that this man wishes to marry his daughter. So he tells the man to marry her." People today tell this story to illustrate the traditional ways: "Dubeday always drove dogs (dog team pulling a toboggan). He lived at Hungry Hall right at the mouth of the Rainy River. He used to wear deerskin pants, and a moose hide coat all trimmed with muskrat fur, and his cap was of otter skin, and his mitts were of muskrat fur. This was how he dressed in the winter. And he would always drive some dogs. .... One time he visited a place called Yellow Girls because he heard of a girl there who was very smart. She could do all kinds of beadwork. When he saw her he wished for her. He went to that place and gave an otterskin, one beaverskin, a blanket, gun, and canoe to this old man (the girl's father) and asked for his daughter. So the girl was given to him to marry. And he did marry her. The old man gave him a blanket, shot-gun, and canoe (because he was pleased with the marriage), and so he came away with his new wife." The story does not tell whether the man had consulted with the girl before making his proposal, but the attitude of the story-teller is that the girl was quite willing.

Sometimes parents act to oppose a child's marriage. A girl's parents may refuse the proposal of a boy or his parents. This is a delicate matter because the rejected people are likely to feel shamed and to retaliate with bad medicine or by drawing a knife or a gun. The girl's parents seek to mitigate the shame and vengeance by presenting large gifts to the boy or to his parents, and at the same time they keep the gifts made to them at the time of the proposal. It is not always possible, however, to conciliate the rejected party. A girl may be the slighted party. Thus there is the tale of a youth who had long been courting a girl, but who seemed to have no thought of marrying her. As fall drew near and the girl's family prepared to leave for the isolated trapping grounds, the girl's father invited the young man to accompany his family, that is, to be a son-in-law. The youth refused cavalierly, without even offering a conscience-gift. The old man brooded over the shame of the rejection, and all during the long winter pursued the young man shamanistically with famine and disease.

The efforts of a mother to impose marriage upon a daughter who has borne an illegitimate child have been described. Such a marriage arrangement is not of the same order, however, as those just mentioned. It is an effort to patch up an awkward and undesirable situation, rather than to initiate a desirable one. Despite the discredit a delinquent girl has brought upon her family and herself, her irregular past is little deterrent to love-inspired offers of marriage. Girls who have been sexually promiscuous and even incestuous and who have borne illegitimate children all marry. In most instances marriages are made, as well as dissolved, without intervention by the parents, and only on the basis of personal desires; therefore the fact that a girl has a "past" is in itself of little import. Men are never denounced for amorous adventures, which are considered rather as delightful, wicked testimony to their charm.

Economic security is a very important consideration in marriage. The parents, especially, keep economic values constantly in mind. They look for industry and skill in the respective occupational fields, and in a man, for supernatural power. They look for an even temper in a daughter-in-law. Parents consider the future as well as the present. They feel that in their old age they will have all they can do to maintain themselves, and so they dread a possible day when a married daughter, suffering from lack of food and clothes, will turn to them for assistance. There are many stories of parents who have been appealed to in this way and who have aided only their daughter, not their son-in-law. Myths describe malevolent behavior directed against a dependent son-in-law, usually by his father-in-law. Parents hope and expect to be supported at least partially in their old age by the grown children, in return for having fed and clothed them in youth, and to this end the selection of a successful son-in-law is good insurance.

Even though Thunder Woman eloped, her mother was pleased "because her daughter was dressed good". This meant that her son-in-law was able to trap steadily and successfully ... Another man was retained as a son-in-law after the death of his wife because "he was a hustler" as a hunter... Keeshka and her young daughter Gaybay lived alone for many years after the death of the husband and father. They supported themselves well enough, but when Gaybay reached nineteen years, her mother said to her, "If you had a man, we would not work so hard to get food for ourselves. The man would always support us." Gaybay herself was reluctant to marry, and refrained from associations with men. Her mother, therefore, undertook to betroth her. "She made up with the parents of a young man whom she wished her daughter to marry. And they too said that they wished for her daughter, for she was a good worker. So she told her daughter 'You must not object. Marry this young man for he is a good hunter, and he will be good to us.'"

... A dying man told his daughter that he wished her, for her own sake, to marry a young man whom he favored and in whose care he could leave her. He seemed to believe that the young man was kindly and a good hunter. His daughter Ice-Woman scarcely knew the young man and did not like him, but she agreed, to please her father. So the old man gave all his possessions to his son-in-law, including the very personal and useful canoe, shot-gun, and blanket. However, Ice-Woman behaved only perfunctorily to her husband. "She slept with him and sat with him, but she never spoke to him although he tried hard to make her like him. She never offered to go out with him either when he went paddling, and she never said anything when he went gambling or dancing. She was entirely separated from him." ... It has already been noted that occasionally a man arranged a war-party with the intention of awarding his daughter to the most distinguished warrior. Such a son-in-law was desirable because his prowess testified to supernatural power which could protect him in economic fields as well as in warfare. A warrior had to be a hardy, courageous person, skilled in precisely those ways that are useful in hunting and trapping. Sometimes at the Victory Dance a girl was awarded by her father to a distinguished warrior even though the father had had no part himself in the war-party.

Parents sometimes arrange a marriage that is primarily a payment for services. This takes place when a girl who has been desperately ill is cured by a medicine man. The parents then hand the girl over to the doctor; their view is that without him she would have lost her life, and since he brought life back to her, she belongs to him. This is no euphemism on their part; it is believed quite literally that the doctor succored her with his power, poured his supernatural power into her, and so she belongs to him just as his very doctoring power does. At the same time, since a girl is desirable in herself, she is viewed as a munificent gift which properly rewards a great service... Great Mallard Duck was a medicine man who already had two wives. One summer he was in a village where a young girl was being fruitlessly treated by many Indian doctors. Her illness continued, and her parents finally called Great Mallard Duck. "They told him that if he could doctor her back to life he could take her for his wife." And so he did.

The attitude of prospective mates rarely reflects the parents' fine concern for economic security. Young men and women prefer to arrange their own marriage, largely on the basis of attractiveness and sexual charm. Lovers have a completely romantic attitude that counts the world well lost for love. This view is so important that it sometimes leads girls to flout marriages that have been forced upon them by the parents. So Gaybay simply ignored th eyoung man whom her mother brought to the house as son-in-law, and won her end, for after ten days the husband left ... Similarly Ice-Woman had nothing to do with the husband whom her father urged upon her... Eternal Man simply fled from the man her parents accepted as a son-in-law, got lost, and married the charming stranger who rescued her.

For the same reason, girls ignore the parents' express prohibition of marriage. Thus **Bluesky** had a psychotic hatred for any man who belonged to the category of son-in-law or prospective son-in-law. She said she wanted to protect her daughters from unworthy men. She continually abused the husband of one daughter, and the lover of another. However, the unmarried daughter paid no attention to her mother's wishes, continued to see her lover, and after she became pregant married him.

Many marriages take place without reference to parents. People who are romantically attracted sleep through a dawn into the married state, without notifying the parents verbally or by gifts. These marriages are from the start private, independent affairs, and are usually contracted with equal good-will by both parties. Parents or other guardians sometimes are offended by such a procedure. **Bluesky**, a very high-strung person, hanged herself after her daughter married without notification. The father, however had no objection to the marriage ... Old Mrs. Greatbear raised a great commotion when she found her granddaughter **Blue Star** married. Blue Star was heiress to a pension allotted to her deceased father by the Government, and gossip said that her grandmother disapproved because she feared losing control of **Blue Star's** income... In most cases, however, the parents' resentment seems to be an expression of sheer wounded pride.

Sometimes a proclamation of marriage is made by some relative after the marriage, or open sleeping-through-the-dawn, has taken place. One pregnant girl who fled from her wigwam because of her mother's hostility, was taken by her lover to the wigwam of his parents. There they slept through to the next morning, and were awakened by the shouting of one of the man's male relatives, "So-and-so came home with a wife last night! So-and-so came home with a wife last night!" The proclamation is of no import; it is simply evidence of a prize piece of gossip.

A suitor's craving for the person he loves or simply lusts after, sometimes becomes so extreme that he overrides the objections of parents and even of the desired one. Such suitors are medicine-men and medicine-women; their amorous conduct is consistent with their general arrogance and malevolence. They are usually successful at least in initiating the marriage. In some cases this success is said to be due to the use of love magic, but generally it is simply that the weaker individual yields to fear of sorcery. If shamans are repulsed, their shame is greater than that of the average person in the same degree that their power is greater. Their vengeance is proportionately violent; they punish recalcitrance with winter starvation, *windigo* insanity, general paralysis, amentia, senile degeneration, "twisted mouth", death in various forms. In the following story, although the proprieties of marriage proposal and gift were observed, the marriage was brought about only through fear of a shaman's revenge. Painted Bow was sickly in her youth and went four times through the newly introduced *mide* ceremony, hoping that this new rite or treatment would cure her. At her fourth ceremony, the head shaman was Shandioo, a man "old enough to be her grandfather. She was about eighteen years old at the time and was a nice-looking young squaw. Shandioo fell in love with her and wanted her to be his wife. But even after they were through (with the curing ceremony), she did not realize how this old man felt towards her. Only after she was asleep in their wigwam did she know that someone was after her; and several nights later she knew it was this old man. So when he would come there at night she would crawl away from where she was lying, and she would go to where her parents lay, and crawl in between them. Her father would kick her, thinking she was a dog. She would not say a word, and he would keep on kicking her till she would nearly fall into the fire-place. So at last her father took notice that she was always crying and sad and wouldn't eat. She would not do any work because she was always kind of hiding, and when night came she would sleep in a place where no one could find her. (Until that time) she was a smart girl, always getting birchbark, cutting wood, making mats, but this she ceased to do. That was why her father took notice of her being sad and quiet. He told his old woman (wife) that she should try to find out what was

5

wrong with the girl (only people of the same sex can talk intimately).
So her mother told her that she wished her to help her set nets.
They did this. She had a good chance then to ask the girl what
it was that had hurt her feelings, and asked her to speak frankly.
The girl said, 'The reason I am like this is that I'm ashamed that
an old man wants me for his wife. I'd sooner die than marry him,
because I hate him. And another thing is that I am afraid he will
use his bad medicine on us and have death come upon us.' The
woman told her daughter that what she said was true, 'He might
make you crazy, or destroy your only brother through bad medicine,
and if we married you to someone else, he would do it just the
same.' They went back, and when they reached the wigwam, her
father was sitting with his head down and tears in his eyes. And
he looked up, and all he could say was, 'Oh, my poor daughter'.
Then she went into the tent, and she saw two brand new Hudson
Bay blankets, and a new gun. While she and her mother were
setting nets, this old man had come and asked her father if he could
marry her. But the father did not answer him. The girl started to
cook their supper, and while she was sitting there she made up her
mind to kill this old man when he came back that night. She heard
her parents talking, and she saw her father come out with a big
bundle on his back. He took it over to the old man's wigwam and
tried to talk to him, but the old man shoved the bundle away. He
didn't want it, and didn't speak at all. The father just left the bundle
and came back to his own wigwam. That night she sat up holding
an axe, ready to kill him any time he came. She waited and waited
and at last fell asleep, and when she woke it was daylight. She got
up less sad, because she thought that the old man was not going
to bother her any more. For about ten days she was happier and
less afraid of this old man. But one night after she had gone to bed
and fallen asleep, she woke and found that someone was sleeping
beside her. She knew it was this old man, so she started to cry. She
did not know how to move, or how to get up. Every time she
moved she fainted (people always become more or less paralyzed
with terror when near a medicine man). She fell asleep again. In
the morning her mother spoke to her while she was crying, and told
her to get up and cook for the old man. She got up and cooked and
fed him, and all the time she cried her heart out. She never spoke
to him or sat with him. She always had her back to him, and he
never bothered her any (never made sexual overtures... The
narrator describes his wealth, derived from his prestige as a versatile
shaman, and from his hunting prowess. He was often away from
the wigwam, busy with his doctoring). So she was with him seldom,

and she hated him with all her might. The things which her father had given, the old man returned. At last she stayed with him so long that she gave herself up to him and lived with him (sexually). (Then the old man used the girl as his assistant in shamanistic practise. After five years the girl bore a son). She always lived near her parents. Her husband was good to them all. But she kept away from people because she was so ashamed to be seen with an old man for a husband. (This is not altogether a dread of actual age and consequent senility, for this man was an outstandingly able hunter, and esteemed for his general alertness; it is a dread of lechery, and also of sorcery, for "old man", said in a certain manner, means "sorcerer".) She always stayed in their wigwam."

Since male shamans outnumber female shamans, and are reputed to have the greater relative power, it is they who symbolize the offensively individualistic conduct, who typically insist upon personal gratifications at all costs. Individual women behave in this way when they can (see story of the shamaness Iron-Woman, pp. 62—63), but any man with supernatural power is *expected* to; it is his prerogative. Where normally a man has only one wife, the shamans have more than one. Polygyny itself serves to emphasize the superiority of the male shaman over the female shaman, for even when the latter does choose to commandeer a husband, she cannot have more than one at a time.

The high-handed behavior of the shaman suitor always arouses resentment on the part of the girl, her parents, and her young lover if she has one. Sometimes the resentment is discharged in violence and the shaman is injured, though the girl and others may be killed in the process. At Northwest Bay there was a great diviner, whose standing was amply evidenced by the tributes of food, whiskey, and goods that the Indians brought him at intervals. "When a young girl was sick he would tell the people that she could live if she married him. Once a couple gave him all kinds of goods, piles of stuff, and lots of groceries, to get him to tell whether a certain girl would live or not. A lot of people were there to hear him. So he started, and he said that the girl would get better if she married him. A young man was present who wanted to marry this girl because he loved her. But the girl had to obey her parents and marry the old man if he saved her. The young man got mad, and while the old man was divining, the young one, who was drunk, went to the back of the (divining) tent... (He looked through the back wall, and saw that there were no supernatural visitors in the tent as there should have been, but that the diviner was employing only sleight of hand to obtain his effects. The young man tore

5*

down the divining tent and exposed the shaman.) That was the end of the old man's divining. He didn't live long after, and the young man married the girl."

Another case had a tragic outcome. Pahwah was a great medicine man, in much demand and collected heavy fees. When he doctored girls, he desired no other fee than to have them in marriage. He secured three wives in this way. The third wife was a girl he had been called to cure at Shoal Lake. "She was about eighteen years old and he was about forty. He saved her for himself and married her. One of his grown sons was in love with her. He became ashamed of and resentful of his father for continually marrying new wives. 'Why don't you ever think of us when you save a young girl? You should save one for us to marry.' The father answered, 'You should try to save one for yourself. I saved all these girls and they were given to me to marry. If you want a wife, go and save one for yourself!'" The son and his young step-mother became deeply attached to each other, "and the girl was so much in love with him that finally she didn't know what to do. At last, after a month of marriage, she hanged herself with her leather strap. She didn't like the old man, and yet she didn't like to wrong him, so she just killed herself. She had gone away early in the morning, probably because the old man had bothered her. The young man told his father, 'Next time you doctor, don't ask for a girl. Get goods and food. Young girls do not like to marry an old man like you. You just spoil them (that is, 'You cause their deaths')."

In still another case, a bitter feud, deaths and suffering resulted from a medicine man's claims upon a girl. Great Mallard Duck cured a girl of grave illness and consequently took her as his wife. But "there was a young man who had his mind set upon marrying the girl. He hated the old man for taking the girl as his wife, and he said he would get even with him some way (the stereotyped shamanistic threat). The young wife was very unhappy but she stayed there as she feared that otherwise the old man would do something awful to her. The old man and his other wives were very good to the young wife... In the fall they moved to the husband's hunting grounds. He was a good hunter, and brought home all kinds of meat. His family had three wigwams. In one wigwam the young wife stayed with the old man, and in each of the others was a wife with her children. All that winter they lived very well; they had all they needed of fresh meat and furs. But about February something happened. The old man went out hunting, but he failed to kill anything. At last all the meat was gone, and they had nothing to eat. All the animals were afraid of him (because they would not stay to be shot or trapped). He could not even snare a rabbit. He became weaker every day, and after days of walking around with nothing to eat, he was so weak one morning that he could not get up. He spoke to his wives and children and said, 'Now my children, I can't do anything for you any more, so get ready while you are strong enough to walk, and go elsehere to try and make a living for yourselves. Leave me here to starve alone. If you do not go, you also will starve here. Our starving is the doing of someone whom I angered. (This is understood to be the defeated suitor who had threatened vengeance.) If you stay with me while I am starving, I might become a *windigo* (and eat you up)!' His (guardian) spirits no longer came to him and that was why he was so sure that someone was using bad medicine on them." The family stayed, however, until one desperate day a wife left with her children. Some days out of camp, they killed a bear and other meat. They returned with the food, and discovered that seven out of the camp of sixteen persons had died of starvation. The dead included the young wife and the husband. The survivors broadcast the news in the spring. "The father of the young woman knew that it was the young man (the defeated suitor) that had done this to the seven. He was very angry, and grieved for his daughter. He determined to revenge himself upon the young man. Once he saw him talking and laughing. He got so mad (mere casual laughing always infuriates a shaman who is passing by and who feels excluded) that he took his axe, went up to him, and said, 'You are the one that killed seven Indians and you were the cause of my daughter's death. I hate you for that, and you are not fit to live, so I am going to kill you right here.' He hit him on the forehead, and killed him. That was the end of him. The Indians had a big meeting and decided that no one should say anything about (voice objections to) the old man's killing, for the other had destroyed seven lives, and it was fitting for him to die too. But the father of the young man was also angry and killed the old man by his bad medicine, and it went on like that between them until the white people came, and that was the only reason why they learned to be good friends."

The insistence upon nursing one's self-esteem by gratifying whims of all sorts is emphasized in the satisfaction of marriage desires, and leads readily to violations of the marriage prohibitions. Sections in Manitoba and in northwestern Ontario favor marriage between cross-cousins, but forbid it between other relatives. In other regions, as Emo in southwestern Ontario, there is a blanket tabu on marriage between all relatives. Also, everywhere members

of the same sib are considered to be brothers and sisters and are
forbidden to marry. However, forbidden marriages do occur
among relatives of all categories except those of actual parent and
child, or of actual brothers and sisters; and even among these
groups occasional incest occurs (See *Ojibwa Sociology*, part 3,
Marriage). Incestuous, forbidden marriages function essentially
like proper marriages. The pair that lives together openly is
considered husband and wife, though of a harmlessly scandalous
sort, and the children are legitimate, though they bear a certain
malicious stigma. In the early days of the marriage, the bold pair
are maligned in whispers as "dogs" or "animals".[1] Their young
children are similarly compared to some animal form; if they are
the offspring of sibmates (people who inherit the same totem
name), they are likened disdainfully to their eponymous totem
creature, and called "bears" or "lynxes", i. e., "not-human". But
the disdain matters nothing, and after some years it is forgotten.
Girls of such a union are sought in marriage, and boys of ability
acquire the same renown as other boys, conventionally born.

Marriage is a mode of life that all are expected to adopt. Yet
not all care to do so, and this private inclination, too, can triumph
over the institutional requirements. Some girls delay marriage
until late in life; others never marry at all but remain single, and
live alone apparently without any homosexual intimacies. These
girls are never called "old maids" or considered to be eager but
frustrated women; they are called only "women who live alone."
However, their reluctance to live in the normal way is reprehensible,
since its motivation is reputed to be unworthy pride or snobbery.
People say, "She thinks no man is good enough for her"; they are
offended by what they understand her attitude to be, and want
to see her punished. Some myths are concerned with the theme of the
beautiful girl who did not care to marry, thereby aroused the
resentment of her suitors and sometimes even of her brothers, and
who was finally humbled by shamed and vengeful suitors. Abstinence is never confused with chastity. Abstinence is considered
a negative attitude of insulting indifference; whereas chastity
is a positive attitude of desire held in leash.

The life of Iron-Woman is generally taken to exemplify the
undesirable character of abstinence. She was a renowned shaman,
the only child of a great medicine man who had taught her all his
wisdom. She remained single for forty years, her sole interests

---

[1] The species of animal varies with the offender's sib: an offender of lynx
sib is vilified as "lynx", one of beaver sib, as "beaver", etc.

being trapping, hunting, and the many games at which she excelled. She never desired a lover or husband; "she thought they were not good enough for her." (It is probable that she did make this remark, for it is typical of a shaman's arrogance.) Her parents, too, did not care to have her marry. But at forty she fell in love; "she wished for a young man about twenty years old." Since she herself was no longer young, she decided "to use love medicine on him. And sure enough, not long after that the man started to come to her. He was a nice looking young man and his parents thought a lot of him. He was respected by other people also. When his parents knew he was after this woman, they tried to stop him, but he would not, or could not, for such is love medicine. And the parents of the young man hated her very much for she was too old for him. Also his sisters and brothers hated her. But he turned against his own people because he was so crazy for this woman. ("Crazy" here is used literally, for love sorcery has a profoundly mesmeric effect, leading a person to extreme lengths which are ordinarily foreign to him. She and her parents moved away from the village, and the young man followed her. So she married him. A day later the parents of the young man went to fetch him, but he would not leave his wife. So the two old women (the mothers) had a great old quarrel. His mother said, 'Your daughter is old enough to be my son's mother, and it's a shame to have her ruin my poor boy'. And the young man told his mother to get into the canoe; he shoved his parents out into the water and told them to go away.". . .

Love medicine returns to its "owner" when its mission is accomplished, and its evil power brings misfortune to the owner. This was the case with Iron-Woman. She had by her young husband three children all of whom died in early infancy of horrible sicknesses. This was the retribution for Iron Woman's prideful abstinence, for had she married in youth she would have needed no love medicine and would not have suffered the consequences of its use.

The abstinence of some girls cannot be explained in terms of pride. They are generally shrinking, "shut in", and fearful of men. They are abstinent in spite of the fact that the guardian urges marriage. Sky Woman was a talented and warm-hearted person who had fled her home at the age of nine, frightened by violent quarreling between her parents. She had been adopted by a loving, lonely old woman, and lived with her for sixteen years. The couple lived alone, and were isolated during a great part of the year. They supported themselves my male and female arts, and wanted for nothing, not even for the power to cure illness, which Sky-Woman possessed. Sky-Woman "was a good quiet girl. She never went with any young man, or spoke to one. Her grandmother told her one time that she should now get a husband. But she said, 'I don't care about having a man to bother us!' She said this because she remembered how her mother and father used to fight, and she thought all men were alike and beat their wives, and so she never wished for anyone. Her grandmother made a bed for her on the other side of the fireplace (so that she could sleep there alone and entertain a man unembarrassed), but she never slept there. Always she slept with her grandmother. So she stayed single for about twelve years (after the first menstruation)." After her grandmother's death, she lived alone, disconsolate. She refused to live with anyone else. Her married sister lived near her one summer, and "her brother-in-law used to bother her an awful lot. He wished for her. One night when she was alone, he came there and wanted to sleep with her. But she took a brand that was still on fire, and hit him with that and sent him out. So she made up her mind to go away from there, because she didn't want her brother-in-law to bother her." But soon she did marry, since she was lonesome. She was then in her late twenties, "not what you would call young."

Gaybay lost her father when she was twelve or thirteen, and for the next seven years lived alone with her mother. The two supported themselves, and lived comfortably on the proceeds of the fur they trapped. When Gaybay was already "about nineteen years old, she had not yet gone with any man. She was an odd kind, a quiet girl. When she was among people she always removed herself from sight. Even in the tent she never talked up to people. She never went with girls either. She went around with her mother only. And her mother used to talk to her often, telling her to try to get married. But she refused to talk about the matter. Once when they were among Indians (the village season, in summer), a young man came to the tent, to try and court her. But she jumped out of her bed, and ran to where her mother was sleeping. Her mother said to her, 'You mustn't do that when someone wants you. You have to get married anyway, and people are making fun of you.' But she would not obey her mother, and would not listen to her at all. She said she was awfully scared of men. The old woman told her daughter, 'If you had a man, we would not work so hard to try and get food for ourselves. The man would always support us.' So one time she discussed the matter with the parents of a young man whom she wished her daughter to marry. They said that they also wished for her daughter, for she was a good worker. She told her daughter, 'You must not say anything. Marry this

young man, for he is a good hunter, and he will be good to us.'
Gaybay did not answer her mother at all. The next day the old
man took his son's belongings to the girl's tent, and the young man
went along. He stayed there about ten days, and all that time she
never spoke to him. At last he picked up and went home to his
parents. He never bothered her again. The old woman was very
sorry for the young man, and she told her daughter not to do that
again." Eventually the girl married several times, but never
satisfactorily, for her husbands were lazy or brutal or died pre-
maturely. The girl's mother came to believe that all this trouble
arose from the fact that her daughter was really not suited to
marriage. So she reversed her earlier admonitions, giving this
advice to women, "Mothers, never tell your daughters to marry
when they don't want to. Let them stay single if they want
to."

Small-Warrior-Woman's "quietness" was even more marked.
She hated and feared her step-father and her mother's co-wife.
There was continual scolding and sulkiness in the household.
The girl begged her mother to desert her husband, to live alone, but
her mother refused gently, saying, "One day you too will get
married and know what it is. You will not want to leave your
husband." When she was about sixteen, she fled in panic from her
step-father's attempt at rape. After that, in the village she was
very sober among the young people, did not "talk cross-cousin",
and none of the young men ever approached her. Some time later,
her step-father attacked her again; then she and her mother left
the man and lived alone. She married a young man, but after
two months chased him away because he was lazy and used to
fight with her. "So she was pleased now that he was gone," and she
lived with her mother. Several years later, the mother died, and
left the girl desolate. "She was always alone in her own wigwam.
No one ever helped her with anything. She just made a living
for herself alone. She never had much. She missed her mother
very much." Years later she died. "No one knew what happened
to her because she was always alone, but her canoe was found on
the lake. The wind must have blown her over, and she must have
rownded. She had never married again, nor had any children.
And she was no kind of *manido*-talker (visionary)."

Some men are permanent bachelors, and abstinent, but they
are not criticized as abstinent girls are. No stories are told of such
men. Indeed, no thought at all seems to be given to bachelorhood,
whereas tales of abstinent girls and bachelor women go on forever.
This is consistent with the double standard of conduct which

requires that a girl's private life be minutely regulated, but which permits a man's to be left to his own discretion.

Sometimes the matter of marriage was taken altogether out of the girl's hands by an enemy warrior who captured her and tried to keep her for his own. This was a fairly uncommon but recognized procedure among all the tribes of the region. Some captive-wives tried to escape, and succeeded by killing the enemy husband, or with the assistance of an enemy co-wife. Others reconciled themselves to their lot. A tale is told of one such woman, whose conduct is believed to have launched the classical enmity between the Ojibwa and the Sioux. She was captured by a polygynous Dakota (Sioux). Later her Ojibwa husband and brothers notified her that they had come to rescue her. In her loyalty to her abductor, or in her perfidy, she betrayed her brothers and husband, caused the death of her brothers and had her husband left for dead. The following year the Ojibwa husband led an attack against the Dakotas, and the feud between the tribes continued thereafter.

The pretentious marriage form is polygyny.[1] It is usually the shamans (men with power to cure, power to divine, power to lure game, others with war-like powers, etc.) who are distinguished by polygyny. Plural marriage is a sumptuary display on the part of men because the provider of the household's food, clothing, and small luxuries is the man, the husband claimed in common by the several wives. Among the Ojibwa, there is no public verbal boasting, such as is licensed among neighboring tribes; but the possession of plural wives is a tacit boast of some force. Outstanding ability to furnish provisions is a gift of the supernaturals, acquired in a vision; and this association of values awes and wins a wife, and also keeps her. Ordinary men are rarely polygynous. In the first place, they will not usually attempt to live beyond their means, for even their best standard of living is but slightly above the subsistence level. In the second place, should they splurge polygynously, they very shortly find themselves corrected, for the earlier wife leaves. The first wife leaves because the presence of a second wife shames her. She knows that her husband has taken another wife because of some personal allure, and this preference constitutes a reflection upon her own charm, upon her unique place in her husband's regard. In true European narcissistic fashion, a sexual partner pins his or her self-esteem upon the other's reaction; and when this reaction is no longer exclusively favorable, as is evidenced by a man's efforts to be polygynous,

---

[1] Polygyny has been made unlawful, but it is still practised in certain regions.

the wife's self-esteem is punctured, she his shamed, and she retaliates by deserting. Even the wife of a shaman, to whom fear is very vivid, occasionally deserts because she is outraged by her husband's plural marriage. A woman's feeling of "shame" is aggravated by the talk of the villagers. They consider that the first wife has been set aside by the succeeding one, and audibly speculate about her sexual incompetence and about her husband's sexual needs and escapades. If a woman stays with her husband under these conditions, the villagers take it as acknowledgement of her inability to get another man. So it is sweet to the wife to revenge herself both upon husband and gossips by leaving.

Thunder-Cloud was happily married to an ordinary man named Friendly-Place. They lived comfortably, for the man was a good hunter. After about eight years of marriage, the Indians convened near their home at Nor'west Angle for their first treaty payments. "There were lots of Indians gathered there from all over the Rainy Lake, some from the Rainy River, and Friendly-Place went around visiting and was never home nights. In the daytime he came home, but only to sleep. His wife never cared. She thought he was out only to see what was going on. But in time she noticed that he acted queer with her (did not have sexual intercourse). About ten days after treaty, he told her that he was going to War-road (village on the American side of the Rainy River). After his departure, some women told her that he was after a girl whom he had met at treaty time. The next day she saw a canoe coming with her husband and a woman in it. He left the girl down the bank in the canoe, and he came up alone with two pieces of print. The wife was sitting finishing off a cedar bark mat, and he threw her these two pieces of print. She did not scold him, but she took the print and pretended that she was glad about it. He said he was hungry and she gave him something to eat. She pretended to know nothing about the girl in the canoe. She just talked and laughed with her husband. About two hours later, the man got up and went over to his mother's tent. His two sisters ran down the bank and got the girl's bundle and brought her up to the tent of the first wife. The wife told her sisters-in-law that there was lots of room in the tent for the girl. The girl was so awfully scared that she sat down outside. The first wife pitied the girl, and didn't say anything to her. When night came they went to bed; the man lay down where his wife was, and slept with her; so the girl slept alone. The wife didn't say anything to him; she pretended that she didn't care. In the morning the man went out and got some fish, so they had fish for breakfast. They were out of meat, so the wife said after breakfast, 'Why don't you go out and see if you can kill a moose so that we may have some meat ?' Her husband answered her, 'We (meaning 'you and I') will get ready and go.' But she said, 'You have another partner, why don't you go with her ? I'll stay home for I am more accustomed to the things around here and know what to do.' She got them ready and told them to take the big canoe so they would bring a lot of meat home. Before they got into the canoe he ran back. She was in the tent, and he came in and kissed her and told her, 'I love you more when you are so good-hearted, and I will always be your husband, and you will always be the boss. Whatever you say will be done, and if she (the second wife) wants to be mean with you, I will take her back home.' This is what he said to her, and he and the girl went away. As soon as they were out of sight, the wife got herself ready too. She took the best of everything. They had just bought a pair of red blankets at treaty, and she took those. She took one of their new canoes and a gun, everything she needed, and she returned to Grassy River where her mother and sisters and brothers lived. About ten days later, the husband came there alone, to persuade her to return home. She told him that she was not going with him because he did not need her any more—he had another woman in her place. Then he said he would go back and return the other woman, and afterwards come and fetch her, and everything would be the same as before. She said no, everything would not be the same because he made her feel shamed when he took another woman while she was still alive; he was never to return again, he was to forget her. He said that he would come anyway and find her no matter how far she went." But her husband never did get her, for the humiliated woman soon left the neighborhood and married another man.

There are many stories of the bitter enmity between co-wives, founded on shame, and often resulting in desertion. **Johnny**, the chief of Hungry Hall, was married to Giantess. "When treaty was first given out at Nor'west Angle, he fell in love with another girl named Grey Girl, and married her. He went back and forth between his two wives staying with his new wife a while, and then returning to the other. The women never saw each other. He went on like this for quite a while, until the treaty arrangements changed. Now, all the people from Lake of the Woods, and from Hungry Hall up the Rainy River had to go to Fort Frances for treaty. So all the Indians met in Fort Frances on July 15th. The blueberries were ripe already. **Johnny** went with Giantess. His second wife was already at Fort Frances. The chief and his first wife got off, and he took his things up, and of course she took her things and

went up also. The Indians were gambling, so she sat there, but
the man went to look on. She did not know where they were going
to camp. There were tents all over. She got up and walked to the
nearest tent, and as she was looking through, Grey Girl splashed
boiling blueberry jam on her face. She was badly burnt. She had
not known that this woman was living in the tent. Her husband
had to call an old woman to put medicine on her face, neck, and
ear. Johnny had intended to keep his two wives if they could get
along together, but they couldn't. The young girl was jealous
of the main wife. The first wife became mean after she was burnt.
She made her husband promise that he would not return to the
second wife, and he agreed provided she would not gossip about
the quarrel. ... Some months later, the Indians held a dance.
Johnny was getting dressed, and he scolded his wife because she
had not made him a pair of new moccasins. Spitefully he went
out to his young wife and got moccasins from her. Of course the
first wife did not like that, because he had broken his promise to
keep away from the other woman. After her husband went to the
dance, she could see Grey Girl going in to the dancing place...
Giantess packed her things and got her canoe ready. After she was
ready, she sharpened her butcher knife ... people saw her doing
this ... and she walked to the lodge where they were dancing.
The lodge was of birchbark, and Grey Girl was sitting with her
back to the bark wall. Giantess lifted the bark up and spoke to
her, 'My, you hurt me badly the time you burned me. Now it's
my turn to hurt you.' So she cut her face from her nose to her
ear ... she cut her cheek right open, and cut a piece of her nose
and ear off. She said to her, 'I am leaving you with my husband.
You can have him all to yourself. I can go and get a man who is
not some woman's husband.' Then she went down the hill and into
her canoe, and she went away down the river."

Sitting-Woman was the second wife of Bigsby. His first wife
had been her elder sister, Rabbit, who had deserted him years
before. The elder sister was a charming, flirtatious woman who
used to return to the village at intervals for titillating experiences.
Once when Rabbit was without a husband, Sitting-Woman was
certain Bigsby would take Rabbit back as a plural wife, and therefore
left him abruptly and would not return.

The wife of a shaman must be strongly motivated to desert her
husband, because she knows well that the man has the power and
the will to injure her frightfully in revenge for the slight of as-
serting her will in defiance of his. Yet desertion does occur, though
not as frequently as in the case of ordinary men and women, and

it is often precipitated by the wife's smarting under polygyny.
"When Woman-Covered-All-Over was a girl, she and a young
man were in love with each other. But her parents wanted her to
marry an old man (euphemism for shaman). She did not care for
him, she was in love with a young man. The old man did everything
to win her love. He used all his bad medicine (love medicine) on
her, and all at once she could not help loving him. She knew that
he was using medicine on her because she was so crazy for him. She
did whatever he wished, and went wherever he wanted her to. So
her parents told her to marry him. She did, and lived with him
for about ten years. Then she turned against him, for he married
her older sister. The older sister had been a widow for two years,
and then he got in with her and married her. He wanted the two
sisters for his wives. He was a great shaman, or *manido kazo*
("one able to talk and treat with the supernatural") divining by
polter-geist methods and curing by sucking and blowing, and he
knew all kinds of herbal medicine. He was a good hunter ... he
used to kill moose and bears, and he always had a lot of fur to sell ...
he was a hustler. But she turned against him because he married
again, and left him, and went to live with her parents. For three
years he used to come there and ask her to return to him, but she
would not. Finally he came and told her that if she would not
return to him, he would give her bad medicine that would make
her as helpless as a baby, unable to walk. So she got sick and was
helpless for eight years. Her mother had to care for her like a baby;
by the ninth year she could crawl around, and by the tenth she was
able to walk. Then she got married right away to another man."

If a shaman's wife does not dare to leave her husband, or wish
to leave him, she may yet suffer all the shame and jealousy of a
wife who does desert her polygynous husband. Pahwah was a
noted curer. Once he cured his wife's younger sister, and the
patient was given to him as wife. "His first wife got awfully
jealous of her sister. She used to paint her face with coal (so they
would not see her in the dark) and watch them sleeping."

The very ghost of a deceased wife once acted toward her successor,
who was also her younger sister, like a jealous co-wife. The younger
sister was walking alone along the road when "she heard Someone
saying, 'Eh! do you love the man you are married to?' The frightened girl said, 'No.' But It kept on saying, 'Yes you do, yes you do.'
The girl tried to deny it, she was so frightened now. The One was
right behind her talking to her, repeating that same thing, 'Do you
love him?' And when she said, 'No I don't', then It would answer,
'Yes you do.' She tried to walk a little faster ... she could see the

wigwam now, and a big fire. Still the One kept on talking to her ...
she knew it was the ghost of her sister ... and she was awfully
scared. She got to the door of the wigwam, and as she lifted the
blanket to go in, It pushed her and she fell right into the fire. The
old woman (her mother) was cooking some fat, and it was boiling.
The girl fell and upset the grease, and all she could say was, 'Oh,
it's my sister that's doing this to me! She's been following me all
the way, asking me if I loved the man.' That was all she could say,
and she died. The man got mad, for he had learned to love his new
wife very much, and he jumped up and ran outside to where the
body of his first wife lay (it had been kept intact over the winter,
frozen). He kicked it and hit it, 'So you are alive, eh? For all the
trouble we went through carrying your old body along, you've
destroyed your sister too!' And with that he let it go, and went back
to the wigwam. He was so sad to see the burnt body of his wife.''

A shaman's co-wives sometimes reason themselves into a jealous
toleration of one another. Thus the first two wives of Great Mallard
Duck, the medicine man, were able to live together peacefully
because each realized that she had been given in payment of the
debt of life itself, and furthermore that even had Great Mallard
Duck wished, he could not have refused her as wife for fear of
offending the parents who had magnanimously made the gift ...
When their husband took a third wife, the first two were able to
extend their toleration to her as well.

Co-wives who were at first institutionally jealous of one another
may become mollified in time, and learn to appreciate one another's
personal qualities. Star-Kin-Woman was hated most cordially
by the first wife of her polygynous husband. For about five years
there was no lessening of the elder wife's carping and gloom. Then
gradually she became gentle, and ultimately loving. Eventually
Star-Kin-Woman felt compelled to desert her husband because
he was attacking her adolescent daughter. "As she was packing,
the elder wife came up to her, begged her not to go, not to leave
her ... she said she would miss them so, would be so lonely, she no
longer wanted to live alone with their man ...''

There are cases where co-wives get along pleasantly from the
start. The basis of such a relationship lies in the friendly nature
of the first wife—a person to whom sociability is more important
than the customary shame. Such a wife is not necessarily indifferent to her husband, only she has not dramatized the marital
relationship in the conventional way. She simply likes,the company
of another woman. Sometimes this liking, or a promiscuously
friendly attitude, finds another unconventional expression in

cooperative relationships with the co-wife. Ordinarily the wife of
a polygynous husband conducts her housekeeping and other
responsibilities independently, as though she were the only wife;
each wife occupies a separate lodge or a distinct compartment in
a lodge, and completely duplicates the activities of every other wife.
But in these unusual, friendly cases, the wives to some extent pool
their work and resources. They privately modify the institutionally
unitary character of polygynous marriage — its functioning as an
aggregation of monogynous marriages — and make of it a cooperative
organization. This private variation of the polygynous marriage
has, of course, no social sanctions behind it, only unreliable personal
sentimental ones that any accident can alter . . . Shaboyez acquired
two wives at different times in recognition of his warlike accomplishments, one of his wives belonging to the neighboring Cree people
and one to the Ojibwa. The wives got along together beautifully.
"They never quarreled, they liked each other a great deal. The
first wife did not have any children, but the second did, and the
first wife took care of the children just as much as the mother did."
. . . The shaman Great-Standing had four wives. He was a huge
man and ate gargantuan quantities of meat, ten rabbits at a
breakfast being his ordinary meal. He employed his four wives
primarily as cooks. "He just kept those four women busy cooking
enough to feed him." The man must have appeared ludicrous to
his wives, for they fell into a comradeship whose chief basis was
private ridicule of their husband. They also exercised a discrimi-
nating forbearance towards one another. One fall starvation struck
the family. Great Standing was in a furious temper, and the wives
sat about idle and forlorn. Finally Great Standing resorted to
talking to the supernatural, and was rewarded. "When daylight
came, he went straight to a cedar swamp with his gun. One cedar
was lying there with roots up, and he said to it, 'Come out! Quickly!'
and a big bear put its head out, and he shot it and killed it. He
went home. His wives were sitting all around the fire with nothing
to eat, and he spoke to them and said, 'All right, old women, run!
And the first one that gets there will be the one to have the bear
(titular ownership, for institutionally wives do not own in common,
only individually).' So the women got up. They all seemed to obey
his orders, whether it was because they liked him or because they
feared him. So they ran. One of his wives was kind of sulky and
jealous, so the other three women let her get there first. She was
the youngest (and newest) of the wives."

Forever-Standing had two wives, and was able to support them
because of his success in hunting. The wives were friendly, and

even united against their bad-tempered husband when he abused one of them. They never competed with each other, and one never sought to play the husband against the other. One wife, Two-Skies, was unfortunate with her three children, for they each lived only to an early age and then died. Perhaps because of this, "her husband always fought with her ... he kicked her and was awfully mean to her. Then his two wives would get after him and they would lick him ... Finally Two-Skies parted from him."

Chief-Earth-Woman married her lover-companion-in-arms after a war raid. Her husband was already married to a conventional quiet woman. The first wife accepted the distinguished co-wife without comment. It may have been that hostility was precluded by the Amazon wife's prestige and supernatural qualities. When the first wife "saw her husband coming home (from the warpath) with this girl, and coming right to her wigwam, she was just as happy as the rest (the villagers who were rejoicing over victory and dancing the Victory Dance). She danced away with the Sioux scalp that her husband had secured and brought home." People cheered Chief-Earth-Woman, and she danced around with her captured scalp and her song of success. She and her lover received feathers for their deeds, and then went to his wigwam as man and wife. "They lived happily. He had children by his new wife, and his wives never quarreled."

Some shamans and other men of means choose to avoid the responsibilities of polygynous marriage, but feel free to satisfy promiscuously their sexual whims. Marten had two wives, and was not interested enough in the display possibilities of sex to acquire more. He delighted rather in terrorizing his neighbors, one result being that young girls were so transfixed with fear as to succumb to him for a night. He used lurid methods of sexual excitation, and was considered bestial, but his general behavior seems to have been motivated sadistically rather than sensually ...
Ahtushkish was a wellknown man belonging to the neighboring Cree people. He was well-liked, and was especially attractive to women. He was physically pleasing, gay, daring, and played the fiddle. As a Hudson's Bay trader, he continually crossed the country to pick up the Indians' furs, and therefore he had the opportunity to relieve the monotonous life of many a woman alone in the wigwam while the husband was out on the trails. "Once he stopped and slept at an Indian's wigwam, and a girl was given to him to marry. He did marry her. He took her along and brought her to the Hudson's Bay Post and made a home for her there. He would go out trading and leave her there. After four years they

6

had three children. (There follows the story of an unmarried girl
who came to Ahtushkush with their illegitimate child. She proved
the regularity of their relationship by the numerous gifts he had
given her. He provided for her until he married her to another man.)
So he got out of this. He continued to go out trading all the time.
On one of his trips he came to another wigwam where there was
an old man and his two wives. One wife was a very young girl.
The old man was all kinds of a *manido kazo* (capable of a variety of
shamanistic activities). The young wife had been given to him
because he had doctored her when she was very sick. When the
trader went there, the girl fell in love with him, and he flirted with
her. (This distinction between the girl's "falling in love" and the
"man flirting with her", i. e., "man using her lustfully, rather than
sentimentally", is not conventional, but is made discriminatingly.)
He used to go there often. All winter he went there and when spring
came, and the ice was just about breaking up, he went there for
the last time. When he left for home, the girl followed him and
caught up with him before he reached home. So he went along
with her and told her to stay somewhere else. He left her in one of
the houses, and he brought her groceries and goods for her to wear.
He went there often. (After a time) the girl came to him with a
baby and said it was his. He gave her clothes and money and told
her to go away. Finally she did as he said. (Shortly after, a young
girl was brought to him by her mother, carrying his baby. He
recognized his responsibility, and supplied the girl with money,
but he did not marry her) ... Once, when he was going among the
Cree as a trader, he met an old man (shaman) who had three sisters
for wives. The youngest of the three was the one who liked him,
and a sister helped her to go away secretly with the trader. They
went away ... but he did not marry the girl after all. That was
the great style among the Cree, for a man to take away another
man's wife, or for a woman to take away another woman's husband.
The trader was a regular flirt, but he really loved only his wife.
He had eleven children by his wife, and seven by other women ...
(Though he did not marry the women who bore his illegitimate
children, he recognized his paternal relation to the children of these
women. For) ... his children that he had by other women all came
to him, and his boys worked there with him for the Hudson's Bay
Company" ... It does not seem that he avoided polygyny because of
pressure from his wife, for she was always cheery and indifferent to
his amours, contented with his generous support. He simply did not
care to encumber himself with an assemblage of women; he wanted
only one woman at a time, for pleasure and company, and when

he was not at his own home, he picked up a woman at each stopping place on his route.

Paybahm also flirted promiscuously, though without the excuse of loneliness and homelessness. He and his wife and children lived in a village to which they returned each summer, and it was part of Paybahm's summer sociability to make love among the women. However, he never took a second wife. He liked his wife, although she was fearfully jealous, and battled continually with him and his mistresses.

Women cannot have plural spouses simultaneously, but only successively. Polyandry is not even tabued, it is just so ridiculous that it is beyond consideration. When occasional polyandry does occur, or is but adumbrated, it is jeered at for its sexual implications. People wonder how the wife divides her favors, whether the husbands attack her simultaneously, whether they quarrel over her, whether she is physically wearied by them, what kind of men can endure the divided ownership of a woman, which man fathered which child, what was the influence on the foetus.

Only one case of unmistakable and long-continued polyandry is known. It took place under unusual circumstances, and was maintained because of aberrant attitudes. Earth-Eternal was married to Small Ice and lived at Hungry Hall. They were both quiet, unassuming people and worked very nicely together. One spring they went on their trails after bear, "and as they were getting to a trap, they saw a big bear trying to work out of it. The bear got away before the man had time to shoot it, and it grabbed him and threw him about six feet, striking his gun away. The woman fled with her son to the canoe, and waited there for her husband. She waited and waited and at last thought that the bear had killed him. As she was sitting there, she heard a yell and knew it was from her husband. She got out of her canoe, went back to the bush, and commenced to call, asking if he was living, and he yelled back, 'Yes, but not for very long.' She ran to her husband and found him nearly crushed to pieces. He said to her, 'Run for the gun.' After she got it she asked him where the bear went. He said it left him nearly dead. It had just tossed him around. The man had pretended he was dead, and the bear had smelled him and left. As the bear walked, his claws dug deep into the ground he was so mad. The man tried to crawl. The flesh of both his arms was torn deep, also his body, his hind part was gashed, and on his side near the stomach he was almost torn open. That was what nearly killed him. At each move, he bled terribly. The woman made some kind of carrier, and carried her husband down to the

6*

canoe. He was like a baby on her back. She put him in the canoe and paddled to the nearest place, where an old white man lived, named Randalls. She thought the old man could do something to stop the blood flow. The old man came down when she pulled ashore, and sure enough he helped her. He took the man out of the canoe and washed the wounds, and bandaged them. After he finished, he said to Small Ice, 'I will send you to Kenora to the hospital, and you will stay there until you get better. If you stay there, and while you are gone, I want your wife to stay here. I will have her as my wife and will pay her so that she will make a living for your boy.' About three hours later, the steamboat came, and it took the man down to the hospital, and Randalls went with him. Before he left Small Ice told his wife, 'You can stay here while I'm away, and work for this man, and if he wants to marry you, you may marry him because I won't get better anyway. Just be good to my boy. And even if I do get better it will be all right because no Indian could make me better anyway (this skepticism is not uncommon, and is no sign of cultural breakdown).' The woman stayed at Randalls' place but she did not go into his house while he was away. She and the boy took care of the cows, pigs, and chickens. No one lived close by. Only across the water were there other farmers, and about a mile away on the same side people were farming. From across the water someone came to milk the cows while Randalls was gone. When Randalls returned he told her that her husband was all tied up and put on a nice bed, and that the Indian agent was going to look after him, and if she wanted to see him sometime, she could go on the steamboat to visit him. 'But I want you to stay right here and work for me while he is away.' She did not answer anything, and started to cut poles for a wigwam. The man came over and asked her what she was going to do with those poles. She told him she was going to make a wigwam, and he helped her. When she finished her wigwam, Randalls asked her if she was going to stay there, ans she said, 'Yes,' but he would not let her, and asked her to stay at his place, so she did. This was about four days after her husband left. She told him that there were still some bear traps on the trail. She went with him to see them, and they brought home two bears. She skinned them, dried the hides and the meat too, and cooked it, and Randalls ate the meat as any Indian would. He helped her with everything, and when he went to town, he brought back shoes for her, and print, and some other things. She was now getting well acquainted with him, and he always came and hugged her while she was working. She knew now that he was after her, but she did not mind as her husband had given his permission (to live with the man sexually).

"One day as she was living there with the white man, the steamboat stopped, and a man yelled, 'The man who was at the hospital died. He lost too much blood!' So they thought her husband had died. She cried an awful lot, and Randalls tried to comfort her and cheer her up. At last she decided to marry him. He told her they would go to Fort Frances on the steamboat. When the boat passed, they got on and went to Fort Frances and she was baptised and they were married by the church. He bought nice clothes for her and for her son. Now she was Mrs. Thomas Randalls, and her boy was baptised with the name of Billy Randalls. When they reached home, her husband asked her if she would like to visit her husband's grave. She did want to, and again they went on the steamboat, to Kenora. She saw the Indian agent and asked him where her husband was buried. The agent said, 'He is not buried yet and I don't think he will be buried because he is getting better. He is still in the hospital. That was a different man you heard about. He shot himself and died from loss of blood.' She did not know what to do now that she was already married to Randalls. She went to the hospital and saw her husband, and she took her son. The man thought it was nice to see his wife and son dressed like white people. He was pleased to know that his wife and son were kept right, but she did not have the heart to tell him that she was married to Mr. Randalls. Randalls bought nice clothes for Small Ice and gave him some money, and told him that when he got better he was to come to his house and stay there with them.

"They returned home, and she stayed there as his wife, for he thought a lot of her and loved her. But she was sorry and lonesome for her husband. In the fall about September, just when the boat was going for the last time, Small Ice came back. He was not quite well though he had stayed at the hospital all summer. He stayed there at Randalls' and no one ever objected. When spring came, he was better. He helped Randalls put out his crop and helped him with everything else. The woman cooked for the two men, washed for them, mended their clothes. She was good to both of them. A year later she had a little girl by Randalls. At that time the Indian slept upstairs, and she and Randalls downstairs. They used to have a nice time talking. Both men were good to her, and liked her very much. Next winter Randalls went away to the (lumber) camp, but the Indian remained and took care of the cows, pigs, horses, chickens; and he lived there with his wife. She had a little boy by him. In spring, Randalls returned. He did not say anything when he knew that his wife had had a baby by her other hus-

band. Again they started plowing; the Indian did the sowing, and
the older boy was now big enough to help. They made a fence,
Randalls holding the posts while the Indian pounded them in. The
people who saw them made fun of them, but they did not care as
long as they got along. In the evenings they would sit around on the
hills, watching the people passing by. The Indian went out moose-
hunting, duck-hunting, and fishing, and brought all the game home
to his wife. Randalls worked, and brought home lots of money to
his wife. The next child she had was a little girl; so that was two
little girls she had by Randalls, and three boys by the Indian. But
her children were all baptised and went by the name of Randalls.
Randalls knew that the boys were the Indian's, but he did not mind.
He cared for all of them just as though they were his own, and he
also cared for Small Ice. He never said a wrong word to either the Indian
or his wife. But when the two girls got big they started to tease the
old man, Small Ice, until at last he picked up and left. He had
stayed for fifteen years with his wife and the other husband. He
took his oldest son, Billy Randalls, with him, but he left the other
two boys. When Randalls knew he was leaving, he tried to coax
him back. But he never returned for good (because of shame); he
stayed only for short visits. When Randalls went away to the
lumber camp as cook, he asked the Indian to mind his farm. He
did, and stayed there all winter, but as soon as Randalls returned,
he left again. For about twenty years, he went back and forth to
see the Randalls. (Neighbors moved in and coaxed the woman to
drink. One winter while the Indian was living there, minding the
farm, she got drunk at a neighbor's, so sodden that she stumbled on
the way home, fell down, and froze to death. Her husband was not
with her, having remained at home.) Randalls was called home,
and only after he had come the woman was buried. So the two men
were left widowed. After the burial Randalls said to Small Ice, 'She
was your wife just the same as mine, and that's why I always left
her with you. Why didn't you take care of her while I was away?
You could have stopped her from drinking, and if you had looked
for her and brought her home that night she would not have frozen
to death. I'm very sorry to lose her, for I loved her very much. I
will miss her an awful lot.' Small Ice did not say anything for he
knew it was true, and he felt sad himself. Then Randalls told him
again to remain as he was going back to camp to work.''

This case was atypical if only for the reason that the living
economy was sedentary; the men's chief occupation was the supervision of Randalls' farm, and they lived therefore in one neighborhood. But polyandry is not feasible under the Ojibwa hunting

economy, for adult males individually own their hunting and trapping territories, and these are necessarily far apart. In the Randalls story there were many unusual features. Small Ice was under the deepest obligation to the white man—obligation for his very life—and this is a debt which an Ojibwa never forgets. The benefactor was in addition an esteemed white man, whose whiteness marked him as "supernatural", and brought the Indian under his influence. Randalls on his part must have been a forbearing soul, and also sensible of his obligations to Small Ice. The men never felt themselves a threat to each other; to the Indian, the white was a benefactor-in-extraordinary; to the white man, the Indian was a devoted assistant and the direct source of his domestic felicity. The woman, too, did not behave typically; she was not shamed over being at the disposal of two men, yet she did not have the irresponsible attitude of a wanton. She did not think of playing one man off against the other for her own profit; she felt equally responsible to both; and since a white man had initiated the situation, she probably felt that it was legitimate.

Such a marriage is not known in true Indian surroundings. Domestic isolation, and the tremendous susceptibility to shame, shatter such situations in the bud. One of the men, or the woman, must depart. A wife herself could have only contempt for one who would consent to be a co-husband. While co-wives are conventionally equal in status, male co-lovers or co-husbands can never be. A man whose wife takes another man as husband is succeeded by that man, not associated with him. To be succeeded or replaced in love is to be defeated in general, to be shamed. To be sure, co-wives are faced with the same emotional problem, but the forms dictate that their resentment is improper; whereas with men such an attitude is obligatory. A man cannot admit that another is more desirable than he, has greater powers or charm. Despite his obligation to Randalls, if Small Ice had had more spirit he would have chafed under the polyandrous arrangement. It was probably made tenable for him by the small margin of Randalls' being a white man, and therefore superior to Indians.

Albert exemplified the typical attitude toward polyandry. He fled from his beloved wife as soon as he realized that she had entertained a lover, and retaliated by divorcing her and taking another wife. The misdemeanor had occurred during one of his frequent and lengthy trips to the trapping trails. He used to be gone for ten or fifteen days at a time; and it was during one such absence that a passing fur trader stopped at his camp and lived with his wife for nearly a week. Sexual misdemeanors, with polyandrous foreshadowings, occur in the summer when a number of people gather in the village. One summer, the wife of Peshegos carried on a love affair with another. Peshegos thought he could circumvent the other man by moving away with his wife. "He said to his wife, 'Get ready, we will move away from here'. He knew that this other man was after his wife. So they left by canoe, and as they were going along, they saw another canoe behind, so they waited. Here was the man with whom the woman had been flirting. Peshegos said to him, 'We will go ashore here. You can have my wife. I won't be mad or sorry. But one thing I want you to promise, take good care of the baby. Only if something happens to her will I be mad.' (By feigning indifference to his wife, Peshegos saved his pride and slighted the suitor.) The woman (who was thus discarded) got out of the canoe. This other man sat down. He was rather afraid of Peshegos (for only a brave man, one with power, discards a wife). Then Peshegos went away. He just took his little boy. The woman stood there looking at her (departing) husband, and the man spoke to her, 'Huh, I suppose he's leaving you for good.' And she said 'Yes, and it's all your fault.' He said, 'Well, come along with me,' and they returned to the Indian camp and married." Sandy Black irregularly took a second husband during the absences of her husband Arnold. Arnold used to work on the river steamboats. During one of these periods, an American Ojibwa visited Little Forks where Sandy and her parents lived. He stayed with her, and consequently was considered to be her husband. Sometime later, Arnold returned from his season of work. He knew nothing. "What could Sandy do? She had to sleep with Arnold, so the American left. Then once Arnold got drunk with John Small, and John told him, 'Your wife is a female with two males...!' So Arnold left Sandy, and she had no man at all."

Marriage by levirate or by sororate is an enjoined form totally removed from the sphere of personal feelings. Often this obligation forces a woman into a polygynous marriage which it is a serious offense to repudiate, but which is repudiated nevertheless by both men and women. This marriage belongs to a category different from that of the usual initial marriage. It disregards marriage as an expression of personal desire, to stress the concept that the initial marriage is perpetual, not terminated even by the death of one of the contracting parties. This remarriage according to levirate or sororate is influenced by the sib organization. The sib organization provides that if a spouse dies, his or her place is to be filled by a sib-mate, preferably but not necessarily related by blood. A sib ceremony must be enacted before the widowed spouse can be remarried legitimately. The sib of the deceased takes the attitude that the surviving spouse has "destroyed" the deceased as though by sorcery, and has therefore offended the sib-mates of the deceased. He (she) must compensate the sib for its loss by paying heavy damages, and must further absolve himself or herself by a show of good behavior for several years (the mourning period). Until a survivor has paid these damages, he is indebted to the sib of the deceased. The survivor's payment and protestation of good behavior constitute the ceremony by which the sib reinstates the widowed spouse in its good graces; and the sib emphasizes the reinstatement by shortly remarrying the survivor to a sibmate of the deceased. (*Ojibwa Sociology*, part 3.) In the folklore, even a supernatural sanction for the sib rite is found, for the ghost of a deceased spouse tries to kill the debtor who has shamed the ghost by re-marrying irregularly.

Just as individuals flout the regulations of the initial marriage, so they ignore their indebtedness to the sib, ignoring thereby the sib's right to supervise their succeeding marriages, and slighting its gift of levirate-sororate remarriage. Marital "debtors" are liable to severe physical punishment from members of the "creditor" sib, especially from the actual siblings and other close relatives of the deceased; also, they are stripped of their property. Indebtedness is, in fact, so common that the very ones who punish a debtor are often themselves indebted to another sib; but this circumstance does not check their wrath. A high awareness of the social importance of cancelling the sib debt parallels an equally strong impulse to flee the debt when personal inclinations so dictate. A punishable debtor is one who carried on a flirtation during the period set aside for mourning, or who marries without having passed through the sib rite. He (she) is punished by the creditors whenever they encounter him. Sometimes the guilty debtor submits to his punishment quietly, and feels keenly the public exposure; but others, men and women alike, are defiant and resent punishment. An occasional outcome of the second attitude is shamanistic feud, initiated by the debtor who resorts to sorcery.

Two-Skies was mistreated by her first husband, Forever-Standing, so she deserted him. After some time she married a young man, good-natured but shiftless, and she had to support him. About four years later, she and her second husband visited Hungry Hall, the village where Forever-Standing lived. When she arrived there, he demanded her back, and retaliated for her desertion by scaring her second husband away and causing him to freeze to death. Then she had to re-marry the first husband. In time, he died. Two-Skies and her co-wife stayed with the parents and siblings of the deceased, working out their indebtedness in good behavior and drudgery. In the fall the entire group went to the hunting grounds, where they nearly starved because of bad medicine sent against them by the parents of Two-Skies' deceased second husband. Two-Skies injured herself and therefore was left alone at the camp while her husband's relatives departed in search of more fruitful territory. They had told her they would return for her, but when they had not come after five days, she left. She visited the parents of the young second husband, and they were glad to see her; then she stayed with her own parents. She was bitter against the family of Forever-Standing for their insolent treatment, and she decided not to finish the payment of the sib debt. Two years later she and her sister went to Hungry Hall to visit the grave of her first husband. When his brothers and sister saw her, they attacked her, plundered her possessions, tore her hair. They were furious because she was living in comfort and had not reimbursed them. They reduced her to such a desolate state that she had to borrow a canoe from some villagers. When she departed, she left the challenging message that "she would marry the first chance she got and wasn't going to give them the pile of stuff they wanted." A year later she married an elderly widower. He was a great shaman, much feared by all. He was reputed to have an unrivaled command over the most disastrous of bad medicines, and he taught all his knowledge to her. She lived with him many years, during which time the creditor relatives of her first husband gradually died from horrible deaths. "Some became blind, some crazy, some crippled, some just got sick and died." They all died in the mysterious, systematic manner that evidences bad medicine. So Two-Skies secured her revenge, having completely lost sight of the sib's institutional rights and of the fact that her own conduct was reprehensible.

There is no social control over marital separations, as there is over marriage by the kin and sib groups; from the view point of the community there is no concept of separation, but only of marriage. As there are no mechanisms for divorce, it can only be private. Consequently the only endorsed remarriage is the one that follows upon the death of a spouse and is of the levirate-sororate character. Ideally, the conventional remarriage is not an additional marriage, but a patching of the first and only marriage at the point where one spouse failed it, so that it can limp on forever.

But the conventional remarriage, like the conventional marriage, in many cases does not find favor because it is at odds with personal whims. Remarriages are almost invariably additional marriages, and like other irregular marriages are always recognized. Women remarry unconventionally as often as eight times, sometimes remarrying a former husband.

Widowhood and divorce provide the woman with the widest liberties she will ever enjoy, if she wishes to assume them. She is free of any supervision, for the marriage that removed her from her parental home conferred an irrevocable title of adulthood. If she prefers a single to a married life, she will not be judged arrogant as she would have been in her youth. She has a choice between supporting herself and her children alone, in her own domicile, and joining her parents or other close relatives to whose domicile she will contribute her labor in return for raw materials. The first alternative is preferable to most women, for there is a certain shame, or liability to shame, in an adult's dependence upon a family not strictly his own. The first alternative requires the assumption of male techniques in hunting, trapping, fishing, canoe-making, and supernatural powers, in addition to the numerous female techniques. A number of lone widows have been noted for their competence in bisexual tasks. A widow can become as distinguished a personality as a man, and it is during this period that many women manifest shamanistic abilities.

Illegitimacy is frequent among widows. It is reprehensible and punished by the creditor sib, but the unconventional widow manages the situation with a coolness or a defiance that is never seen in the delinquent young girl. The widow, with her greater sexual sophistication, engages deliberately upon prospective illegitimacy, having decided that the personal satisfactions will outweigh institutional censure. Also, the widow is capable of supporting her child, as a girl is not, for she has broken her dependent relationship with her parents long ago, established her own domicile, and is economically independent.

A widow's private remarriage, like a divorcee's, is always at her own discretion. A few unconventional widows never remarry. This results only from the woman's personal preference, for the Ojibwa scene is flooded with male protestations of romantic love and offers of sentimantal marriage ... Sky-Woman married late in life, after the death of her grandmother. She was widowed in early middle-age and chose to spend the remainder of her life alone, although she was desired in marriage. This was consistent with her early behavior, when she had been explicit about the fact that she did not care for male companionship: indeed her husband had had the quiet, complaisant traits of her grandmother. After her husband's death she had a dream visitation from her grandmother, felt a new assurance, and lived alone, following the bisexual occupations she had learned in her youth... The mother of Blanketed likewise never remarried. She had been widowed as a young woman, and alone reared her three young children to adulthood. She was a courageous happy person, skilled in bisexual occupations. She was so contented and competent that her children never wanted for anything; "they were always happy; the only thing they feared was the Sioux." And even when their village did suffer a Sioux attack, the widow again proved her resourcefulness, even saving whole families. For these deeds she won the title and feather of bravery ... Keeshka was widowed in her ripe youth. She was fully aware of the economic advantages in marriage, and indeed insisted that her daughter marry but she herself never remarried ... Marsh-Woman deserted her first shaman husband for another whom she loved passionately. The latter was injured by the first jealous husband, crippled so badly that until his premature death Marsh-Woman had to support him and their daughter. Though desired in marriage after his death, she steadfastly refused to remarry. She lived alone with memories of her unfortunate lover-husband ... Often widows have certain objectives so clearly in mind that they are willing to wait years for the suitable remarriage. Ice-Woman as a girl married the man to whom her dying father had betrothed her. She disliked the man and felt no remorse at his early death. She returned to live with her widowed mother, and the two got along splendidly. After some years, her mother remarried, and urged her to do the same. "Ice-Woman answered that she would not marry again to please another ... she would marry the man that she herself liked, and if she could not find anyone she liked she would stay single forever." She remained single for about thirteen years, and then married a man whom she loved and trusted. "Only then she knew what love is." ... Two-Skies remarried when she found a person capable of aiding her in her vengeful designs against her creditor sib. After his death she did not remarry ... Deceased's husband was killed in a bitter feud. After his death, Deceased did not care to remarry. She was occupied with thoughts of revenge upon the widow of the man who had killed her husband, placing the blame for the murder at this woman's door. She camped alone in the bush with her children, and during the next seven or eight years she bore four illegitimate ones. At the end of that time she married, unconventionally but desirably, a man who was the chief of Hungry Hall, and a great shaman. After fifteen years of happy marriage, the shaman died; and because she liked him so well and desired to make a public demonstration of her feeling, she made a conventional marriage to his brother ... Beehgokway never remarried after the death of her husband, but this did not deter her from bearing children. With her two legitimate children, she lived alone in the bush, quite capable of rearing them unaided. At one time she lived near a logging camp. The camp cook liked her and was good to her, provided her with food and other luxuries, and so she bore him two illegitimate children. She did not marry him, but tenaciously retained his two children.

A widow sometimes approaches the father of her illegitimate child in the hope that he will marry her. But she does this only when she really desires the man, and it is personal desires that determine the man's response. One summer the shaman Coming-Cloud left his village for another and stayed away all season. The following year he returned to his own village, and the people felt relieved as they depended upon him for certain ceremonies. "Later, in the fall, a (widowed) woman with a humped back came to him. She had a child of his and she was bringing it to him. The man went down to the river and took his baby and the humpy-back woman. The baby was all beads." The description of the baby's luxuriant appearance that follows implies that the illegitimate mother came to her man proudly, not beseechingly in the manner of an unmarried girl, but full of respect for herself and for him, and certain that he would not refuse but could only desire to take her and her baby into his home. Yet marriage was not originally intended, or the baby would not have been born illegitimately. "It was tied in a cradle, it wasn't laced. But it had two wide cloths, and they were all beaded, and even the cloth with which she carried it on her back was beaded. On the cradle was tied some porcupine heels, and some little beaded bags containing the navel cord, and all kinds of round sticks which were little nets. The baby was fixed fine. Coming-Cloud took them to his shack and had her for a wife."

Divorce is nearly as common as marriage. Some people are divorced not once only, or even twice, but seven or eight times. Everyone who divorces, remarries. Divorce implies that common interests are at an end, either by consent of both parties, or by the decision of one spouse alone. Divorce in Ojibwa approximates the status of "desertion" among us. It is institutionally ignored. No one has the right to interfere seriously with the affairs of another couple, or of another domicile, and this policy of non-interference applies also to the concerns of a separating couple. There is, therefore, no influence to counteract the momentary distempers which usually cause marriages to break up. An Ojibwa never lost caste because he was known to have separated from a number of spouses. No one has the right to censure a deserter publicly, for public rebuke is an infringement upon self respect and causes personal shame. Pat Red Hawk's first wife denounced him publicly before the Indians gathered from miles around for their annual payments; and all Pat's relatives and sib-mates were overcome by shame. They were shamed, that is, by the rebuke, not by the fact of separation.

A foreign influence has recently entered in the form of the Canadian Government Agent, to whom the Government has delegated the role of peacemaker. The Government insists that Indian marriages be monogamous and permanent; it enforces its will with threats of jail and withheld subsidies. A number of persons continue in the old tradition, especially those living in the hinterland; but those living on the more civilized reserves (the location and grouping of a reserve are those of the aboriginal summer village), especially the young couples, are now made to "stick together because of the Government." In other respects, all unions are as troubled as in the orthodox days. A new morality, however, seems to be developing in response to Government pressure, so that the young people, even those who themselves have deserted several times, say, "Nowadays they don't respect a man who changes his wife." This new morality has a certain foothold in the older traditions that a deserter should leave the vicinity of his or her spouse. Today when the Indians are restricted by the Government to one reserve, after the first marriage a deserter cannot esaily remove himself from the spouse's presence (and resentment), therefore all separations and remarriages take place on the same reserve.

Divorce, or desertion, is carried out in varying ways. The most "respectful" form requires husband and wife to talk over the plans for separation, or one of them to openly threaten separation. This form involves the minimum shame for the deserted spouse, for he or she at least knows in advance what is going to happen. Often a person learns first from others, through gossip, that the spouse has deserted for good and perhaps is already married to another. This is taken to mean that the deserter has no concern at all for the deserted one; and in this society which has cultivated so keen a sensitiveness to shame, it is a severe blow ... Albert left his wife when he discovered that she had casually betrayed him. He departed in stony silence, without a word of explanation. He went to the nearby village at Warroad, Minnesota, and asked a girl to marry him, still without a direct announcement to his wife.

The girl agreed, but her father and brothers objected, claiming that Albert was still married. The girl ignored the objections of her family, and lived with Albert, but after a time he listened to the girl's father and brothers. He went to the camp where his first wife lived with her children, "and brought her back to the place where he got her, Garden Island. He left her there with her parents, and left her for good." . . . Friendly-Place offered to return his second wife, if the first wife would return to him . . . Pat Red Hawk and his wife lived at Hungry Hall. Without his wife, Pat accompanied a group on a visit to the Manitou Reserve. There he remained and lived with a daughter of Chief George. After a time, his first wife was informed of his betrayal by Manitou visitors to Hungry Hall. For revenge, she struck back at him with verbal contumely. . . Thunder-Cloud heard of her husband's threat to beat her, so she never returned to their wigwam, but left without notifying her husband and walked one hundred-odd miles to her natal village. Later, both she and her former husband married others. In the same extra-insulting way —without notification — she walked out on her second husband when he took an additional wife. . . Ahtushkish also quietly "picked up his things and left his old woman," who not long after married another.

Desertion sometimes takes an extreme form, where a husband abandons his wife under cruel circumstances. A man's work carries him to isolated regions, far out on rivers, and to uninhabited islands, or deep in the woods. Often, he takes his wife along for company and assistance, and this arrangement enables him to desert his wife by abandoning her to probable death. A woman has no such opportunity to torture or surprise her husband, though sometimes in a rage she attempts to kill him outright. Husbands who desert in this way, and so cause the wife's death, claim a certain immunity from blood revenge by the wife's family, for they assert that the wife was lost in a storm or in some other way. Hawk-Woman was a gentle wife who suffered much at the hands of her husband. He delighted in torturing her, he beat her, until she cowered far away, left her periodically for another woman, watched her grief without rejoinder, and at last returned to her only to turn on her again with kicks and repeated desertion. The woman continued quiet and receptive and faithful. One spring they went out moose-hunting. "They traveled by canoe up the Lake for two days. The third night they stopped on the shore. The next day they killed two big moose, and she cleaned them, and dried the meat. So they (separately) went up into the woods to get some

birch to make a birchbark wigwam, and also birchbark for a canoe.
She came down with her load of birchbark, and saw their gun there,
so she took it along and went back for another load. When she
returned, their canoe was gone, also her husband. So she was left
there alone with no canoe. But everything else was there ... her
kettles, tea pail, knives, all her clothing and blankets, and she also
had the gun. She walked along the shore thinking that her husband
was out paddling, but it got so dark that she returned to the wigwam
and went to bed. The next day she waited, and still he didn't
come. Then she knew that her husband had left her there for good.
She made up her mind to stay until death came to her. She made
birchbarks, tanned the moose-hides, and pounded meat, and then
she got some cedar and made the frame of a canoe. She stayed
there and did all her work, made mats, and all kinds of things.
She had her sewing with her. One evening she went around the
point of the bay and sat there. She saw a moose in the water.
She waited until it came closer, and then she shot and killed it..."
The tale continues, describing her further capable conduct in this
difficult situation, doing the work of a man and of a woman as well.
Later she was discovered by a young man, who married her, and
from him she learned that her deserting husband had "told her
people (relatives) that he lost her, and that he hunted and waited
for her three days. He had lied to them about the place where they
had been hunting, so all the people had gone to the place where
she was supposed to have been lost, and searched for her, but they
finally gave up and thought her dead by that time. Her husband
had married again."

Gaybay was a far more spirited person than Hawk-Woman, but
she had the same difficulties with her husband. "He was a hustler,
but he was awfully mean to her. He used to lick her an awful lot.
Then one time, about three or four months after they were married,
they went out hunting on the lake, just the two of them. He got
mad at her and started to give her a beating. He kicked her and
clubbed her until she could not breathe at all. When he thought
her dead, he threw her over on a rock and covered her up. He came
home and brought the news that he lost her, but he did not tell
just where. Then the old woman (Gaybay's mother) got into her
canoe and went along the shore. Gaybay had only pretended she
was dead (so that her husband would not beat her any longer).
After he was gone, she crawled out and washed her face. She was
aching all over. She was on an island with no way of getting to the
mainland. She had nothing to eat, no axe, and nothing to cover
herself with. She could hardly see. Both her eyes were swollen

and bruised. She was there about three days, and was about starving. She kept shouting for help. This old woman was going along the shore, and she heard someone yelling on the island, so she went to it. She had with her a young girl, and when they got to the island, there was Gaybay sitting on a rock, all bruised and swollen. The old woman got out of her canoe and ran to where her daughter was sitting, saying, 'Oh, my poor girl, such an awful life you're in, to be treated like this by your man!' And she said, 'Yes, mother, and you always told me I would live well if I married a man, any man. Here I am, bruised and half-killed, and nearly starved...' So she took her daughter home, and when they got there, the man was already gone. He never showed up, for he really thought he had killed her."

A form of divorce is found occasionally, though chiefly in the memories of informants, which is identical with a form found among neighboring Plains tribes. This is the dance of divorce, or the "throwing-wife-away-song." Among the Ojibwa, the dance is viewed entirely from the man's viewpoint: it is a public occasion upon which the man displays his "bravery" in discarding something that is dear to him. The designation of bravery is awarded for any display of fortitude: "throwing away", or risking, one's life on a war-party in pursuit of scalps or horses, throwing away much money or furs in gifts at a give-away dance, a woman's yielding her illegitimate child to its real father. And since a wife is usually, or has once been, the love of a man's heart, the ceremonial throwing-away is indeed so extravagant, so gratuitous an act that it merits the term bravery. However this bravery is viewed with disfavor by the Ojibwa. It is "crazy" to give away something for nothing, and the title of bravery in this context is considered "nothing". Besides, women, and most men, too, have a concept of personal dignity that is altogether opposed to such cavalier disposals. No woman belongs to a man to the chattel-like degree that sanctions an arbitrary disposal of her. A man may attempt this, just as he may attempt to take the life of another person, but the woman has the right to retaliate, just as have the relatives of a murdered person. She may retaliate with bad medicine, or by spurning his favors when he solicits her again. For the very men who "throw their wives away" are so little committed to the Plains logic of the act that they forget their claims to bravery in their desire for the discarded woman and in their efforts to take her back as a wife. A story is told of one "crazy" man who became affected by megalomaniac ideas when he was drunk, and if he was attending an Indian dance at those times, he would order the singers to play the "throwing-away" song, and

7

would dance around, proclaiming the availability of his wife and
his own bravery; but the next night he was always found under
one blanket with his woman.

Young Man seems to have been a pathfinder in ceremonial
demonstrations of bravery. He was one of the first Ojibwa to risk
his life in pursuit of a mere pony that had been stolen by the Sioux,
and also one of the first to "throw away" his wife. He practised
the Plains type of bravery gestures in company with another that
is more congenial to the Canadian Ojibwa and Cree — attesting to his
bravery by stealing the affections of another's wife. His life was,
therefore, a succession of bravery episodes in the cultural terms of
two distinct peoples. "Young Man had a pony. Very few Ojibwa
had ponies then. Only the Sioux had ponies. One time his pony
was missing... he had lost it. He felt very bad for he loved it.
He looked for it but could not find it anywhere. So he said to his
family, 'I am going out to look for my pony. I will not give up
until I find him, and I will not come home without him. If I'm
killed, well, you will know.' So he went away." After many adventures, Young Man returned with his pony and an additional one he
had captured. "He was praised for his bravery, going to the Sioux
country all alone, and coming back with two ponies. Whenever he
danced, he would hold one finger out on one hand, and two out on
the other hand. That meant that he had been alone and had brought
two ponies home. He risked his own life when he went there. He
used to tell how he did it... When they danced he always made a
speech about it. Once a man gave him a (sacred) song which meant
that he, Young Man, had stolen a horse from the Sioux, and he used
to dance when it was sung. Once when it was sung, he was given
a belt with horse-hoof marks on it. (These gifts entitle the donors
to a share in the bravery, although it is a small share. They are
buying bravery stocks from the great bravery capitalist.) He made
nice signs with his hands as he danced. Right after that the 'part-
ing-with-wife-song' was sung, and he danced to that too (being by
this time intoxicated by bravery). He said, 'No man can do anything to me that will make fun of me (i. e., that can shame me. This
is simply an arrogant expression). The reason I am dancing this
song is that I part with my wife.' His wife was right in the dancing-
place listening to him. And he did part with her. He didn't part
with the woman because she was old or because he didn't like her.
It was just because he danced that song. He was so brave that he
didn't care. Soon after that he married another woman. He took
her away while she was yet staying with her husband, as he (Young
Man) was not very old (and women could still fall in love with him).

He did it just because he was so brave..." Peshegos carelessly discarded his wife after she betrayed him. This however was a spontaneous move on his part, motivated by the need of guarding his self-esteem, and bore no conscious or cultural relation to the conventional "throwing-wife-away." Nor did Small Ice think of himself as discarding his wife when he yielded her to their savior, Randalls.

People desert one another on any conceivable pretext, or on none at all. Much cultural pressure, as evidenced by tales, genealogies, and prevailing attitudes, is directed against institutionalized permanence in marriage. People marry where desire directs them, and remain together as long as inclination and habit dictate. The causes of divorce are often stated in terms of mere whim. The casual character of marriage and desertion is exemplified in the history of Kath, who had a checkered career leaving husbands and being left by them. Her first marriage, when she was about fifteen, was to a white man, Sam Hunter, who kept the local Hudson's Bay post. After fifteen or more years of marriage to Sam, "she said that she would rather go back and be an Indian than live in a store with a white man," and went off with an American Ojibwa whom she met at an Indian dance. So Sam was abandoned, and alone, as the couple had no children. Life with Sam had been unexciting in its calmness, but it became quite the opposite with the Ojibwa husband. "He used to give her an awful beating, kicking and fighting her. She stayed with him about three years, and then she left him too. She married another (American) Ojibwa, and after she had lived with him for two years, he became mean, even worse than the other Ojibwa. He used to fight her, and one time he burned her on one side of her body. Some kind women treated her arm; it was badly peeled. She had nothing to lay her head upon, she was so poor. She had no clothes, and nothing to eat, but just what people gave her. Only when she was getting better did she remember Sam Hunter, and she thought she would return and ask him to take her back, if only as a servant to feed his pigs. So she started off, walking from Leech Lake to Grand Forks. She had nothing but ten pounds of maple sugar in a birch container, and some matches. These she carried on her back, and one old spare dress. She traveled with only her underskirt on. She had no shoes, or anything on her feet. And as she was walking along she saw all kinds of wild beasts, bears, lynx, moose, deer, wolves, and snakes, and other things she was afraid of. When night came, she used to climb a tree, and put sticks across, and sleep there. She had a little axe with her, and in her story she used to say that none of these wild beasts were as bad as

7*

the (American) Ojibwa Indians. As she went along, she used to kill
a rabbit, and roast it and eat some of it. This was in the fall when
low-bush cranberries were ripe. She ate cranberries with maple
sugar. That was all she had to eat. One time she came to a place
where she had to walk in water for three miles. I guess the water
was way past her knees. This was on a muskeg (marsh land). After
she had walked three days, she came to a logging camp, and when
she came near one of the shacks she heard someone inside. She
looked in through a crack, and saw a big bear. So she went into
another shack and closed the door, and watched the bear go out.
The shack she had gone into was the cook shack, and the shack the
bear had gone into was the bunk house. After the bear had gone
out, she ran into the bunk house and found some old pants, coats,
socks, and Canadian moccasins. She put on the pants, coat, moccasins, and socks, because she was ragged and covered with
scratches. She took a plate, cup, knife and spoon, and a piece of
tablecloth and started off again. She went the way the bear went,
and she got to a river. She knew this was Willow Creek. She saw a
little boat, and another big boat. She threw the little boat in, ran
back again to the shacks and took a frying pan and all the food she
could find. Then she started in the small boat. As she was going
down the river, she saw the same bear on the shore, going the same
way. She yelled to the bear and said, 'Are you going where I'm
going?' And the bear ran into the bush, just as much frightened
of her as she was of him. So she got to Big Forks River. She knew
then that she would reach Little Forks. She used to say that she
cried an awful lot on her way, thinking about her Ojibwa husband,
and about her hard life, and about Sam Hunter. It took her another
four days. She made a paddle for herself, and she had to portage
once, dragging her boat. So she came to Big Falls, and she had
to walk in water dragging her boat along. When she came to the
foot of the rapids, she got in again. There was a bay and a point,
and as she was going around the point, and into the bay, she saw
someone coming in a boat. She was frightened (that "someone"
might be her deserted husband; she was in a near-hysterical condition throughout this divorce flight) and she couldn't do anything
but meet the one that was coming. It was a white man, and he
grabbed her boat, and asked her where she had come from. She
tried to tell him by signs how many days it was since she hadn't
had anything to eat. He said he was trapping bears, and he gave
her a lot of bear meat, tea, sugar, lard, and bread. He let her go,
and she went away, landed, and had a good meal of the food this
white man had given her.

"She slept on the way four times. She came to the mouth of Big Forks River, and out on the Rainy River, and she had to go three miles up the river to where Sam.Hunter had his store. She didn't cross to the Canadian side (where Sam's store was), but she kept going along the American shore until she came right opposite his store. She camped on the American side, and sat there and watched him walking around. She saw a woman and a child about three years old. There was a new house, and a larger store. When Sam Hunter saw that someone was camping across the river, he got into his rowboat and went across. When he pulled ashore he saw Kath sitting there. He asked her why she had run away, and where her (first Ojibwa) husband was. She told him (lying from shame) that he was dead. He said that he had married four years after she left him, and that he had a little girl three years old. He told her he would give her clothes and something to eat, and told her to go where her mother was. He said she should come to his store just as though she were intending to buy. She did. His wife never paid any attention to Indians who came to the store, so Sam had a good chance to give her two pieces of print for dresses, and white cotton, shoes, stockings, hat, shawl, and a blanket. He even gave her thread, needles, underwear, a sack of flour, tea, sugar, lard, baking powder, pork, everything. She started the next day down the river. She used to say she was so sorry that Sam Hunter was married! She cried after she got into the boat ... why did she leave such a good husband, and go through such a hard life with the Ojibwas, and now she had no husband at all? Three times married, and never a widow!"

She clothed herself with the goods Sam provided, visited old friends, and stayed in her mother's village. She lived with her mother for a time, but left to stay with another old Indian woman because her step-father pursued her lustfully. Soon Sam Hunter's wife died, and he remarried Kath, who was now happy to stay at the store. Sam then fell ill of a lingering disease which consumed all his capital and caused trade to fall off. After four or five years he died, and Kath was left destitute and a widow. Not long after she married another American Ojibwa named Cheeta, from Red Lake. "But he couldn't take her away (to his own home) because she didn't want to go to Red Lake (i. e., she didn't want to leave her village where she could be assured of some protection by her relatives). She was afraid he would be mean to her. So one fall he went away. She didn't know he had left her until someone came from Red Lake and told her. He told my grandfather that he was going out trapping and didn't know whether he would come back because he couldn't get his wife to go with him. So **Kath** was single again for a year.

"Then a man from Duluth married her. He was a halfbreed named Baptiste Coola. She went with him to Duluth, and was gone for quite a while. Some people visited Duluth for their treaty money, and one of them, a girl from Fort Frances, took **Kath's** husband away and married him. So she was single again, and came back by canoe with other people. She stayed around Fort Frances a while, and got entangled with a man from Port Arthur (Lake Superior). She married him and went away to Port Arthur, and was away for a year or more. She returned from Port Arthur on the Canadian Pacific Railroad and went to Rat Portage. From there she returned by boat to Hungry Hall. She was there a few months, single, then married again. He was a lazy man. She was awfully poor. She lived just on her hunting, trading, and fishing. She lived with him for two or three years. Then he got kind of mean with her, and every time he came near her, she fought him and told him she didn't want him any more. So she left him too." After this, Kath became a distinguished shaman, presumably as a reward for all her hardships. She became well-liked, renowned, and wealthy. Some time passed, and she married again, her last husband. They lived happily until her death. She justified her many marriages and divorces by divine sanction, and in the ritual invocation that precedes certain practises and that recounts the powerful vision, she would say that "she had dreamed to have eight tom-toms (for doctoring), eight rattlers (for doctoring), and eight different husbands." ... Kath's behavior seems to have been spontaneous with her, not conditioned by childhood experiences with her parents, for her mother, Deceased, was a devoted wife to each of her husbands and was never divorced, but remarried only after widowhood.

Rabbit was a flamboyant young woman who divorced for no weightier reason than the love of flirting. "She got married to a man named Bigsby. She had a little boy, and when her little boy was old enough to walk around, she started to quarrel with her husband. She wanted another man. One night she dreamed (sacredly) that her father was supposed to do all sorts of *manido kazo* such as the *ogima* ('chief') dance and other kinds. She went to her father and told him to do this (behest of the supernaturals) and her father did it and people came from all over. At this dance **Rabbit** had a good time flirting with the man she wanted. She did not want her husband at all. When the 'chief' dance was over, and the people were returning home, she ran after this man and left her two year old boy behind." Two years later, the deserted husband, **Bigsby**, was given his wife's younger sister, Sitting Woman, in marriage, and they had a child. "It was a little girl. The old man gave another 'chief' dance that summer. **Rabbit** came there with her third husband. You see, she did not stay with the second man long, but she married his (cross-)cousin, and had a child by him, and it died. That was three different men she had married, and she did not stop flirting at all, though she was married. She was always dressed nicely, like a young girl. (Matrons prove their single-minded devotion to husband and home by paying little attention to their ordinary dress. Men have the same attitude, therefore a married person is suspected of irregular erotic interests when he or she dresses up on ordinary days. Widowed persons during their mourning period exaggerate this convention and are extremely slovenly. **Rabbit** therefore wore her heart on her sleeve by being careful and charming in her dress.) Lots of people were there (and were curious about **Rabbit** and her younger sister). Sitting Woman was very bashful because she was married to her sister's first husband, but when the dances were over, **Rabbit** went back with her third husband. Either she did not bother with her little boy (by the first husband), or the man would not let the boy see his mother.

"A couple of years later, her (third) husband died, and she was left a widow. She paid the sib debt but did not remarry conventionally. She married another woman's husband and went away with him all summer. The son that she left with her first husband was now ten years old, and her sister had three children by **Bigsby**. **Rabbit** had now married four times. Her fourth husband left her; he only stayed with her the summer and then returned to his other wife. **Rabbit** went back to Kenora. One time **Bigsby** went to Kenora, and as he was going back and forth between the boat and the store, he saw a woman coming towards him. It was **Rabbit**. She asked him if he would not ask the boss of the boat to let her get on so that she could return to Long Sioux (where she was born). So **Bigsby** asked and was told she could get on. The boat started out. **Bigsby** used to sit around on the deck and sleep there. In the afternoon he took a nap, and all at once **Rabbit** came and lay down with him. He got up and walked to the other side. When the boat got to Long Sioux she got off with her things and followed him right to his home." The possibility of jealousy, closely allied to shame, was always latent in the marriage of Sitting Woman to the deserted husband. She was a little ashamed of having been assigned to, and having accepted, the man deserted by **Rabbit**. She always shrank

from her sister when the latter came to the village in the years after
her desertion. So now, when Sitting Woman saw her husband
return with Rabbit immediately behind him, she surmised that the
two were reunited. Her old shame, and the usual resentment of
polygyny flared up. "She got mad. Bigsby tried to tell her that
he had not brought the woman there, that she had come of her own
will. He said he wouldn't marry her anyway. But Rabbit thought
he would take her right back again. She put her things on the other
side of his bed (the arrangement entokening marriage), and this
only made Sitting Woman worse. That evening Sitting Woman
gathered all her things and took her three children, and went to her
aunt's place. When her husband followed her and tried to coax her
back, she would not come back. She said she hated her sister and
didn't want to stay with her. (This hatred meant jealousy. The
antagonism had developed at the time of Sitting Woman's marriage, for in previous years she and her sister had been devoted
companions.) So Bigsby went away. A year and a half later,
Sitting Woman married another." Bigsby stayed single for three
years but the unceasing pursuit of Rabbit eventually wore down
his resistance and he remarried her.

When a woman deserts from a polygynous marriage, it is usually
because of jealousy and shame... "Thunder Cloud lived with her
husband about ten years. They had no children. He was very
jealous. Once she met a man (accidentally) as she was going down
the bank and this man went into her tent. Then Great Bird, the
husband, came, and when he saw this man in the tent he got jealous.
The woman was not even in the tent, but other people were. He
stabbed the man with a knife in the ribs, and he said he would stab
her too. Some of the women told her this, so she never went back
into the tent. The women got her ready, and she walked from the
Manitou to Hungry Hall with nothing to eat." Thunder Cloud's
resentment of her husband's unfounded jealousy, and her fear of his
violence were so great that she braved the terrors of starvation,
cold, and Sioux warriors rather than return to him... The jealousy
and grief that led Tuhpuhsi to desert her husband are described later... Men do not flee from the wife's wrath or jealousy,
but Ahtushkish did desert his wife after her insane and unfounded
resentment of her daughter had caused the latter to flee from home.
He left not because he feared his wife's jealousy, but because he
was annoyed and because home had lost its charm after the ten-
derly loved daughter had gone.

Jealousy took a violent and unfounded hold on Blazing Sky.
"When he was young, he was a big flirt. He used to flirt with all

the young girls, and he even tried to make up with young married women. Sometimes the married women ran away from him, and sometimes he found one that did not run away, and then he flirted with her. He always watched to be sure the husband was out of the way. Then he would go and sleep with the wife while she was alone. Blazing Sky was always afraid that the husband would know he had slept with the wife; but he was never caught. One time he fell in love with a girl and married her. The girl was very quiet (demure), but he was jealous of her. He could never leave her, thinking that she would sleep with some man, or talk to another man. Even when she went out chopping wood, he followed her, and watched to see if she was with some man. But he never caught her, for she never looked at another man. Then when she got home he would say to her that she had been with some man. When she went to pick berries (a woman's occupation exclusively) he walked around watching her all day long. He never did any work himself, as he was always worried and jealous. He never went to hunt ducks, or did anything, unless his wife was right beside him. He was too jealous to let her out of his sight even for a little while. One time as they were living in a big tipi with his sister and her husband and another couple, early in the morning he woke and saw his wife was gone. He looked to see if his brother-in-law was there, but he was gone too. He thought to himself, 'Now I know that she's out with him.' He got up, and as he was leaving the tent, he saw his wife busy making a cedar mat. He looked around to see if his brother-in-law was there, but he wasn't in sight. He went out and started to beat his wife. She yelled, 'He's beating me! He's jealous of his brother-in-law!' All the people jumped up and tried to stop him. His sister told him that her husband had gone hunting, that he had gone out early that morning. But no, he would not believe her. He wanted to have it that his wife ran after his brother-in-law. He said he was going to leave her, that he did not want to stay with her any more as she was too crazy. (He could fend off the shame of the other's rebukes only by increasing his arrogance and causing another to be shamed. By shaming his wife, he restored his own self-esteem.) Then his wife said to him, 'You can go away if you want to. I don't want to stay with anyone that is jealous of me all the time for nothing.' So he got ready. He took everything they owned and didn't leave her anything." His jealousy and fear of being shamed, seem to have been deep-rooted reactions, for in his subsequent marriages he behaved repeatedly in the same way.

Women often desert a husband when they have conceived a passion for another man. Some men desert their wives for the same

reason; others formed a polygynous marriage when this was feasible. In these days, however, when monogamy is enforced by the
Government and men are as restricted maritally as women, the
alternative of polygyny is no longer available. Women who desert
for love make their plans secretly, to avoid intervention by the
shamed husband... Marsh Woman was a Cree. These Cree border
the Ontario and Manitoba Ojibwa, and their customs are nearly
identical with those of the Ojibwa. "Once many of the Indians (the
West Ontario Ojibwa) went to the Cree to visit them, and Chief Eagle
Wood went along. They stayed over there quite a while. Chief went
with Marsh Woman, who was married to a Cree. Both her parents
lived with them. She did not have any children although she had
already been married six years. She did not care for this Cree man
as he was mean and jealous of her all the time. Every night Chief
went to her tent when her husband was not home, and they used to
talk and make love to each other, as they were deeply in love. One
morning the Ojibwa got ready to leave for home. Chief also got
ready. He was all alone in his canoe. He was heavy-hearted at
leaving his sweetheart behind, and she felt the same way. All day
long she sat around with her head down, looking in the direction
her lover had gone. That night he made up his mind to go back and
see her once more. As he got to her tent, he saw her sitting outside.
Her husband was not home, so he went up to her. She was so glad
to see him, they grabbed each other, and he asked her if she was
lonely, and she said 'Yes.' And he said to her, 'I am very lonely,
and I realized that I could not go back without you. Can't you think
of some way by which we can have each other ?' She said she would
find a way, and told him to hide there that night and all the next
day, and she would manage to see him again the next night, and
then she would tell him what to do. He stayed somewhere in the
bush, and she went to see him that day and also that night. She
had a talk with her mother. She told her that she did not care for
her husband as he was mean and jealous, 'and I've made up my
mind to go with another man that I care for. Do not worry about
me if you lose me tomorrow morning. I will be alive, but I'm going
to do something to make people believe that I'm dead. Do not get
scared but pretend that you are lonesome. I will see you again
sometime. I love this man, and he cares for me.' Her mother said
that she would do as she was told, and that it was all right.

"So that evening she set a fish net and they all went to bed.
Early the next morning before daylight her mother spoke to her
and said, 'Get up now, my daughter, and go see your net. It's
daytime now.' She got up. Her husband woke and asked if he could

go along with her, and she said, 'No, I'm all ready now and don't
want to wait for you.' She went out, got into her canoe, and went
where her net was. She took it out and washed it clean. Her lover
was already on the shore. Then she came ashore, and she tipped
over her canoe and threw her paddle out on the water, and also her
dress which she wore. Then they went away. Chief had his canoe
farther along the shore. They got into his canoe. She had a few of
her things with her. They paddled all day and all night. When the
Cree people got up and had their breakfast, the old man, her father,
said, 'I wonder what's delaying our daughter? She's staying away
a long time. It's a wonder you never worry about her. Where did
she set her net?' The old woman told him. So he got into his canoe
and went, and when he got there he saw the canoe floating around,
also her paddle and her dress. What else could he think but that
his daughter was drowned? And so he came back. He yelled to the
Cree Indians saying, 'Oh, my friends, my daughter is drowned. Go
and see the canoe floating!' He got out of his canoe and ran to the
bush crying. The old woman jumped up and ran to the bush too.
She could not cry for she knew her daughter was not really drowned,
but she tried hard to pretend she was lonely. All the Indians got
busy and looked many days for the body. They hunted for it in
the water, but they could not find anything. The old man was
very sad and downhearted. He took it very hard at meal-times (when
ritual offerings of food are made to the ghost of the deceased). He
could not eat, he was always crying; but the old woman was not.
Well, she had nothing to cry about, for she knew her daughter was
alive. Then one time when they were going to eat, the old man burst
out crying, and the old woman said to him, 'Stop your crying or
else you will die of a broken heart.' The old man said, 'Yes, I will
die of a broken heart for she was the only child I had and I cannot
live knowing that she died suffering like that.' The old woman said,
'Do not cry any more. She's living and we will see her soon.' So
the old man stopped crying and believed what his old woman said.
And of course some of the (other) old women overheard her saying
that. The old man told the people, 'You might as well stop looking
for the body. We may find it sometime when it floats up.' So the
people stopped looking for it. Finally one of the other women told
the husband what she overheard the old woman saying, that her
daughter was alive somewhere, so the man did not bother thinking
that his wife was dead. These two who ran away did not stop where
the other Indians were camping. They went right on ahead and
reached the place where his own people and parents were. Of
course his parents knew that he had taken this woman away from

another man, but they did not mind it as they liked her. She was nice looking, strong, and a good worker."

Other enamoured women desert without the sound hopes of Marsh Woman, but simply on the off chance of marriage... Several women deserted husbands for love of gay Ahtuskish, but he did not marry any of them though he did find them husbands. The people do not brand Ahtushkish's conduct as irresponsible, for marital responsibility is not recognized as the motivation of an adult's life. It is so thoroughly recognized that a person follows only his private inclinations, that even the longing sweethearts of Ahutshkish did not insist upon marriage after he had definitely refused. To him, marriage involved other values than a flirtatious interest in a girl and acknowledgement of his relationship to her child. He felt no more responsibility toward these women, than the women felt toward their husbands whom they betrayed casually and as casually deserted.

A husband's physical cruelty is often advanced as a reason for the wife's desertion. Deceased's daughter left three husbands because they used to fight with her, using fists, feet, and burning brands ... Two Skies left her husband because he fought with her and kicked her on the buttocks... Catfish Leonard's wife deserted for the same reasons. The children of both these women were still-born or died in infancy, and the women attributed the fact to the buttock-kickings they had received... Hungry Loon's first marriage was a history of physical cruelty. "When she was about 26 years old she met a man from Leech Lake. They used to have an Indian war dance long ago, and at one of these dances she fell in love with this man. Her mother did not want her to marry him. One night she got ready. She got all her things, and canoe, birchbark, and some things to eat. She even took her father's gun. And then she ran away with this man. They went to Leech Lake by canoe; it took them about ten days to get there. They killed moose and dried some of the meat. They had lots to eat as they traveled along. They got to Leech Lake, and her mother-in-law did not like her. About fifteen days after she got there, her husband became awfully jealous of her, and gave her a dreadful beating just for nothing. She didn't deserve it. You know how it is when a stranger arrives in a place: all the people wanted to see her, and the men passed close to her tent to see her because she was a nice looking girl. She had long hair; when she was sitting on the ground, her hair used to lie right on the ground. And she was whiter than any of the other girls. After her beating she first thought of what her mother said to her. She used to go in the bush and cry. Her husband fought her and kicked her, and she had such lovely hair that he just pulled her by it and dragged her around. After about a year, she became the mother of a little boy. Two years later, she had a little girl. Her little girl died when she was two years old. About a month after the little girl died, her husband gave her another good beating. She went back in the bush crying. Some woman came to her and said, 'Why don't you try and go home?' She answered that she didn't know which way to go, that she didn't know the place. So she stayed there. Some old people lost their daughter, and then adopted her as their daughter. So she stayed with them and half left her husband, but still he stayed around her all the time. Once he went to her and said that if she would get ready he would take her to see her mother. He said that they would travel through Big Forks, through Rainy River, and out to Lake of the Woods right through to N.... (their destination), if she promised to come back with him. So she promised to come back with him, but in her heart she knew that she would not. This was in the spring after they got through making sugar in May. When they reached N...., her mother and father were glad to see her. Everyone welcomed her with joy. Lots of people missed her hair, but she never told who had pulled it out. Her husband became mean to her again. He never fought her there (on her own home territory), but he was sulky and mean, and in the fall he begged her to go back with him. But she wouldn't go. He said to her, 'All right. If you don't want to go, I will take another women with me.' She said, 'All right. You can do it.' She had grown to hate him. She didn't care whether he left or got married. He went away with one of her cousins, her father's brother's oldest daughter."

Some men claim that they deserted a wife because of her sterility. This prejudice is altogether an individual one, for in case after case men have been devoted to a barren wife, or to one who could bear only one child. Some women feel their sterility keenly, grieving about it, and occasionally taking the husband's illegitimate child as their own. Other women have accepted the fact without any disturbance. It is considered desirable to have children, and a woman's chief function is to bear them. Sterility is unfortunate and bad in theory, because it is a deviation from the biologically normal; but the sterility of a specific woman is not necessarily branding in her husband's eyes.... Marsh Woman's Cree husband was fiercely attached to her though she bore him no children in the six years of their marriage; and her second Ojibwa husband was equally attached to her though she succeeded in bearing him only one child... Kath was married to eight men in succession, none of whom complained of her sterility. . . . Nor did Giantess' husbands complain of her's. . . . Iron Woman suffered from an affliction worse than sterility, for each of her three children died in infancy, supposedly as a result of her life-long practise of bad medicine. Her young husband never resented this, and refused to avail himself of her permission to marry a younger and fertile woman, but remained with her devotedly until she died. . . . Gaybay was married five times. She bore only one child, and that was in her fifth marriage. However, she was never considered undesirable because of her apparent sterility, and her fifth husband "thought a lot of her" though she had only one child. . . . Thunder Cloud did not bear children until she was married to her third husband, yet her first husband, with whom she lived ten years, and her second husband, with whom she lived eight years, cared for her ardently; and her apparent sterility was no deterrent to the third marriage. . . . Ice Woman bore only one child during the many years of her happy marriage. . . . Tuhpuhsi was secretly worshipped by her second husband long before they finally married. They lived happily together and the husband's affection remained constant even though Tuhpuhsi was sterile.

No conventions sanction desertion of a barren wife, and in individual cases sterility is a matter of complete indifference. In a man's opinion, a childless marriage is always due to deficiency in the woman. . . . One man at Lake of the Woods beat his wife often because she could not bear children. "Hawk Woman was a good woman, honest and brave, and a good strong worker. She did everything for her husband, kept him clean, and worked for him. But he was mean to her because she didn't have any children, and that was why he was always beating her. But she couldn't help it. She wanted children just as much as he did. She used to cry an awful lot wishing she could do something to have children. He did everything to her. He used to leave her to marry someone else. Then he would come back again whenever he was pleased to do so. And she would be just the same (i. e., even tempered); she was never mad or jealous. . . ." Hawk Woman believed that the sterility was her husband's fault, and told him so. He declared that he would leave her and prove his virility. He did leave her, and lived with Katie Skies, thirty-two years his junior. Katie did not conceive, but an extended trial was prevented because the Indian agent compelled the deserter to return to his wife. Later he abandoned her on a deserted island. She was found by a secret admirer who gladly married her, and who was never disturbed by her sterility during their long life together.

At Hungry Hall, one man left his wife because of her suspected homosexuality. The woman was reputed to be the lover of her niece. Each of the women was married. "Their children looked so queer" (hydrocephalic) that the husbands of the women called a diviner to ascertain the cause. It was revealed supernaturally to the diviner that homesexual relations of the two women caused the children to be sick. The husband of the niece thereupon beat his wife; and the husband of the aunt deserted his.

Women sometimes leave their husbands in order to protect a daughter or sister from rape, or to avenge injury or shame which has already occurred. Thus one woman left her husband in order to protect her young sister, Little Maid, from her father-in-law, Marten ... Coming Cloud, who seduced and later married his step-daughter, was left by his wife in retaliation for the shame he had brought upon mother and daughter, and for having caused the girl's death.... Great Buffalo Woman's mother left her husband because of his repeated attempts to rape the daughter. When he tried to protest his innocence, she poured upon him the fullness of her contempt: " 'Shut up, you dirty dog! (This is Ojibwa equivalent of our vilest curses.) It's you yourself that's bothering my girl every night! You should be ashamed of yourself, doing that!' He came crawling in and sat down beside the fireplace. The mother hid his old blanket so he had no cover all night. Great Buffalo and her mother never slept, and in the morning the mother spoke to her, 'Get up now, and go right out. Take all your things along. Put them in your canoe and wait for me.' She did as her mother told her and soon after her mother came down with a bundle of her things. (The co-wife) came running down and begged them not to go... Great Buffalo's mother said, 'I cannot stay here and let my husband ruin my only daugheter. So I'm leaving here for good. I hate that old fool!'.... They left for their old home. Soon after they arrived there, the old man came chasing after, but the mother took a big stick and sent him away, hitting him. She even threw him in the water and pushed his canoe out. He had to swim for his canoe and hold onto it.... She told him never to come there again and never to bother them, and this he did."

The miscellany of "reasons" for divorce can be continued almost endlessly. Thus Thunder Woman's mother left her husband because he refused to forgive his daughter for having married without his permission. Gaybay's first husband left after ten days because she was cold to him.... After two months Great Buffalo Woman chased away (from her mother's home) her husband because he was "lazy, cranky, and jealous.... One time when she could not stand it any longer she took his blanket and other things and threw them out, and said to him, 'Get out and stay out! I don't want you to stay here and be mean to me! We do not need you here because you're no good anyway, and you're always jealous of me for nothing!' So the man went out... he was ashamed... he got in his canoe and went right home.".... Kota left one husband because he was lazy and she had to work too hard.... Shame in some form is a frequent cause of desertion "They were a newly married couple living among a lot of Indians. ("A lot of Indians" is the village, and sociologically is a correct designation for an Ojibwa community.) Once the Indians all got ready to go and battle with the Sioux. The woman said to her husband, 'Why don't you go, you too, with all those men?' The man said, 'I don't want to go with them. I will go after they return.' So he was left behind, and the woman was ashamed of her husband; she thought him a coward. When the men returned, they brought some Sioux scalps, and had their war dance. After that he got ready and went, and was gone quite a while. When he returned, he brought a scalp, and they had another war dance. The woman noticed that her husband never took off the band which he wore on his head where his feather was. One time she was combing her husband's hair, and smelled something rotten (gangrenous?), so she looked close and saw that it was his own scalp that he had cut off and brought home. Then she knew that he really hadn't gone to the Sioux Indian country. The next summer the (Ojibwa) Indians prepared for another battle, and she prepared too and went behind. But when the Indians ran towards (attacked) the wigwams of the Sioux, she ran too, and she killed one Sioux and cut off the scalp and came away. She stayed behind again; she was afraid of the Indians, and also afraid that the Sioux would overtake them on their way back. The Indians did not know that she had gone along with them, but when the men returned, then they knew that she had been along with them. She jumped off her horse, took this Sioux scalp, and threw it at her husband. 'Here, take this, and mend your own scalp where you cut it off last summer! I was so ashamed of your cowardice!' and with that she left her husband. She did not live with him any more."

Divorce, with its absolute want of institutional restriction, depends even more than marriage upon temperamental reactions. Sometimes the deserted spouse accepts his status immediately, or becomes resigned to it. This is especially true of women. But when the deserted one is the husband, his typical reaction is to contest the woman, to counteract the shame of her desertion. If she has gone off alone, he follows her and pleads with her to return. If she is adamant, he threatens her. The more he is a man of spirit—sensitive to shameful thrusts, readily suspicious that he is "being made fun of," jealous of his self-esteem—the more violently he threatens his wife. The bitterness and malice that are exhibited by a deserted man are extreme. If the wife has gone off with a lover, the husband's shame reaches a peak more quickly and he deliberately resorts to physical and magical retaliation upon the pair. Deserted women typically are not as violent as men, and do not resort to the same extremes of retaliation. They frequently show no overt reactions, and remarry without reference to the desertion. This difference in the behavior of men and women is characteristic of the differences in early training. From the day of birth the boy has been taught to place his pride much above that of any woman, and if possible above that of all other men. When a man reaches the latter viewpoint, he has developed the inordinate egotism of a shaman. It is consistent that a deserted shaman reacts even more violently than do other men to a shameful situation like desertion. The woman, on the other hand, has not been trained to guard her self-esteem, and even in a shameful situation her aggression is moderated. A man vents his resentment upon both the deserting wife and her lover, whereas a woman confines herself to her own sphere—that is, to her rival—and even in this situation does not dare to match herself against a man. Shaman-women compose no control group, for they generally come to shamanhood in middle life when the "foolishness" of desertions is over. The few women who were shamans in youth—Sky Woman, Iron Woman, and Half Sky—married only once and were never divorced ... In this situation, as in others that confront men and women alike, the fundamental response is similar and is purely individualistic; it is the manifestations that differ between the sexes. Men—and especially shamans, whose personality is the apotheosis of Ojibwa manhood—cannot submit passively to opposition or failure, but express their mortification and resentment in the most overt manner possible. Women, to whom the extremes of emotion and behavior are foreign, accept the shame of desertion and make the best possible adjustment to it; the behavior is still in individualistic terms but it does not have the scope nor the power of the men's reactions.

Some women are far from passive, however. Thus Giantess left her husband when he took a second wife. But before she left she took her revenge—not upon her husband, but upon her rival. She publicly gashed the second wife's face from one ear to the nose, and scorned her as "one who took away another woman's husband".... The wife of **Hoffman**, too, was shamed and resentful

8

because her husband courted many women and made no effort to
hide his philanderings from her. She fought with her husband, but
chiefly with his mistresses or even with those whom she only
suspected of adultery. Several times she slashed the faces of women
"because she was jealous and ashamed." She was so aggressive in
defending her honor that even her Amazonian daughter scorned
her.

Often two people remarry after they have separated, at the
initiative of either spouse. The first resentments are forgotten or
have been transferred exclusively to the rival. A reunion may, of
course, be merely a prelude to another divorce. Thus Mrs. Red Sand,
the younger, leaves her husband Tom periodically, and returns to
him after some months. Tom has become so accustomed to this that
he simply waits for her return. Mrs. Leonard used to flee from her
husband Catfish because he beat her. He would find her at her
father's home and carry her back. Then she would desert again,
and Catfish would repeat his pursuit.

Some men are at first indifferent to a wife's desertion, but later
go into a frenzy of jealousy and bitterness upon discovering that
the wife is happily remarried. The very deserter may become jealous
of his wife's new happiness, and fight to deprive her of it. A wife's
contentment is a challenge that must be overthrown if possible.
A man's fury may find violent expression in attempts to kill the
new husband and to abduct the wife, or even to kill the wife.
Sometimes the husband succeeds in killing the lover and taking
back his wife; or he may instead be killed by one of them. Some
women have a similar emotional reaction to a husband's successful
remarriage, but they do not usually resort to violence in their
efforts to displace the rival.

Hawk Woman was abandoned by her husband, Cranes. Clearly
the man did not want her, for he took pains to abandon her
on an unfrequented island, and he directed the Indians to search
for her in an altogether opposite direction. Nevertheless, when he
heard that she was living happily with another man he tried to
disrupt the marriage and injure the second husband. Hawk Woman
and her second husband, Harold, "happened to make their wigwam near Cranes.' Cranes' (second) wife was filthy and dirty
looking, and they already had three children, and their bedding was
old and dirty, for his wife was lazy. But Hawk Woman was always
smart, and kept everything nice and clean. Often other women
would say to Cranes that he had made an awful mistake when he
was mean and left Hawk Woman in the wilderness to die, and now
although he had another wife he had to live in dirt. Many a time

when Hawk Woman was home alone he would come there to bother her, or try to make her husband jealous. But Harold never was jealous and never said anything to his wife because he trusted her. He knew she was true and honest to him (this is not a typical state of mind) and he liked her too much to hurt her feelings. One morning all the people were leaving for a different place. Hawk Woman got up early and went to see her net. Cranes and his wife and children had already left. She caught some fish and came back and cooked her man's breakfast. After they were through eating they got ready. They took all their things down to their canoe, but when they got there they found that the canoe had been slashed twice. They were left with no canoe, but some of the old women (the mother and aunt of the second husband) got to work, sewed up the canoe and seamed it with pine pitch, so then they were able to go." They traveled until they overtook the other Indians. There the rival husbands met again, and Cranes commenced taunting. "He made fun of the canoe that was cut up. But as Harold was getting into his canoe, he said, 'Cranes is always running away from me!' Cranes said, 'Yes! and I was the one that cut your canoe!' Of course Harold got up, ran into the water, grabbed Cranes' canoe and pulled him out, dipped him in the water three or four times, knocked him in the face, and then let him go, saying that he should not dare to do anything further to him or tease him any more." They met at still another camp, but Cranes this time camped apart. "The men were playing all kinds of games such as lacrosse and the moccasin and hand games. Every time they played lacrosse, Cranes made it a point to hit Harold; then he would deny having done it. Harold said nothing to him because he didn't want to have another row as his people were always telling him to behave. So he never paid any attention to Cranes although the man was always teasing him..."

Tuhpuhsi suffered cruelly from the indifference and subsequent desertion of her husband, Buhnah. (See story in Part 5.). Although she remarried and was happy with her second husband, whom she loved, she harbored a deep resentment against the first husband. She expressed this by trying to shame his second wife and thus to wipe out her original humiliation...

The much-married daughter of Deceased was rather milder in her protests when she found her first husband, Sam Hunter, comfortably re-married. Simply, "she cried, and she used to say that she was sorry Sam got married."

Bigsby though a man made little protest throughout his rather hectic married life. He did not over-react to any of the com-

8*

plicated domestic arrangements in typical fashion. However, his conduct was characteristic enough of him personally. There are always a few such men who go their quiet, unassuming, and conscientious way and who are not valued greatly by men or women... Maggie's husband is of the same quality, and of him she says quite pertinently, "He's so quiet, he's hardly a man. He doesn't come near me (sexually) from one month's end to another. But he's a worker."

Friendly Place's behavior towards his deserting wife was also atypical. For although he felt humiliated and tried to make his wife return to him, his attitude was humble. He was really sorry for the slight he had inflicted upon his wife and wanted her back because he valued her personally, not simply because she had defeated him.

The exaggerated forms of revenge which are employed by a shaman who has been insulted are exemplified in the following story. "This is a story of a woman called Eternal Man. She was an (Ojibwa) Indian girl, the youngest of three daughters. Her parents were both living. Her oldest sister was a woman who did not obey her husband; she was always flirting with other men. Her husband was always after Eternal Man, and he also wished to marry her. She did not care for him, she hated him, but her parents and sister planned for her to marry him. Her sister said it was all right for them both to marry the same man. Eternal Man did not know what was being planned until the time her brother-in-law went to the Hudson's Bay Company. They used to get some Hudson's Bay rum when they sold their furs. So he brought some rum home and gave it to his father-in-law. He also gave him a gun, blanket, and other things, and asked him if he could marry his young sister-in-law. The old man thought it was all right. They were living in one big wigwam and the father moved Eternal Man's belongings to the other side beside his son-in-law, and told her to marry him. They were all drunk now. She did not know whether to obey her parents or not, for she hated to be his wife. The old woman said to her daughter, 'I will not force you to marry him. It's up to you. If you like him enough, marry him. Do as you like.' When her mother said that to her, she made up her mind that she would not marry him. When night came, her brother-in-law asked her to sleep with him and she did lie down for a little while. He was very drunk, and when he started to bother her, she rose and prepared to leave. She took a knife, axe, and some matches, twine for rabbit snares, and an old skirt. So she went out. She also took a little pail from outside. Then she started off in the night. She did not know where she was going, but she kept right on. She did not care where she was going as long as she was leaving the one she hated. At the coming of daylight she lay down and fell asleep. She slept for a long time and when she awakened she did not know where she was. She had not brought even a mouthful of food to eat. She did not know how far away she was from home. It was cloudy and it looked like rain. She started off and walked all day, and towards evening she stopped and made a birchbark windbreak, just a short one, and when night came she put this birchbark over her head and slept. The next morning she started off again. She did not want to kill herself. She thought only that she would wander around the woods so she would never again see her father and sisters and brother-in-law (all of whom had alarmed and shamed her by this forced marriage). She felt sorry only for her mother for she knew that her mother would be very lonely.

"She walked for three days and it never rained once. Finally she came to a clearing where some men were making a road. It was the track for the Canadian Pacific Railroad line. She was dreadfully afraid to see anyone, so she went back into the bush again and slept there that night. Next morning she could hear the men working with their shovels, so she walked in another direction. About past noon she came to a lake, and she stayed right on the shore in a little bay. Only then she knew she was very hungry and had nothing to eat. It was now the fifth day since she had left home. As she was sitting there wondering what to do for food she saw a bird flying over her; it had a fish in its mouth, and as it flew past her, it dropped the fish and she jumped up and grabbed it... it was a sucker. She cleaned it and cooked it in her little pail, and started to eat it. She missed salt very much, for the Indians were already using salt. When she was through she fell asleep. Next morning she made another birchbark, so she now had two. Blueberries were nearly ripe and with them she thought she would not starve or die. Only she was awfully afraid of bears and she often saw them, but they never seemed to take notice of her." (These episodes with bears and the bird during the difficult divorce interim all have mystical value, provoking stress visions comparable to those of troubled childhood. The listeners realize this as the story is told.) Her further wanderings are described. A self-outcast, she lived from hand to mouth stealing food and utensils from shacks along the railway construction and from Indian camps. A young man found her, guided by a vision, conquered her fears, and married her. The young couple were deeply in love, and lived happily. They went trapping, and when they had caught five hundred muskrats, they went to Kenora to sell them.

"She was quite happy to go back to her own country for she used to live in Kenora. They went into the Hudson's Bay store and bought things. Then they went outside and idled around. While they were sitting there they saw some canoes coming, more Indians coming into Kenora. She did not care to see her brother-in-law (her first husband), for she was awfully afraid of him, but he was the first one to arrive. She paid no attention to him, did not look at him. (In the man's opinion, Eternal Man was his legal wife, for he had gone through the ceremony of betrothal. Therefore her desertion did not nullify the marriage, but was an act of divorcement.) But when he saw them sitting there he came right up and gave her a slap across the head. She fell to the ground. He said, 'It's about time you thought of coming home,' and was just going to give her another slap when her (second) husband jumped up and told him to stop. 'It's enough that you scared her away. That's why she wandered around for such a long time without any food.' The first husband stopped, frightened. Her (second) husband took her by the hand, led her into the store, and told the men to get a policeman. The policeman came and took the other man to jail. He cried like a child and pretended that she was his wife. But she had already told her (second) husband about it. After her brother-in-law was taken away she went out to see her parents. They were all glad to see her again, for they had thought her dead. They cried with joy to see her alive. She and her husband stayed for ten days in Kenora, and when they returned north, she took her parents with her and they stayed with her until they died. Her mother told her that when they missed her that morning, they thought she had just gone to the bush, but when evening came they all got worried, and next morning her brother-in-law commenced searching for her. Each day he searched, and each day he came back without her. One day he came home and made them believe he had found her, but said that she wouldn't return with him. The following day he left with some clothes, food, and blankets and stayed away for a while. He made them believe she had a wigwam there and wanted to stay there alone with him (all this to save his face before the family). But finally he told the truth, and his wife was very mean to him after that (for he lost caste in her eyes as one who had been rejected, and also he was the cause of Eternal Man's departure). Then they thought her dead. This was what her mother told her. (The brother-in-law was now deserted by his wife, Eternal Man's elder sister, who married a brother of Eternal Man's second husband. The family was now reunited, and the brother-in-law totally rejected. The girl and her second husband were shamans of the *wabeno,* or fire-juggling, type, and periodically gave *wabeno* dances.)

"One time they held another *wabeno* dance and people from many different places came. Her brother-in-law came too, just to insult them. He acted bold and said that they were pretenders not real *wabeno*s. One time when the men were idling together, he was bold enough to the young man, 'I will come and visit you (supernaturally, and with fatal intent) this fall. It will be a joke if I have your body for my (medicine) sack.' He meant to kill him. The young man answered, 'It will be a bigger joke if I get the best of you.' The young man went home and told his wife that the reason her brother-in-law was against him was that she had once left him, but she told her husband not to mind. Sure enough, that fall balls of fire appeared and night owls, and other signs of bad medicine. It went on like that all fall. One night when a ball of fire was coming towards them, her husband took his clothes off and went out to meet this fire naked, and he killed the fire. After that no more of the brother-in-law's bad medicine came there. About ten days later they heard that the brother-in-law had died. So that was the end of him. The second husband did not use any bad medicine to kill him. He just killed the fire and so killed him too."

Ahtushkish made the mistake of seducing the wives of two shamans. Ahtushkish was so notorious that his very name was an impudent challenge to these men. In each case the shaman ignored his culprit wife and focussed his attention upon the man. Ahtushkish was sent among the Indians to buy up their fur. "The first wigwam that he came to belonged to the old man (i. e., shaman) whose girl wife he had taken away. Ahtushkish said, 'So all the Crees are here again?' The old man said, 'Yes we are here. Come in.' So he went in and sat down. The old man took a knife and said to him, 'Where did you take my wife?' He answered, 'I didn't take your wife away. She followed me herself, and I'm not married to her either.' The old man stabbed him with the knife. He jerked down and was stabbed on his hind part, and just as the old man went to stab him again, he kicked him on the throat and the old man fell over. Ahtushkish jumped up and took the knife, and was going to grab the shaman when someone held his arm. The blood was just streaming down his pants. He went out of this wigwam and went home. He was sick for a long time. His wife never said anything to him. She was well contented with what she had. She didn't care what her husband did. And the girl for whom he had been stabbed was already working for some people quite a distance away.

"When winter came he went out trading again. Two of his children died at the same time (this implies the evil machinations of the shaman). And one time as he was going from his home to the store he met a big dog who started to fight. They fought for a long time. At last he licked the dog, tore him to pieces, and after he had torn him to pieces, it proved to be nothing but a rotten log. The old man (the deserted shaman-husband) did all these things to him with his bad medicine. That winter as usual he went all over trading with the Cree people. Other stores and fur traders were now settling there. In the spring, after the lakes opened up again, he was told to go and meet the Crees as they came in with their furs. He went alone, paddling, and he met the Crees camping on an island. He camped there himself, and bought all their furs. This same old man happened to be there again. Ahtushkish wouldn't buy his fur, but the old man got one of the men to sell his fur for him. They all stayed there over night, and when morning came all the people went away to the Hudson's Bay Post. When the trader went down, he found his canoe cut in pieces. Everybody else had left, so there was nothing for him to do but stay there. He was on an island, with no way of getting home. One of the young girls overheard the old man telling his old woman that Ahtushkish would surely die now because he cut up his canoe. The Crees camped again and when it was getting dark, the girl made up her mind to return. She got into her canoe and went back. The trader was busy sewing up his old canoe, and she spoke, 'I came back for you. So hurry up. The people will wonder where I've gone to.' The trader put all his things into her canoe and they started paddling. When they reached the Crees' camping place, the trader asked the girl what she wanted for her pay (every service must be paid for), and the girl said she wanted the very best goods he had, and a pair of buttoned shoes. So he gave her enough for a dress, and the shoes, and lots of tobacco (an important native medium of exchange), and she lent him her canoe with which to go to the Hudson's Bay Post. (The girl was now left without a canoe for her own transportation, so she requested her grandmother's permission to travel in hers, and in payment for this privilege she gave her grandmother some of the trader's tobacco.) When the people came in sight of the store they could see the trader walking around, and the old man wondered how in the world he ever got there. All the people said, 'Oh, look, the trader got here before us.' The old man was so stunned he never even spoke. He went ashore and camped away from the people, and said, 'It's a wonder how he ever got here. I wish I knew who helped him (so as to punish that person).' The girl and her grandmother went up to the store and the boss of the Hudson's Bay gave them a lot of groceries and goods, for the trader had told that his canoe had been cut up, and who had rescued him, and the storekeeper also made the old man pay ten dollars for the loss of the canoe. The old man got still madder. The trader went to the shaman's wigwam and taunted him, 'I have come here to tell you that if you want to destroy me, take a gun and shoot me, if you're man enough (for a shaman generally does not shoot, preferring to kill by surreptitious sorcery). I will not try to shield myself. If you were a man of my own age, I would fight you, but you are too old. I will not do you any harm. So I've come here for you to shoot me. I don't want you to use any of your bad medicine for you cannot destroy me like that. If you were a man I would have beaten you up as soon as you came ashore, after the way you treated me, cutting up my canoe. But I will not do that to you because you are too old for me. And the canoe didn't belong to me either. I will not moan or do anything (cowardly) if you shoot me; instead I will shout aloud (the war whoop) to show I'm a man.' And the old man said to him, 'All right, I will let you go. I never realized before that you thought of me like that... and I would just like to see you beat me up!' Again the trader said, 'Yes! I could do that! But I don't want you! I'm here only to see if you are brave enough to kill me. After you kill me, you also will be killed, so if you want to die, you too, go ahead and shoot me! I *did* marry your wife and had a child with her! She followed me herself. I didn't bring her away, and I'm not staying with her any more!' The old man said he would leave him alone. While the Cree were on their way home, the old man drowned. His own people (close relatives) said it was the trader who did this with his bad medicine. But it was not true, for the trader did not know about the old man's drowning until later on, and nobody could say he knew any bad medicine... only, he was such a flirt. Nobody saw him go after the old man, for the old man was with his son when he drowned..."

About three years later, Ahtushkish caused the youngest wife of a shaman to desert her husband. "When the old man learned of it he got mad, and said, 'I will sicken the trader so he will never be able to take a wife away again.' He was a worse (more powerful) old man than the first, and he paralyzed the trader by his bad medicines. The trader could not move at all; only his head was not paralyzed. He was that way for nine years. He was nursed like a baby. And after all, he did not marry the girl for whom he was paralyzed. He was not a very old man when he died... he was about forty years old. So that was the end of Ahtushkish."

Sometimes the deserted husband is as fiercely motivated as even a shaman might be, but lacks the latter's ability to execute his revenge. He then secures the services of a shaman to avenge him. Albert's son-in-law was one such bitter but impotent husband whose shaman-father made his son's cause so much his own that he directed sorcery not against the deserting girl, but against her father, Albert, who was a rival shaman. "Albert 's daughter got married to a man from Kénora. She married him in the spring, and in August, after the blueberry picking, they parted. She went home to her own folks. That fall her husband went to look for his wife, but she wouldn't go back with him. He felt awfully ashamed when he left Albert's without his wife. He went home and told his father he felt awfully ashamed... About this time Albert went to his trapping grounds with his son. They were there a long time but they couldn't kill anything, and they ran out of food. (This is starvation caused by another's malicious sorcery.) He couldn't even kill a rabbit. The son got so weak from hunger that he couldn't walk. There were serious snow storms... The wind blew right into the wigwam and blew the ashes around the fire. This wind lasted four days. On the fifth morning, Albert took some lynx paws, singed them over the fire, and after he got them cleaned he made a little broth out of them. He waked his son and told him to drink the broth, and told him not to sleep as he knew Something was coming towards them. It was still snowing and windy and cloudy. He told his son he would go and meet the Thing that he knew was coming. He took his gun and snow shoes, and went to meet this *windigo*. Of course, as he went along, he sang and talked to his guardian spirits. He came to a place where there was a low bush of oaks. The wind grew stronger as he went farther, talking and singing. He could feel the power in his body. He felt like a *windigo* himself. (A *windigo* in this context is an ice-skeleton giant, with an insatiable cruelty and hunger. He bears enough resemblance to the European ogre to replace the latter in some borrowed European tales.) Suddenly he knew he was meeting the *windigo*. It was so strong and powerful that he lost his senses and almost turned away. But he trusted strongly in his own gods, and trusted that he could master any *windigo*... When he came to his senses he was sitting in the snow almost naked, holding a short diece of oak in his hand. He looked around and saw the snow trampled and the little oaks all broken. He sat there trying to remember what had happened. Already the sun was shining and the wind was going down, so he started on his way to camp where he had left his son. He went along and he picked up his clothes and

snow-shoes, and came to a place where he found his gun. The barrel
of the gun was stuck down in the snow. He never knew how his
gun came to be in the snow; the last he remembered was that he
had it in his hand. It was clearing, and the wind had gone down.
(These are indications of conquest over the enemy.) He had gone
only a short way when he saw tracks of a porcupine (further signs
of conquest, following as it does upon the period of starvation),
and he followed the tracks. The porcupine was on a tree and he
killed it. His luck had suddenly changed, and when he reached
camp, he saw his boy cutting wood. They cooked the porcupine,
and had a feast over it, and he thanked his guardian spirits for
having given him the power to master the false *windigo*. They
started home again, as they were short of everything. It was ten
days after he had mastered the *windigo*. When he reached home,
his wife told him that an old man had frozen to death beside the
water-hole ten days before. It made him think of the *windigo* he
had mastered. He was certain that it was he who had gotten the
best of this other man, the father of his former son-in-law.''

The deserted shaman-husband of Marsh Woman relentlessly
pursued his wife and the Ojibwa lover with whom she had
eloped. His prime motivation was not to humiliate his rival,
however, but to discipline his wife... The people had gathered at
the Hudson's Bay Post in the fall to secure supplies for winter
hunting. The deserted husband "also went there, and he heard
that his wife was there, living with Chief Eagle Wood. Old Berry
was very mad. He took his knife and started sharpening it. Somebody saw him doing it and warned Chief. Chief was sitting with
his wife and others in his wigwam. All at once Old Berry came in.
He was covered with a blanket, and he said, 'Here you are, you
dog!' He took Marsh Woman by the hand. He had his knife in the
other hand ready to cut her. Chief grabbed her other hand and
said, 'No, you cannot take her away from me.' And Old Berry
answered, 'Well, you can have half of her, and I will have the other
half,' but as he lifted his arm to halve her, a woman jumped. This
woman was Chief's aunt. She grabbed Old Berry's hand with
which he held the knife, and she threw him down where she had her
bedding and picked up a little axe, and said, 'You sit right here.
I want you to stay right here and live with me. You owe that to me,
as that first wife you had (an Ojibwa woman who had died) was my
sibmate and although she is dead you did not give me anything (in
cancellation of the ritual indebtedness). So you've got to marry me
and leave those two alone, and if you don't do as I tell you, I will
cut your back open with this axe' (an extreme execution of her

right to punish a sib debtor. The entire proceeding is especially humiliating to Old Berry and farcical to the others because both he and Marsh Woman are Crees, and the Crees, though in most respects nearly identical with the Ojibwa, do not recognize the sib system of remarriage). He promised he would do as she told him, and would not bother the others any more. For more than ten days he stayed there with this woman. Marsh Woman and Chief also stayed in the same wigwam. People made fun of him and the men used to laugh (for he not only had to surrender, but he had to watch his wife in the arms of another). He became ashamed, and one day he sneaked away from the woman and went back to his own country. So no one bothered the couple any more. After they had been married for two years, she had a baby girl. Her mother and father were with them now (having left Old Berry with whom they had lived until the hostilities just described).

"Chief got sick, paralyzed in his legs and one arm. He could not move at all, except for the one arm. For ten years he suffered like that. Also, his aunt died soon after Old Berry left. These were all the shaman's bad doings, through his dreams and bad medicine. Marsh Woman worked hard to make a living for her husband and child. At last, after ten years of suffering, Chief died and was buried, and of course it was all her fault...

"One day, as she was sitting outdoors, she saw Old Berry come ashore. He did not go to her wigwam, but he visited the other people who were camping there. Then he went away. He visited there often. She became frightened of him... she was afraid that he would bother her. And sure enough he came again, and that night he entered her wigwam while she was asleep. She woke, knowing that somebody was there. She got up and found Old Berry, her first husband. She asked him what he wanted. He did not say anything, but tried to lie down with her. She said to him, 'Get out of here, you old fool! I hate you because you brought so much suffering to my poor man, and at last you killed him. So I don't want you to bother me at all!' He said, 'We will see about that. I'm not going to leave you alone. You will have to marry me. If you don't, you will be sorry as I will do something to your beloved daughter. Tomorrow you wait for me right here. Don't you dare hide from me. I'm coming here with all my belongings to stay with you for good!' Then she grew frightened, for she loved her only daughter, and her daughter's life meant more to her than her own self. So she said yes to him, and he went away.

"The next evening she went to her mother-in-law and said, 'I want you to come and sleep in my wigwam. I want you to watch what I'm going to do!' So her mother-in-law came over. After dark the Cree man arrived with all his things. The old woman was already in bed. He came in and sat down beside Marsh Woman and started to bother her... he wanted to make love to her. She was so mad, and made up her mind to get rid of him some way for she really hated to lie down with him, and she knew very well that if she sent him away he would destroy her daughter. So she said to him, 'Leave me alone and go to bed if you want to stay here.' So the man did lie down. She reached for her little axe and hit him on the forehead, and killed him right there. She just split his forehead open. The old woman jumped up for she saw what her daughter-in-law had done. She did not say anything to Marsh Woman, but Marsh Woman spoke loudly and said (so the whole community could hear and be sympathetic witness to the act), 'I hate you so much, that's why I'm killing you. I don't want you to kill my only child, after you've killed the others. It's enough you killed my husband.' Then she got up, and someone came and threw the Cree out. So he was buried. She was very glad she got rid of him for he was such a bad man... All the people were on her side.''

Peewahsheek's husband fumed for a long time because his wife deserted him. First he tried to wound her by marrying her cousin. "But she didn't care what her husband did. The man and his second wife were gone all day and all night, and the next day. That night when Peewahsheek was sleeping, this man came to her tent and snatched her little boy. Just then she woke, and she knew right away what had happened. She jumped out of bed and ran out but the man was already in the canoe with the little boy. Peewahsheek and her parents followed, but they couldn't find them as it was pitch dark, so they went back. She was very downhearted. The boy was only four years old, going on five, and she worried much about him because there was no way of hearing how he was.

All winter she cried for her son, and sewed beautiful garments for him. In the spring she set out on the long and difficult trip from her Canadian home to the Leech Lake village where her husband was with their son. It took sixteen days of steady walking to make the trip. When she arrived at Leech Lake she stayed at the home of an old couple that had adopted her. She didn't see her little boy, as her husband's wigwam was four miles away, and she didn't like to go over there. Her adopted father went and said to her (former) husband that he should bring the little boy back to see his mother.. she had come far enough to see the boy. The man was quite surprised to hear that Peewahsheek had arrived in Leech Lake. He did take the little boy to see his mother. The boy was six years old and his father said, 'This is your mother.' The little boy said, 'Yes, I know this is my mother. I've been lonesome to see her for a long time, but I suppose you're not lonesome to see her because you used to fight her.' Peewahsheek gave her boy the things she had made for him: moccasins, beaded leggings, and coat made of rabbit, pants, and shirt. Then the man took the little boy home. After that, he brought him often to see his mother. She stayed with her adopted parents, and helped make sugar. The husband got so that he was not afraid to leave the little boy there. Peewahsheek saw her cousin (the second wife) who was abused just as she had been. Peewahsheek stayed there waiting (secretly) for the lakes to open so she could canoe back. Her (former) husband and his wife went away to hunt muskrats and the little boy was left in her charge, so she had a good chance to get away. Her adopted parents gave her a canoe and got her ready. She started off and paddled all day. In the evening she stopped and was sitting on the rocks when she saw a canoe coming. It was her husband's brother and his wife in search of her. She hid, and they passed by. She stayed there all the next day and in the evening they passed, going back. Then she started off again, and that night came to a camp. She got out of the canoe and went to the shack. There were two old people there. The old woman was very glad to see her and her boy, and told her that these other people had been there and had told them not to let her go by for she was kidnapping the boy. But Peewahsheek made them understand that it was her own boy, and told them that she had run away from her husband because he abused her. She showed them her head with all its scars. They told her to go, and gave her lots of food. So she was off again... she paddled all night and all day. Her little boy was happy to be with her."

She had further adventures on her flight, and visited other camps of Indians and of whites who had been warned of her coming and from whom she had to hide or make explanations justifying her flight. She paddled steadily and made some difficult portages, and eventually reached Kenora and the Indian agent. She stayed there four years feeling that the neighborhood was some protection against her husband's expected kidnapping raid. She put her son in the Government school as an additional safety measure, although she disapproved of the school itself.

"One time when she was getting birchbark, she met this man (her husband). He asked where the boy was, and she got very mad. She had a little axe in her hand and she made a gesture of hitting him. 'I would like to kill you!'... and did not tell him where the boy was. However he learned where the boy was, and watched him playing football. The boy saw his father, and ran into the school. But the man was permitted to see his son for twenty minutes and he gave his boy twenty dollars... Then one time Peewahsheek was washing her things on the shore. The man came there and said that he was suffering because she was not good to him. She answered that she did not want to have anything to do with him because he had made her suffer when she lived with him. She told him that he had pulled all her hair out, and that was enough for her; and even her cousin (his second wife) was almost dying at that time because of him. So he cried, and left her alone. Later she married a white man, a cook in a logging camp and she stayed and helped him... A little later she became lame. It was this man (her first husband) who caused her lameness. Her (second) husband took her to Winnipeg and she was cured, but she always limped a little after that."... It is seldom, however, that one spouse strikes at an offending husband or wife through the offspring, as Peewahsheek's husband did.

In a highly individualistic society such as this of the Ojibwa, where there are super-sensitivity to affront and violent expressions of protest, and where a person's wishes are at all times supremely important, it is not surprising to find a preponderance of stormy marriages, frequent divorces, and violent interludes. There are milder unions, also — ones in which there is little friction and ones which, though turbulent, do not lead to divorce. These are in the minority. At Emo, a reservation containing nearly three hundred Ojibwa, long genealogies were obtained which gave innumerable accounts of marital separations; apparently there were but seven men of the preceding generation who "had just one wife and stayed with her." The recently instituted Government control may affect the nature of marriage and divorce, and consequently an important cultural expression of the Ojibwa temperament.

In general there is great inconsistency between the theory and practise of Ojibwa institutions. For example, visions vouchsafed a person are supposed to remain a secret possession, yet most people learn one another's visions even to the details. Again, the war-party is supposed to be a close-knit group organized under the direction of one man and responsive to his every command; actually each man is his own captain, and the nominal leader can be displaced by a competent subordinate. In contrast to these, marriage relations are strikingly consistent. Marriage is theoretically the union of two people who like each other deeply, and in practise this is borne out. Divorce is supposed to be a natural consequence of indifference, or of offense, and this also is normally the case.

Most people are quite explicit about the motivations and details of marital and sexual life. There is rarely any hesitation in relating situations which have brought shame or rejection, or in telling of romantic episodes and memories. The life histories that people spin about themselves, and even about others whom they know only through hearsay, are most eloquent in those passages describing relations between the sexes. To the Ojibwa, these relations are not a simple succession of incidents, but exciting plots, all the emotional possibilities and psychological subtleties of which are analyzed in the telling.

Thoughts of romantic love are everywhere. The men, especially, are romantic. Freedom of sexual expression has not in any way interfered with the imaginative love constructs with which we are familiar in our own tradition. Occasionally an individual treasures the memory of a loved person for years, even though the person is married to someone else. A number of native myths involve sentimental love; and European tales dealing with a knight's chivalrous quest of a prisoned lady have been borrowed and are popular. There are native love songs; and jazz songs that deal with love are quickly annexed. Generally speaking, women take a passive role in a romantic relationship, just as they take subordinate parts in other relationships with men. They wait for the men to make sexual overtures, to confess feverish longing, and to suggest marriage or elopement. Suicide, or more often attempted suicide, over disappointed love is a familiar resort among women. Men seem to be more articulate than women about love. It is men who are said to be proud of their wives, not women of their husbands... Hole-in-the-Sky is a veritable gallant, and makes a point of being gay and charming to women and of flattering them inordinately. He has dreamed of women who revealed themselves as his guardian spirits. He has had deep attachments to a few selected women who came into his life at different times. He has never forgotten the first girl he loved and who ran away upon their marriage day; he fancies her as she was in her youth, with all her qualities magnified and the hurt to him consequently increased... An ardent nature may cause a life of jealousy, vengeance, and maliciousness in all its forms, but it is interesting to note that this is not necessarily the outcome; a life of love and faith is also considered the adequate expression of intensity. Adventures and hindrances are not necessary in an Ojibwa romance, but they are common. What is essential is to have a loved person who can be idealized; and often this is realized in unions that are externally drab.

The courtship of Tuhpuhsi's second husband was conducted in a manner that seems very familiar to us. Marsh Woman's lover, too, used phrases which are well known: "And he said to her, 'I am very lonely. I realize that I cannot go away without you and live alone. Can't you think of some way by which we can have each other ?'"

Eternal-Man was immediately attracted to the young man that found her in the woods: "She was sitting there in the bush watching the camp. The young man saw her from the back, went up to her quietly and spoke to her, saying, 'Huh! where did you come from ?' And oh! she got scared. She jumped up and said, 'Oh, I got lost long ago!' He said, 'Oh, then you must be the girl we heard of who got lost twenty-four days ago, away back across the (international) line.' She said, 'Yes,' and he said, 'Get up and come with me. I will take you.' She liked this man as soon as she saw him; and the man liked her also. She said she would go... She went along with him, and then she grew shy because she was all ragged and hair was uncombed, and she would not go with him any further. He left her there, but first he made her promise not to run away. 'If you do run away, I will go myself and get lost.' He also told her that he wanted her to be his wife. So she said, 'I will not run away, for I like you.'... They liked each other an awful lot, more and more... and he was always so good to her."

Glowing Woman was lost in the woods and wandered for days, frightened and desolate. After her rescue, she married a man who had sought her faithfully. Later she became very ill, and on her deathbed she cried aloud in protest, "Why didn't I die when I was in misery tearing through the woods ? Why must I die now when I want to live ? I am so happy with my man! I love him and want to live with him and with our children. Must I die when I am living happily ?"

Sheebahyash's romantic love for his wife was combined with a passionate jealousy that distorted much of his life. Finally he left her... The next day he thought, "'Why did I ever leave her ? Why am I so jealous of her for no cause ? She is so smart and was good to me... I love her, and couldn't find a better woman. But she will never forgive me! Oh well, I will go to some place near by, and I will hear what people say about her, what kind of woman they say she is when she is single.' He returned to the village where his wife was staying. She had returned to her parents and grandparents after he had left her. He sat around and listened for men's

9

(salacious) gossip about her, but he did not once hear any. He thought
to himself, 'Wasn't I foolish to leave such a nice woman just because
of jealousy, when I should have stayed with her and made a living
for the two of us ?' He was often sorry he ever left his wife." He
overheard more and more testimony to his wife's purity and indifference to men, and his desire for her was whetted. He tried to
approach her, but she beat him off, telling him that she would have
nothing to do with him because he had shamed her publicly by
claiming that she was a loose woman and by deserting her. Then
he began to day-dream about her, and as before, he neglected
hunting and trading to watch her. Finally, "he walked away with
a broken heart. He was sorry, also mad with himself for being so
(groundlessly) jealous. So he did not go near her again. He made
up his mind to try to forget her, which he could never do." He
remarried several times in the vain pursuit of forgetfulness. After
some years he was single again. "He heard that his first wife was
still single; she lived just like a man and killed lots of muskrats.
He tried to make up with her again, but she wouldn't have him at
all. His parents talked to him about her. They also were sorry that
she did not want him. Often they said to him that he had been
foolish to leave her, and that he would never again find another
woman like her. Once he went to her father, and asked him to tell
her to go back to him. The old man said, 'I cannot do anything
with her. It is your own fault. You were married to her once, and
you left her and made her ashamed. So I cannot make her marry
you. If she is willing to go back to you, it is all right with me.' But
his first wife did not want him. His mother and her mother talked
it over, for they liked each other, and said they would love to see
their children live together again. The girl's mother advised her to
go back to this man. She did not answer anything, though her
mother told her that it was not nice for her to do that (repudiate
a man); and that people would make fun of her if she did not marry;
and also that they (the parents) were old now and would soon die
and leave her alone. Finally she said that for her mother's sake she
would go back to him; but deep down in her heart she really cared
for him. When he came to her, she made him promise that he
would never again be jealous of her groundlessly. He did promise,
so they lived together again and were good to each other and were
happy. He was so proud of her, and ashamed of himself. . . ."

Two people who marry because of a mutual passion, stand alone
in the world. Literally, they are the world to each other, for the
affinal obligations that are found in neighboring regions, and in
most parts of the world, are absent in Ojibwa. An individual owes

nothing to the parent-in-law or to the child-in-law except a certain politeness of speech and general deportment (see *Ojibwa Sociology*, chapters 2 and 4). All the important economic obligations are restricted to members of the domestic household. Indeed, there is a latent hostility between households which is not at all set aside in the interests of affinal relationships. This is particularly true of romantic unions where the principals have arranged their marriage privately without the intercession of the respective parents who may not even know one another and who may be totally ignorant of the plans of the young people. This latent hostility becomes active occasionally, and some of the vilest imputations of evil intent and sorcery are cast by a person upon the parent-in-law. Some myths are concerned with a man's efforts to starve his son-in-law to death, and the same actions are attributed to certain living individuals. One woman drove her visiting son-in-law out of her house... This detached attitude toward the closest affinal relative—the view that he is a member of another household and therefore a stranger — expresses itself in another way. This is in taking the child-in-law as a sexual mate. Even the accusation of "incest" loses much of its force in comparison with the feeling that the in-law is a complete stranger.

In certain cases the responsibility for a marriage does rest with the parents. In these marriages there is not the complete isolation described above, for the parents feel certain obligations toward the new household. This feeling of responsibility, where each set of parents treats the new domicile as an extension of its own, arises from the fact that the two households of the parents were originally close, and that the usual hostility was reduced to a minimum. The arranged marriage and parental supervision of the newly married couple are manifestations of the friendship of the parents themselves; it cannot be thought of as prescriptively affinal behavior. Even such a marriage, as it becomes established, gradually loses its sponsorship and comes to function as a self-sufficient, independent economic unit. Often the elderly or devoted parents of one spouse live in the new home for shorter or longer periods, but this is not in any sense enjoined behavior; it is an expression of affection on the part of parents and child. The elders have no voice in the affairs of the young couple, and if possible the two generations conduct their housekeeping independently.

Thus the typical Ojibwa marriage is a lone domestic enterprise. Marital life is the most continous social experience in each person's career. Clearly, it is a very limited social experience, especially for a monogamous couple. But every cultural effort has been made to charge it with excitement and beauty.

9*

Part III.

OCCUPATIONS.

All those talents and traits of character which we think of as functions of a total personality are regarded by the Ojibwa as isolated, objective items which may be acquired in the course of life by individuals who are fortunate enough to coerce them from the supernaturals. In Ojibwa thought, there is no original and absolute "self"; a person freshly born is "empty" of characteristics and of identity. Consequently tremendous pressure is exerted upon a young person to pursue the supernaturals and move them to fill up his "emptiness." The term connotes principally inadequacy in the hunt, war, and shamanistic practise, all of which are essentially masculine occupations. Shamans speak of themselves in conventionally humble phrases as being "poor," "nothing;" they do this partly in testimony to the fact that all that they have and are is a direct gift from the supernaturals. A person may live his whole life in "emptiness" if he is vouchsafed no visions and no talents.

All of this great pressure to secure personal qualities is levelled directly upon the male; it is he preeminently whose personality is of importance. As we have seen, women are given little consideration culturally. To women are allotted the quiet, sedentary, and domestic occupations that are not considered dependent upon supernatural gifts. This neglect is bolstered by the belief that women, because of their harmful blood discharges, must be kept from contact with the bountiful supernaturals. One noted shaman went so far as to say that his supernatural "brother" dreaded a woman's bloomers as symbols of her sex and maleficence.

Prescriptively feminine work is extremely varied. It is learned and practised by every girl, no matter to what extent she may supplement it with male work. She sets simple twine traps about the wigwam to catch whatever small creatures may wander into them; these are usually rabbits. She does this regularly, and it is the first lesson in trapping which she teaches her children. The snared rabbit is skinned, the meat and bones thrown into the cooking pot, the fur saved for weaving into rabbit robes. These robes are pretty and warm, and invaluable to hunters. The woman cuts the fur of one rabbit into a long, thin, continuous rope, which is tied onto another such rope made from the fur of another rabbit; one rope is then used in the weaving as weft, and another rope as warp. They use long strips of grass and cedar bark for weaving also, and make mats out of them to be used on the floor or stood up against the lodge wall. Native or commercial twine is used to crochet fishnets used by women and men.

Women tan deer and moose hides in several different ways, to produce varying grades of fineness and coarseness in texture, and colors that range from brownish tan to a yellowish cream. The desired texture and color are determined by the use to which the hide will be put. Moccasins for serviceable wear are made of a leather that is tanned to a rich tan color and to a coarse thick texture, whereas moccasins used at dances are made of leather as delicate and pretty as a European's kid glove.

Women used to do all the tailoring and sewing, but this work has been displaced partially by commerical products. They still make moccasins and the bead-embroidered "aprons" men wear at native dances. An "apron" is a huge pocket for a man's tobacco, flint or matches, and pipe, slung under one arm by long straps which cross over the opposite shoulder. A well-outfitted dancer wears a pair of such aprons. Some women in the hinterland still make hide garments for their men, cut however after the fashion of European garments. They also make mitts and caps of muskrat hide and fur. In olden times, the women made a long shirt, loin cloth, leggings, and a sort of wind-break rabbit blanket for the men; for themselves they made an extra-long shirt or dress with attachable sleeves held in place by draw strings, shorter leggings than those worn by the men, and a rabbit blanket. "People were never sick in those days. They did not get sick until they commenced wearing White clothes, and the men began to cut their hair." Today many women tailor calico and serge garments for themselves and their young children. They also clean and mend their husbands' garments and adornments. This is quite a gesture among the Ojibwa, for ordinarily the rigid separateness of individuals extends as well to their possessions. The husband generally does not reciprocate this gesture, however.

The "moss-back" cradles in which infants are carried, or were carried until lately, are made in two stages, one of which is men's work and the other women's. The husband makes the wooden frame, the wife makes the leather sack or blanket which is sewn onto the frame, and is laced around the infant. The leather of the sack is now being replaced by velvet, as being more modish. Snowshoes are likewise made in two stages. The man makes the wooden frame, and his wife or sister or mother weaves or crochets the raw-hide (usually moose hide) mesh.

Women of the backwoods still manufacture their own needles and thread, or did until very recently. The needle is made of a marten's penis-bone, or sometimes of tough wood. The thread is made from the long back tendons of moose and deer, sometimes from the tendons of dead horses, occasionally from buffalo tendons, whenever a buffalo strayed into the woods for shelter and was caught there. The tendons are prepared by separating out the component threads, which are then stretched and dried; "and they never break." Some plant products are also used as sewing thread, especially for binding together bark blankets and utensils.

Some women still prepare native vegetable dyes, though these are being increasingly supplemented by commercial products. The native colors are brilliant and fast. They were used chiefly for coloring porcupine quills which were then sewn onto deer hide in blocks that formed geometrical designs of triangles, diamonds, and squares. I have seen specimens of these natively dyed quills that are about a half-century old and which still sparkle though the quills themselves are partly broken, the commercial thread is rotten, and the hide is grey with age. In these old pieces, the native colors were a deep orange-scarlet, a gleaming yellow that darkened occasionally into light orange, and a deep violet or purple. There were also a dark pink and a light bluish green which the Indians consider commerical, but which they think had native analogues.

Women used to embroider hide garments and moccasins with porcupine quill work. Some women still know how to prepare the quills and how to sew them on. The quills are plucked out of a freshly killed porcupine, and steeped in hot water for several days until they become pliable. The quills, which are normally ovoid and resistant, are then easily flattened out by applying pressure with the thumb nail. They are dipped in the dyes, and left to dry. When used in embroidery, the quill is placed in a verti-cal position and each end is passed over and under a fine thread loop.

Quill work has been supplanted by the far simpler bead work. The use of beads was concomitant with the introduction of curvi-linear designs. The old geometric designs have almost entirely disappeared with the disappearance of the quill technique. In bead-work, a varying number of beads are strung on a thread and tacked down with a stitch at intervals. This is an entirely different tech-nique from that employed in the quill work. Embroidery in silks is also popular, and is handled like beadwork.

Until recently, women made a number of utensils out of birch-bark. These included implements for cooking, eating, and storing. The sides were sewn together with native thread, and handles were attached in the same way. Large, relatively decorative spoons were made of wood. Hunters still resort to bark and wood utensils. Bark utensils used to be decorated by the women. They would bite into the fresh bark, and with their teeth imprint geometrical and curvi-linear designs. This is now a lost art.

Birchbark is also used for roofing. This bark is indispensable to the wigwam. It is waterproof, breaks the winds, and is easily portable. Women roll large sheets of it off the tree in early summer, toughen it before the fire and in the sun, correct uneven and weak spots, and sew sheets together end to end to make an ample blanket for the roof.

Women pick berries and cherries throughout the summer months: strawberries, blueberries, gooseberries, chokecherries. Curiously, they are not interested in raspberries. They cook all this fruit and eat it as a simple boiled dish, pour it into soup, eat it with meat or wild rice or fish, and recently have learned to make fruit pies. They also dry the fruit, storing it for future use in the fall and winter. The Ojibwa who neighbor the Cree also make pemmican, and chop dried fruit up with the meat.

Women harvest and preserve aquatic rice, assisted by their husbands. A man poles the canoe while his wife harvests the grain. Each woman spreads her rice on the ground upon a bark spread, or upon a rack, to dry in the sun. Then it is placed upon a rack over a fire, to cure in the thick smoke. The husband then treads the rice, to loosen the husks; then his wife fans the trodden rice. When it is prepared, it is stored in a fawnskin sack.

Women assume the principal role in sugar-making. Most of the maple-sugar groves are owned in the name of some woman. The entire family goes to the sugar groves. A woman, her husband, and her grown children who are as yet unmarried choose certain trees upon which to work alone. Each person drives a cut into a tree and places a pan at the base of the tree to receive the sugar sap. When the pans are full of sap, they are emptied into great kettles or tubs near the wigwam. The woman places the tubs over great fires, and vigorously stirs the sap with a paddle while it boils. Each tub of sap is treated somewhat differently, depending upon its ultimate use as syrup, ground sugar, or block sugar. For example, the sap intended for syrup does not boil as long as that designed for ground sugar, more water is poured into it, it is stirred more, and the fire is not so fierce.

Every woman sets out nets for fish, especially during the seasons of open water. Fish is used for the lighter meals, such as breakfast, also to tide over shortages in the meat supply, or to add variety to the diet. It is considered a most important item. The large organs of some large fish are used as storing utensils; oil, for instance, was formerly stored in sturgeon bladders.

A woman often aids her husband in his hunting. While the husband does the actual shooting, she handles the canoe on duck or moose hunts, and is on the watch for game and for signs of danger. She also performs part of the sacrifices her husband must offer after a successful bear or moose hunt. She cleans the skull of the bear, paints it "prettily" in red and blue circles and stripes, adorns it with bright colored ribbons, slings a small sack of tobacco about it, and hangs it on some tree. She handles the "bell" of the moose head with the same respect, adorns it with ribbons, and hangs it aloft with a sack of tobacco.

The woman cures fish and meat in different ways. Fish secured in winter, and meat also, if there is a surplus, is hung on racks to be frozen, and this weathering alone preserves it. In summer and early fall fish is cured by exposure to sun and smoke. Jerked meat is treated in the same way, but the process may continue through the winter.

Women gather herbs for food and medicinal purposes. The food herbs are chiefly tea-substitutes; they are less in demand now than in earlier days. However each woman is still busily occupied collecting medicinal herbs, of which a great variety are employed. The bark of certain trees is used as medicament and nourishment during times of winter starvation.

Herbal doctoring is practised by both men and women. That is, women do not become eligible for the profession as a simple consequence of their sex; but those who are vitally interested in the work apply themselves to it continuously, and the gifted ones are recognized and are in constant demand by patients. The native pharmacopoeia is remarkably extensive; besides herbs, it includes animal products such as bear gall and certain skunk secretions. There are numerous traditional prescriptions for a great variety of ailments, and new prescriptions seem to be invented daily. Pharmaceutics is the interest of older, rather than of younger women; or it may be that older women have become distinguished through long practise. Middle-aged women spend days grubbing in the soil, and return laden with branches and roots. Their wigwams are hung with sacks containing these materials, waiting for the occasion to be brewed into a prescription. Some women are so interested that they trade with individuals in distant groups of Cree, Dakota, etc., to secure herbs that are not indigenous.

Women are the midwives of the Ojibwa. Men are excluded from a childbirth except for a certain brief magical performance which is resorted to in a desperate case. Midwifery is a highly skilled occupation, depending upon an extensive herbal knowledge, detailed knowledge of the female anatomy and physiology, varied massage techniques, and a cool and resourceful intelligence. This profession, too, is not open to all women but only to those who show marked apitude and interest. Public recognition of a woman's ability is expressed by repeated requests for her services at confinements.

Women, together with children and disabled older men, are important as a chorus to the exploits of the warriors. As the men leave for the war-path, the women are supposed to escort them part way in canoes, cheering them on with songs that promise victory, referring to old conquests, reminding them of unsatisfied grievances against the Sioux, deriding the Sioux. If the warriors return successful, the women are notified of the fact by the men's songs of conquest, and paddle out in a welcoming body, to greet them with songs and cheers and to snatch the enemy scalps. If the warriors return defeated, the women are again notified by the dirges that the men sing, and they remain ashore, singing a mournful response.

Women continually make artistic contributions which are much appreciated, but which are given no formal recognition. Artistic women — in marked contrast to gifted men — are given no title nor are they regarded with the awe that indicates general respect. Many of the native love songs which are immensely popular, known over several localities, and passed down for several generations, have been composed by women. Songs are composed quite spontaneously by women while at their work; they are overheard by others who repeat and add to them, and they are gradually added more or less permanently to the cultural stock. Not much less than one hundred years ago, Two Seated Woman composed a song in quite a homely fashion at her work. Her lover had departed for a time, and missing him, she hummed about him:

> "Now I start to weep.
> My lover went away.
> Without him how will I cross
> When I come to the Path-leading-to-the-river?

He told me, my lover,
'Don't cry, don't,
When I depart for the Path-leading-to-the-river.
Do not worry, do not mind.'

Indeed, I will follow him.
To the Path-leading-to-the-river he went.
But indeed, how will I cross
When I come to the Path-leading-to-the-river?

Ah-h-h, then I will see my lover."

About seventeen years ago, Maggie dreamed, or invented, a most complicated choreography for a group of sixty persons. She also composed accompanying songs: the melodies, the words, and the drum-beats for about eighty songs. This dance organization lasted for about ten years and was then discontinued. However Maggie's songs are still sung at native dances within an area of about one hundred square miles, often by people who never saw her, always by people who are not interested in her personally although they know that "the songs come from her dance."

Women are most important in rearing children. To her daughter, the woman is the model of female accomplishments, and she takes pains to teach her daughter the conventional techniques and attitudes. A father is in the same way his son's guide and teacher, yet the mother is important in spurring on her son. She continually says how proud she would be if he killed a beaver, or a bear, if he was industrious, if he "dreamed, and learned about himself," if he left the country and brought home a Sioux scalp; and when her son has made her proud, even if only in a small way, she lavishes praise upon him and teaches her daughter to admire him.

All of a woman's work is done alone, although certain stages of it may be in the hands of her husband, son, or brother, as in sugar and rice manufacture, the provision of meat and hides, and the instruction of her son. Men, too, work alone and upon individual responsibility. Isolation in work is naturally most marked during the five or six months of winter when the wigwam is set apart from all others, and the family lives as though alone in the world. A man goes on his trails for a week or two and his wife stays alone at the wigwam and works. Her elderly mother, her co-wife, and her grown daughter may be in the lodge with her, doing the same work, but each woman does her task separately, and there is rarely any division of labor. The great division of labor is in the assignment to the men of hunting and of securing raw materials, and the assignment to the women of manufacturing the raw materials. Within these great divisions, it is usual for each person to execute all the stages of any task he is engaged upon. This arrangement furthers the individual's personal initiative and sense of aloneness. The chief exception to this is in the preparation of rice, where a man and woman work simultaneously and cooperatively.

The man's work is much less varied than the woman's, but it is appraised culturally as infinitely more interesting and honorable. It has about it an indescribably glittering atmosphere. It is notable that the culture hero cycle deals almost exclusively with men and with the deeds of men, while women are introduced as the most shadowy of lay figures. Even in the tales of European origin, which are more often about women than the aboriginal tales, women's work is barely hinted at. Women accept these values quietly, and further them by falling into the role of onlookers who watch and admire with bated breath.

Every man must hunt game and birds and trap for fur, regardless of any specific ambitions for glory. Hunting is regarded strictly as a man's sphere, and every man's participation is obligatory. A grown son who refuses to do his quota of hunting is practically left to starve. A married man who is too lazy to hunt can be supported by his wife for a time, but her tolerance will change to scorn, then to indifference, and finally she will desert him. A man who is unsuccessful on the hunt, and who goes with his wife to her parents' wigwam, can expect to be rejected and left to die of starvation. In one case the parents' scorn was so great that they took their daughter in to feed and lodge her, but refused their son-in-law. Folk-tales are concerned with the same theme. From his earliest years a boy is trained in his responsibility, is taught the techniques, is early though gradually thrust upon his own initiative, and is impelled to seek visionary support.

Men's fishing is important, but apparently no more important than women's fishing. In southwest Ontario and southeast Manitoba, men's fishing differs from women's, while in northwest Minnesota the styles are the same. In Canada, the characteristic men's style is, or was, to fish with the lance. During the seasons of open water, a man was paddled by a female household relative while he looked down throught the clear water for sturgeon, pike, and whitefish. Upon syping a fish, he plunged his lance into it. In winter, when alone on his trapping grounds, a man built himself a tiny wigwam over a hole he had made in the icy surface of a lake, squatted over the hole with a torch and his lance, and when a fish came in sight, he speared it. This form of fishing typically is never practised by women. In Minnesota, men fish with nets during July and August, as women do also. Undoubtedly fishing with nets was stimulated by the market which the United States government has created for fish, for a greater haul can be made by net than by lance. The requirements of the Minnesota market have also caused these Ojibwa to cease extensive fishing during fall, winter, and spring to permit replenishment of the lakes by summer.

Men manufacture certain tools necessary for their hunting and fishing. In early days, each man made his own bows and arrows, and men are still alive who know the art. Small but highly effective bows and arrows are sometimes made for boys by grandparents or parents, and nearly all men know how to handle bow and arrow. Today of course, firearms are purchased, and the men are so well acquainted with their principles of operation that they can mend and almost rebuild a gun that has been injured in some way. Steel knives are bought, but when shortages arise the men fashion crude implements of wood or bone; the women do the same.

Snowshoes are even more essential than a gun. Men make the frame out of some flexible and wiry wood like black ash, and women weave the mesh out of moose rawhide. When necessary, men can weave the mesh.

Canoes are considered the work of men. If a man is married, however, or has a strong young daughter or son at home with him, some of his family will aid him part, or all, of the time. Still, canoe manufacture is within the compass of one man, and even women sometimes make their own canoes. A man digs a trough in the earth, in the shape of a canoe, to serve as a mold. Inside this he builds the skeleton of the canoe—bottom, sides, and gunwale—and around the frame he wraps a fine sheet of birchbark. Pitch is applied to the seams. The canoe is placed in the water to remain for some days and be rendered seaworthy.

War has been a pursuit almost as imperative for all men as hunting. It has no direct economic value, but it testifies to qualities which are indispensable in the economic struggle. A successful warrior is one who has been granted specific powers by mighty supernaturals, powers which exactly parallel those necessary to successful hunting. A competent warrior must be able to divine the fate of the war-party, and to arrange his movements accordingly. He must be able to influence the weather: to cause winds to shift in a direction favorable to his party and unfavorable to the enemy, to raise a mist, to make rain fall and erase the tracks of his party. His movements must be so cautious, so finely timed that he can stalk the enemy undetected, as he would stalk game. A warrior who displays all these qualities is called "manido" ("extraordinary, superhuman"), also "brave" for he does not flinch at possible death. One conventional purpose of war is to show off courageous and extraordinary qualities, and to bring back an enemy scalp in testimony of them. But the death and capture of enemies is desired for more than mere display purposes, for the motivations of the feud have been displaced onto the war pattern. Among the Ojibwa, a male sibling or other close relative is supposed to avenge the murder of a person. But outright murder rarely occurs among them, and deaths are therefore said to be caused by the machinations of some sorcerer. Generally a sorcerer cannot be killed. Therefore all the pent-up bitterness against murderer-sorcerers is displaced onto the Sioux who have indeed killed a number of Ojibwa. Consequently when the Ojibwa organize a war-party, the cry is generally to avenge the deaths of brothers, father, or uncles who have been killed by the Sioux. War therefore has been felt imperative for all males because it has offered a test of ability and provided a vent for the obligations of the blood feud. Even today, though war has been abolished for about fifty years, old Hole-in-the-Sky fidgets and sulks in the presence of a Sioux, and mutters bitterly that he wants to kill him "for he knows how many of his relatives the Sioux have killed."

There is no formal centralization of power among the Ojibwa, but to the extent that the sorcerers intimidate the people, they dominate their society. Shamanism is preeminently a masculine claim, but is not considered a vocation of which all males are equally capable. All men are eligible to appeal to the supernaturals for certain shamanistic gifts, but it is not believed that all men can be rewarded. Other shamanistic abilities are acquired by purchase, but this also is selective since not all men have the means of purchase.

Shamanism is a comprehensive term that among the Ojibwa includes several categories. Divination is one shamanistic specialty, and includes several varieties within itself. All divining talents are visionary gifts. The curing of illness is another shamanistic specialty. Two major curing forms—sucking doctor technique, and the Sun Dance—are abilities obtained through the vision. Other major curing forms — *midewiwin* or Grand Medicine Dance, and herbal ministrations — are techniques which are purchased. Two minor curing forms for healing local parts by tattooing are acquired by visions, and two others which consist of herbal ministrations are bought. Sorcery, that is, the supernatural power to afflict an enemy at will, is eminently the power of men, and is secured sometimes

through visions and sometimes by purchase. Weather control is also a
shamanistic procedure learned by vision. Certain male shamans, those
who are eminent as sorcerers and *mide* practitioners, have the right
to conduct burial ceremonies. This is considered a shamanistic claim
because it involves control of the supernaturals. If not approached
by the soul of the deceased correctly, as instructed by the shamans,
the supernaturals are prepared to interrupt the journey of the soul
into the next world. *Mide* shamans acquire by purchase the rare ability of writing certain sacred mnemonics upon birchbark. But as they
frequently employ a female household relative as amanuensis, a certain
knowledge of the hieroglyphs spreads throughout the population.

Certain male shamanistic practises center around war, hunting,
and trapping. These are divining procedures of five different sorts
(polter-geist stunts in a tent; juggling with fire; gazing into a bowl
of blood; scapulimancy; the dread appearance of an amphibious
rodent), and techniques for controlling the weather, especially the
direction and force of the wind, the rate of freezing up the lakes,
and the severity of snowfall. Two or three of the divining procedures are frequently practised by women, however, and transferred
to spheres other than war and hunting. One of these is the *wabənu*
(fire-juggling that must end at dawn). A female *wabənu* assists
her husband if he is a *wabənu*, in giving the ceremonies and in
divining the cause and course of illness. Another divining procedure
allowed to women is a sketchy kind of scapulimancy resulting from
a violated taboo. Beaver bones should be returned to their natal
waters; and when they are allowed to fall into the fire instead
they are scorched into a tracery which the housewife reads for,
omens of sickness and death. The third divining measure, allowed
to all, including women, is similaer to our black cat superstition.
When a certain water rodent appears on land, hobbling along with
its webbed paws flapping away from its body, it is believed to be a
harbinger of death in the domicile by which it stops. Women also
share with men the prescriptive right to secure visions giving
longevity to the visionary, and granting the power to give a name
to a stated number of other persons.

Since the advent of the traders, Ojibwa men have learned how
to barter. They trade furs and meat which they have secured in
hunting, and since the men, rather than the women, possessed the
materials desired by the Whites, they became the traders. Today,
when rice and berries and maple sugar are commanding some white
attention, the women also are learning to function as dealers.

Occasional men, perhaps one or two in a given region, possess the
ability to model in pipe-stone. There is a general sentiment that

this skill is a supernatural gift acquired through a vision. No women seem to have the ability, and today the number of men who model is so small that it is difficult to establish any genealogical lines of inheritance. Jim Horton is the only man so gifted at the Manitou Reserve. His major work, made with only a jack-knife, is a black pipe-stone pipe, the stone stem eighteen inches long, and the bowl three and a half inches high. Around the stem is carved a snake, twined around and around from one end to the other. The scales of the snake-skin, the muscular twists of the coiled body, the details of the fixed eyes, are all carved with loving minuteness and emphasized by judiciously placed silvery coatings of lead. Another impressive pipe was seen at Red Lake, but its owner had died and with him the regional knowledge of the technique. This pipe is of red pipe-stone, somewhat shorter than the one mentioned, the stem being eleven inches long, and the bowl about three inches high. No figure is carved on it, but various geometrically outlined areas are beautifully planed on the several sides; the piece of stone was selected for its handsomely spaced, natural color striations, varying from deep purplish brick to light Spanish tile.

Serious inroads are made upon a fast occupational sex dichotomy because of the Ojibwa respect for ability, and stress upon individualism. There are numerous women with an aptitude for pursuits that are culturally defined as masculine, for they at one time or another engage in these occupations. Everywhere there are some women who hunt, go to war, and doctor as men do. Women who perform masculine work do so with a feeling that they are assuming simply an additional role, one which is defined as unusually difficult but which for them is surrounded by no status aura. People take such women seriously at face value, and explain them as beneficiaries of the supernatural whom their blood discharges did not completely frighten. But the behavior of these women is never taken to be characteristically feminine despite the fact that even the most conservative women usually find it necessary to take up some prescriptively masculine work at one time or another. The cultural view of the normal woman remains unchallenged and finds expression in the training that is usual for girls. Those women whose behavior is exceptional are not judged with reference to the conventional standard but with reference to their individual fortunes only. The conduct of the ideal woman, therefore, and the behavior of any individual woman may be quite at variance.

The attitude towards men's work, on the other hand, permits of no leniency. Boys are consistently trained to a categorical male consciousness—urged to occupy themselves with men's work, stimulated with a variety of incentives, and in every way taught to distinguish themselves from women. Each individual man is measured against an absolute standard of masculine behavior and he is judged accordingly. A man's personal honor rests upon exclusive devotion to the masculine skills, and a man would dishonor and betray his masculinity by venturing out of his field. Ojibwa society is therefore less exacting in its occupational demands for women than it is for men, and since women may learn all skills, or encroach upon all skills, they are much more versatile than men.

The theoretical occupational dichotomy does not rest as a simple function of sex difference, but is employed also to make caste-like distinctions between male and female. The Ojibwa make the generalization that any man is intrinsically and vastly superior to any woman. Naturally the work assigned to men is judged accordingly. Among neighboring tribes, male supremacy expresses itself also in the belief that even the men who repudiate their masculinity and adopt the role of a female, do feminine work better than the best of women. Among the Ojibwa the superiority of men and of the work done by men, find a collateral expression in the unformulated belief that woman who do men's work are superior to other women. Women are not taught any responsibility to their sex group, to its horizons and values, as men are; and when they deviate, there is little thought that they are violating any fundamental canons, or attempting impossibilities or anomalies.

Those women who cross the occupational line and take up men's work, do so casually, under the pressure of circumstances or of personal inclination. They follow up the girlhood training which they received from the lesser avoidance relatives, or are taught men's occupations by specially interested husbands, or are forced to men's work through the exigencies of widowhood, desertion, illness of the husband, etc. They are designated by no special term, there are no alterations in costume or linguistic forms, they are never suspected of sexual irregularities even though some never marry, they have no privileges that do not pertain to the occupation they follow, they are never jeered at. Women regard them as "extraordinary" or "queer." Men regard them rather in the light of the occupation they follow; to them a girl who qualifies as a warrior is considered as a warrior, not as a queer girl.

In the training of a girl, the lesser avoidance relatives are most important in developing her unconventionality, for they employ her as an assistant in their work. A girl who accompanies her father on a duck or moose hunt must learn all the cautions of the hunt except the actual shooting. Personal inclinations may then tip the scales of sex difference. This is evidenced in the case of Half Sky, a girl visionary. She was her father's eldest and favorite daughter, and his constant companion throughout her youth. "She learned everything by watching him"; her interest delighted him, so he taught her the masculine prerogatives of setting complicated traps and of handling a gun. After his death, her heart-broken sorrow righted itself through an identification with him so that she took up the masculine duties and honors of her widowed mother's lodge. She not only could do the work of men but she also felt the responsibilities of me...... Sheeba had also learned a good deal from her father. After her mother's death she undertook to rear her little sister, and taught her hunting in addition to women's trapping and fishing. In time the two girls had a lodge together and lived comfortably by hunting and fishing. The girls ceased hunting, however, after marriage, to follow exclusively feminine work..... It is common to find widows living alone with their children, supporting them with the aid of the elder daughter, as a father would. The two women "hunt like men", at the same time that they carry on the women's industries.... Gaybay was an only daughter who often accompanied her father. When she was ten or twelve years old, he died. She was then old enough and with enough experience to aid her widowed mother in supporting the lodge; so the two women used to trap all kinds of furs for the trade. After her marriage, Gaybay did less trapping since operating an independent trapping line breaks up the domestic household; but she resumed after her widowhood.... If a man's only child is a daughter, it is almost a certainty that he will teach her the work of a man, at the same time that her mother will teach her the work of a woman. This was the case with Iron Woman, the daughter of a famous shaman. She was noted for her "supernatural" ability at all skilled activities: religious performances, games, hunting. Her father had taught her carefully, and had provoked her to prove her superiority over others. She was so interested she never thought of marrying and maintaining her own lodge; besides "she thought no man was good enough for her." Her parents did not coax her to marry; they were interested chiefly in making her their companion in all that they knew and did ... The stepfather, who is the real or titular "father's brother", commonly engages his wife's daughter to assist him, and this often develops into an unconventional training for the girl. The relationship suffers, however, from its tendency to slip into attempted rape, when the frightened girl flies and refuses all further association with the man. An assistantship with the grandfather meets with the same opportunities and disadvantages.

10

It is often difficult to determine the influences which have been decisive in persuading a woman to do men's work. Since no serious institutional obstacles are placed in the path of a woman's assuming men's roles, it is difficult to gauge the positive force of a woman's native bent; it is simpler to estimate its absence, as when a widowed mother refuses to hunt or trap but has to be supported on the doles of neighbors.

A variety of social situations in childhood seems to favor female unconventionality in many individual cases. The instances above illustrate how unconventionality may be the lot of the only daughter, as well as of the favorite, or eldest, or orphaned daughter. Illegitimate or neglected children may fare likwise. Illegitimate mothers marry as easily as more respectable women do, and their children are often dearly loved by the stepfather. Thus, Ahtushkish had no children of his own, but loved his wife's bastard daughter so much that he called her *n'danis* (my own female issue), not *ndoẓ mi kwem* (my brother's daughter, or my rival's female issue) and he took her with him on his less strenuous hunting trips.... Neglected children, whether or not legitimately born, are often adopted by a woman or by a couple in memory of a deceased child. Contrary to many adoption practises elsewhere, neglected children are often taken into the household of adoptive parents and there accorded the finest treatment. In repeated instances, such an adoptive daughter, who is usually the only child, acts as the hunter for her widowed "mother," applying the knowledge she has acquired in youth from the adoptive mother or father. Sky Woman bore this relation to her "grandmother." The grandmother had chosen to live alone after her husband's death, and had therefore assumed and perfected all skills, masuline as well as feminine. Her motivations were solely personal; the only sanction requisite for her occupational irregularities was her own approval. Sky Woman came to live with her grandmother when she was nine years old. She had been reared as the only child in a turbulent and even bitter household, where she was left much to herself, and spent her time in day-dreaming. Her parents were intense people, much absorbed in each other, extremely jealous and given to quarreling. The child had been neglected by them in both their loving and their stormy periods. To cap all, one of her parents used to desert temporarily in a fury, and if her mother were the deserter, the father would set off in pursuit, leaving the child alone. One day, when her parents were engaged in a fierce quarrel, Sky Woman fled from the din. She wandered for days, and kept herself hidden in the bush. A searching party of Indians discovered her, among them the old woman whom Sky Woman came to claim as her grandmother. The old woman treated her gently, and begged her to live with her, promising her fine clothes, food, and love. So the little girl agreed. She found herself in a wigwam without men, with no rival claimant upon the old woman's care and tenderness. Sky Woman thought of her grandmother as the one security in the world. She became fanatically attached to the old woman, abjured her parents, sisters, aunts and uncles, refused to associate with other people, or to consider marriage until after her grandmother's death, and in every way spun her life about her grandmother. The old woman taught her skills to a receptive pupil: life necessities and love shaped Sky Woman's inclinations. "Her grandmother taught her to do everything that the Indian woman does. She could do bead-work on a frame, and also the other beadwork (laying the beads on hide or cloth, stitching them down with thread), could tan hides, weave mats, cedar bags, and yarn bags, also make nets, birchbark coverings for wigwams, and birchbark baskets. She learned how to trap, to set snares and nets. They were both good hunters. She also made snowshoes. So they always had lots of nice things." But Sky Woman went further than this. "In the fall they went to Swampy River. They used to hunt and fish there every fall, and they stayed until the lakes froze up. They gathered a lot of meat, fish, muskrats, and rabbits, and they killed a bear and made lots of bear grease. While they were there her grandmother got sick, so sick that she thought she would not live. So Sky Woman sent word by someone who was passing by to tell the people that her grandmother was sick and might not live.... so that people would know how they were. She never slept, watching over her grandmother. One time she fell asleep and dreamed of the time she had been lost. She dreamed that someone gave her a rattler and other things they use when they doctor, and spoke to her saying, 'Try this on your grandmother. She might get better.' So when she woke she made a little rattler, and started to *nananda wiat* (cure by sucking). When she finished, the old woman seemed to be brighter. That night she started again on *manito kazo* (talking-supernatural, or invoking supernatural) and cure by sucking. Before she was through she heard somebody outside. It was her father and mother and some people coming to see how they were. She did not stop with her *manito kazo*, but kept right on until she finished. Her father and mother made their wigwam close by, and about four days after, her grandmother got better and was up and around, so then from that people knew that she was a sucking doctor and she was wanted from one place to another to doctor

10*

the sick." Sky Woman continued to hunt and fish until she was married, and she resumed after her widowhood. She also continued to cure illness, but did so in response to solicitations rather than in man-like pursuance of a career. Indeed, her curing was so intimately bound up with her experiences with her grandmother that when at last the old woman died, she threw away her curing paraphernalia and claimed that her usefulness was over.

Unconventional girls are not necessarily of marked talent or individuality. They are frequently the product of entirely whimsical situations. A boldness of girlhood which has been fostered by an indulgent father or by the needs of orphanhood, may be suceeeded by a conservative womanhood. On the other hand, a conservatively reared girl may mature into a vigorous woman who voluntarily adopts masculine work. The important factor is that a girl grows up seeing these unconventional possibilities about her, and sees them easily accepted. She understands that the course of a woman's life need not be specialized, as is a man's.

It should be expected, however, that unconventionality is sometimes a consequence of talent and individuality. One such conspicuous case was "a queer young girl who hardly ever spoke, never paid any attention to what was going on, and never went any place where there was amusement". She was the daughter of a diviner and was therefore conversant with the supernatural characters and with supernatural situations. Once during the village season she had a clairvoyant vision of an imminent Sioux attack. She told her father, surprised that the *manito*-men had not already been apprised. He spread the news through the village and tried to organize defenses, but he met with solid opposition from the men. They said that they had no reason to trust the daughter's vision when the seasoned medicine men of the village had received none; again, she was only a girl, and girls could not be seers; besides, nobody knew anything about her, for she was always alone. However, the girl's prophecy proved true.

Those women who adopt men's work are characteristically resourceful and untroubled. Their attitude stands in marked contrast to that of the exceedingly few men upon whom necessity has placed the obligation of women's work. Thus, John Henry Prince and his wife Jean Mary once got lost in northern Manitoba at a time when Jean Mary was far advanced in pregnancy. The day of childbirth approached, and still the couple were not rescued. As the birth pains became more severe, the man began to blubber. His wife expected his assistance, but he had to combat the deep-seated tradition forbidding men to act as midwives, even to approach a woman closely while in her travail, or to talk about the details of childbirth. So John cried, but Jean Mary was impatient with orthodoxy in time of urgent need. As the baby was being born, "she said to him, 'Shut up, and don't sit there crying! Come here and help me as much as you can! It's not you that's having the pains.' So the man came, shivering and crying, and he asked his wife, 'Are you going to live?' So finally the baby was born."

.....And again, a Cree man of the White Dog reserve became distracted when his wife was lost in a storm and he was left alone for the night with their nursing infant. He did not think of calling a neighboring woman to nurse the frantic baby, but he fumed and strode up and down, and finally called upon the supernaturals for aid. "'If there is a god, please show me what to do to stop my baby's crying', and after he had done everything (by way of invocation), he tried to give it something to drink, but he did not have any milk in the house. He walked back and forth there in the house, and at last he said, 'Oh, *manito*, give me milk in my breast so I can stop my baby's crying, or else it will die!' He sat down and started to nurse the baby. At last towards morning he knew that he had milk in one of his breasts. So the baby nursed, and at last it fell asleep."

The importance of personal inclination appears strongly in the tales about women warriors. Native drive is purer in the war setting than it is usually in the economic setting, for it is uncomplicated by the struggle for subsistence. Chief Earth Woman was a conspicuous girl—one of the few girls to seek the enemy on the warpath like a man; she even commanded the war-party, and received the honors of a man. Occasional other girls have accompanied men to war, but under the aegis of the father's vision. Chief Earth-Woman, however, was licensed by her own dream, and on her own initiative overcame the prejudices that bar her sex from warfare. Her enterprise was inspired by love of a warrior, who probably coached her. "She was a young girl, about seventeen years old, when she fell in love with a married man. Of course he was young, but he had a wife and two children; still she flirted with him. Then her lover got ready and said he wanted to go to the Sioux country for a battle. And for four nights the men got ready, and danced. All that time she was in the bush alone, making many pairs of moccasins. Her mother wondered why she was doing this, but the girl never told anybody. When the warriors were leaving, the women paddled along a little way with them, to tease them or splash water on them. This was the way long ago. Then the women missed the girl. She was not around anywhere, and after

they had returned she was not seen either. Her mother looked for
her all over. She missed her daughter's canoe and blanket. So she
did not say anything for she knew that her daughter had gone
along with the men to *an do bà ni* (seek war honors as a novice).
She believed that the girl must be certain of her safe return through
some *manito kazo* (talk with a supernatural), otherwise she would
not have gone. Of course, she did not know that her daughter was
in love with one of the married men who had gone.

"As the men were going along, the lover waited, for he knew the
girl was expecting him, as they had planned to go together long ago.
Then he got into her canoe. When they came to Warroad, everyone
got out and started to walk from there... The Ojibwa always got
out of their canoes there and then walked to battle with the Sioux..
And as they went along, and when they stopped at dinner time, the
leader told all the men to *manito kazo*. Then he asked the girl if
she had come because she knew of something to help her through.
She did not answer anything, but started to *manito kazo*, making
a speech about a little wren. That was the best thing to have a
dream of, especially for war. So the leader said it was all right for
her to go. She always walked behind with this man whom she ran
after. (This was not strictly proper because no sex ideas are to be
entertained on the war-path. On the other hand the two were
regarded as "warriors," not as man and woman.) Then at one place
where they were to *manito kazo*, she said, 'We are in danger. I
think I see blood on our path ahead.'" Because of her prophecy,
one of the warriors who apparently had no visionary powers for
war was sent away from the party lest he be killed in battle. "So
she started to *manito kazo* again, and this time saw no blood on
the path. Then the headman said, 'Tomorrow morning we will
overtake the Sioux.' But she said, 'No, we will not have time to
wait that long as there is a river here that goes into a lake, and just
before noon some of the Sioux will pass here. They are moving
along the river. And that will be the best time to see them.' So
they went to the river and waited for the Sioux to pass, and sure
enough they paddled by. Her lover was the first to kill one, and
she ran and cut the scalp off. He also killed another, and the
other men killed one. So they had killed three men, and they
started home. The women and men (in camp) watched for them
day after day, and one morning, just about noon, they saw the men
coming. They came singing, they sounded so nice, as the new
nado bà ni (warriors) were singing, 'So that's how the Sioux heads
look!' and the older men were singing. 'Chief Earth Woman is
bringing home one Sioux head!' And she too came along singing,

'Yes, it wasn't for nothing that I went after the men! I knew I could go there and bring home a head ... and also a man for myself!' All the men joined in singing with her right away. Also the people who were waiting (for the warriors) sang and rejoiced with the ones that had come home safely, for they knew that everyone was alive." Afterwards the victory dance was held, Chief Earth Woman received feathers as the other warriors did, and married her companion-in-arms.

The desire for glory was not the only motivation which prompted a woman to go to war. "A woman had a son who was sickly. One time she went out with people (western Ojibwa) who were going buffalo hunting. Her son died while they were traveling about. She said, 'I will take my son home. I will not leave him here.' And she carried his body from place to place. She thought, 'If only we see a strange man while we are camping here, I will leave my son.' And sure enough, while they were camping, the Sioux overtook them. The old woman tied her dress up, and she took her gun which was sawed short, and fought all day like a man. Before she started to fight, she untied her son and made the body sit up and she said, 'Now, my son, I will leave you here. You will go along with a strange man (into the next world).' After their great battle was over, they could hear the Sioux men and women crying, for they had killed a lot of Sioux. After the Sioux were gone, she went to the place where the Sioux bodies were scattered and she took the body of a handsome young man, and dragged it to the spot where her son's dead body was sitting up. She made the Sioux's body sit up beside her son's body. She said, 'Now, my son, here is the strange man that I promised would go along with you.' She left the two bodies like that. Then the Ojibwa moved away from there. They had a lot of Sioux scalps, and held a great war dance."

A young man and his wife of the same group of Ojibwa were out alone hunting buffalo, when they were set upon by Sioux, and the man killed and scalped. The young wife was captured and marched along by the party of Sioux. "After they left this place they were tired, and they took a rest and dried the husband's scalp. The woman pretended that she did not care that they were taking her away, and so the Sioux chief thought she liked him. He sent the other Sioux away to hunt for something to eat because he wanted to be alone with her. He asked her to look on his head (for lice), so she did, and she kept on until he fell asleep. She saw that he had his knife in his belt, so she took it and stabbed him near the heart. After she knew that he was dead, she scalped him. She took her husband's scalp and ran away with the two scalps. The

Sioux Indians never followed her. She returned safely to her own people, and her husband's people thanked her for bringing home their son's scalp. They did not want the Sioux to dance over it. They had a feast and a dance over this other one that she brought, and she earned her feather."

Women like this young wife, and the women of the preceding tales, receive the title and symbolic eagle feathers of "brave", *ogitcida*, which is a male title ideally, and grammatically is not conjugated for female sex gender, although sex gender is one of the categories of Ojibwa grammar. The people are untroubled by the contradiction between a woman's earning this title and the conventional belief that war is a male occupation closed to women and inimically affected by their proximity. Although actually women are honored if they have infringed successfully upon the field of men, the distinctions between male and female activities are never lost ideally. The distinctions appear in the very speech forms by which the narrator approvingly describes the irregular activities of woman: thus on the preceding page it is said that the woman hero "fought like a man", and elsewhere it is said of Sky Woman and others that "she hunted all day like a man."

One girl followed the war-path on the spur of a mood that wavered desperately between suicide and braggadocio. She was one of three surviving members of a family of seven, the others having been killed by wolves. She had been raped by her French mixed-blood employer, and expelled from the house by the latter's wife after signs of pregnancy appeared. After the baby's birth, the girl gave the child to his father, a rather extreme gesture for the sentimental Ojibwa, and one indicative of the girl's depression. Then she left the neighborhood to work for some westerly Ojibwa who sporadically hunted buffalo south of the Red River. "She went along helping the people, and she was paid well for she was very smart. The men were bringing back pemmican and buffalo hides to the Hudson's Bay Post. One time some men asked her with whom she had left her baby. She said that she had given it back to the father, and they answered that she was very brave to give away her baby. She said, 'Yes, I'm brave. If there were anybody going to the Sioux country, I would go along.' The men said (tauntingly) that she would not go because she would be too much of a coward, and that she was saying these things only because she was afraid. They were all against her (on personal grounds only). They even said to her that she couldn't take this French half-breed away from his wife when she had tried to do it (although she had not tried, but according to the story-teller had been raped). She did not care what

was said to her. About four days later some men came along who
were going to the Sioux country for a battle. Some of the men of
her party yelled to her, 'Here come the men that are going for a
battle!' They were just teasing her. She jumped up and said,
'I'm going along. I don't care if I get killed either. I was supposed
to die long ago anyway and it was only on account of my brother
and sister that I lived (they had survived the attack of the wolves
for a short time under her nursing). And now I don't care if I die,
because I threw my baby away, and I also disgraced myself by
having the child of a married man.' So she went. The warriors did
not want her to go, but one man said to let her go, that they could
use her for bait. So they did let her go." The girl's further experiences reveal a certain recklessness, a certain bravery and lack
of perspective that must have been fundamental in her character
and which predisposed her to ignore conventions. "When they
came near to the Sioux camp ground they stayed there that night
and were going to wait for morning. They all fell asleep because
the Sioux chief knew that the party was near (and had caused them
to sleep by supernatural means). The Sioux came and circled around
them. The chief also knew that there was one woman there who was
to be used for bait (left behind for scalping, and so occupy the Sioux
while the Ojibwa slipped away) and he told the men not to kill
her. She wakened from her sleep. She knew the Sioux were circling
around them, so she started crawling toward the bush. The Sioux
men were lying down. They made room for her so she could crawl
out. She jumped up and ran, and as she was running along she
came to a hole and crawled in. Soon she heard yelling. She knew
the battle was on. She did not move. She knew she would be found
anyway, and as she sat in this dark place listening to the shouts of
men, something came to the mouth of the hole and crawled in. She
was not frightened. It came closer and lay down. It pushed her
further into the hole. She felt It and It had fur. They stayed there
for a while, then It went out. The noise was quieting down now.
Then It came back again ... she saw It was a big bear. Oh! she
was frightened. The bear came and pulled her out and looked at
her. It walked away, and then came back again and pulled her.
She knew the bear wanted her to go somewhere, so she followed.
It seemed to be in a great hurry... It would look at her, then would
run, so she ran too and finally they came to a lake where there were
canoes. The bear threw one in the water and gave her a paddle,
and pushed her into the canoe and out onto the water. She started
paddling as hard as she could. When she looked back the bear was
tearing up all the remaining canoes and breaking the paddles in

half, and just as he was tearing up the last canoe, the Sioux men came running down, yelling. The bear ran away along the shore, as fast as he could, in the same direction she was traveling. Of course the Sioux did not have any canoe in which to follow her; they just had to stand on the shore and watch her escape. When she came to a rapids the bear was already there waiting for her. She was frightened because she did not know what It meant by this. Then she remembered that when she was a little girl she used to dream (spontaneously) about a big bear which went around with her and protected her from everything. Then (with new confidence) she got out. The bear picked up the canoe and portaged. She paddled onwards while the bear ran along the shore around points and bays and everything. Then she came to another rapids, the bear was already there, and again It took the canoe over the portage. By this time it was night, and she slept in the canoe. Suddenly the canoe jerked, and she woke up. The bear had waked her because it was broad daylight. The bear swam across the river, and she knew It wanted her to cross. After she rounded another point, she came to a big lake. The bear stood in one place and looked across the lake. It was sunset now, and she did not know where to go. Again the bear stood on his hind legs and looked. She also got up and looked, and saw smoke from a fire. Then the bear looked at her, turned, and walked into the bush. She did not know what to do, nor where she was, but she paddled towards the place where she saw the smoke. It was quite dark when she got there. She saw a woman and two men sitting near the campfire. She did not know who they were, and she was afraid of them. She went closer. They were sitting down, talking and laughing. Then the woman got up and came down to get some water. The woman said, 'We might make it to N——— tomorrow.' The girl was very surprised to hear where she was, so far from home. She did not speak, but she went closer and listened to them talking. The woman was saying, 'I am frightened, just as if someone nearby were looking at us.' Only then the girl spoke (but even this speaking up showed temerity on the part of an intruder), 'Yes, I'm near here, watching you. I wanted to find out first if I could understand your language.' They all ran down and asked her where she came from. She told them that she came from Sahging. Then she got out of the canoe and sat down near the fire (uninvited) for she was cold, as this was early in the fall. She had not eaten anything since she had gone to the Sioux country, but she had not felt hungry until now. The woman gave her some hot tea and something to eat. Then they slept. She lay down near the fireplace and slept.

"The next morning they started off. She took some of their things in her canoe. Then they camped again. The woman told her that the young man was her brother, and that he was single. The girl said that she was not good enough for any man, and she told the woman her story: that she had gone to the Sioux country and that the bear had led her away from danger and brought her to this place where she had found these people. The woman said, 'So this woman here was saved by a bear!' After four days they came to the place named C——— where there were a lot of Indians. There she married this young man, and they had a little girl. Both her sister-in-law and her husband were very good to her. When her little girl was three years old she went out picking berries one day and suddenly she saw a big bear coming. She knew It was angry. It came and grabbed her little girl, and right in front of her tore the child to pieces, and then It went away again. She went home crying, and her sister-in-law thought of the story she had told about the bear, and she hated her. The girl could not help the death of the child. Her husband did not blame her, but her sister-in-law did. The girl was very sorry to lose her little girl, and she knew well enough that the bear had killed the child in anger because she had never made the ritual offerings after marriage. Every spring and fall she was supposed to make a little birch pan and put some sugar and other things in it, and put it where the bear could come and eat. But she had not done what the bear had wanted her to do and he had become angry. After the remains of her little girl were buried, she could not stand any more. She had gone through too much. All her life passed in her mind—how her parents had been eaten by wolves, and her little sister had starved to death, and her little brother had died of a broken heart; how she had been raped by the half-breed and had borne an illegitimate child, and then had given her away; and now when she was happily married and forgetting the past, her little girl had been torn up by a bear in front of her. She wished the bear had torn her up too ... she could not go on living ... so that night after her baby was buried she went out and hanged herself. She was found dead the next morning, and she was buried. So that was the end of her."

It is understood, in this story, that the sister-in-law's hatred was occasioned by the girl's having failed to keep in ritual contact with her guardian bear by making regular respect offerings of sugar, and thus by her negligence had invited supernatural punishment. Such carelessness is altogether reprehensible. Ritual offerings are usually the responsibility of men because in general they have the important visions and sacred powers. No man or boy would

forget to make ritual offerings, since they have been trained
since earliest childhood in these forms; a man's failure to make offerings is a deliberate move. But women have not had this training; their acquaintance with the forms is largely academic, and
they usually make offerings only at the request of the husband or
father and as a proxy for him. But a woman who has important
supernatural powers has become sociologically unsexed, and is
expected to function as responsibly as a man, and to suffer the
consequences of neglecting the ritual forms. The heroine had powers
that are conventionally masculine, but she had not had the training
for the behavior that validated them. She did not think of the bear
as her spiritual guardian and as the pledge for a career, but instead
she used him as a tool which she promptly laid aside after the moment had passed; in the same way she had seized upon the war-party
as a device which offered escape from a difficult situation, not as a
step in a career.

In keeping with the indifferent tutelage of girlhood, the behavior
of a woman is typically less extreme or special than that of a man,
and it is also much more variable and unpredictable, both in relation
to other women and to herself. The motivations of men, who all
have the same high stakes in the culture, are stereotyped and in
any one man's life are consistent from one period to another. But
this cannot be said for women. A woman's drive toward masculine
work, which is largely untutored and spontaneous, may lapse under
changed circumstances, and it cannot be assumed that one woman's
motivations are similar to those of other women engaged in the
same work. The case of Cocos illustrates the variations in behavior
that are frequent among women. Cocos, trained by a father who
was bent upon revenge upon the Sioux, embraced the role of warrior
in the conventional masculine spirit of making it a career and a test
of personal excellence, a spirit quite different from the fleeting,
hysterical impulse of the girl in the previous story. However,
unlike a man, by middle age she had become a coward, and fearful.
"This is a story of an Indian girl named Cocos, and her father
named Paybahm. When she was small she often saw her mother
fighting her father, and also many times she saw her fighting
other women, or cutting another woman's face because she was
jealous. She used to think her mother was brave for doing these
things, but she wondered why she was always fighting with someone.
She had an older brother and a younger sister, and a baby brother.
She was the one that stayed at home to mind her baby brother when
her parents went out to set their nets or do other work. One day
when she was still a little girl her parents went out in a canoe duck

hunting, and she was left to care for her older brother who was sick and for the baby who was tied in a cradle, but not laced in, and his little hands were out. All at once four Sioux came running toward the wigwams with clubs. She ran out and hid under a raw moose-hide. She could hear her sick brother moaning under the blows of the Sioux. Her little sister ran along the shore yelling as hard as she could. Her grandmother, who was very old, was in the wigwam too. The Sioux pulled off the old woman's scalp while she was still alive, and after that smashed her head. They pulled the baby out of the cradle and cut him on the elbows which they also pulléd out of joint. Then the Sioux saw the parents coming from the lake. They ran off and left the baby half dead. When her father and mother came ashore Cocos came out of her hiding place. She ran into the wigwam. Her brother was dead, also her grandmother, and 'the baby was dying from loss of blood. So she and her little sister were the only ones still alive. Her father told them to get into the canoe and took them to the other Indians, leaving the dead behind. He described what the Sioux had done. Some of the men went back and when they came in sight of the wigwam they could tell that the Sioux had returned as the old woman's body had been put out on the shore; so they buried the three dead people. But her mother was not any better (less jealous).

"Many years passed, and when Cocos was a young girl, her father got ready to lead a party to the Sioux country for a battle to avenge the death of his mother and sons. He wanted to take his daughter along, and promised her to the first man who killed a Sioux. She too wished to go with him. She was a nice looking girl, brave and strong. And because of her, forty men promised to go along. Cocos did her *manito kazo* and she knew by the little spirits who were her *pawagàn* (guardian spirits) that she could get home safely again. The old man did not say anything to his wife. He let her decide for herself if she wanted to go along with the party ... people would know then if she was really brave; but she did not go. For four days they danced and performed *manito kazo*, and the men who were to go for the first time stayed alone for four days ... no women ever saw them (tabu associated with fear of menstruation). Cocos also was alone (by analogy with the male novices, since she had been unsexed by her vision). She put soot on her eyes (conventional in the presence of the supernatural, or in pursuit of the supernatural) and got ready. Early the fifth morning they started off. She was the only woman who went with these forty men and her father; so at last she knew that her mother was not really brave. They traveled for many days. They walked all night and all morning, and stopped at noon to rest. (Entokening their novitiate) she and the young men who were going for the first time kept to the rear and sat with their backs toward the place they were going. They all had soot on their eyes, and when they stopped they did *manito kazo*. The old man said to the men, 'If any of you have no dreams to help you out, you had better return home, and if any of you have some kind of a big beast for a guardian spirit, you had better go back.' No one ever spoke. Some of the men had cranes and other kinds of birds as guardians. One young man—he never paid any attention to anything—he was always the last one—he did his *manito kazo*, and he had a little humming bird in his dreams...

"They took many pairs of moccasins, as the prairie was hard on moccasins (Ojibwa moccasins are not soled of rawhide, like the moccasins of the prairie tribes, but are of soft tanned leather). They did not take anything to eat, as they could get all they wanted by *manito kazo*, such things as porcupine, skunk, and bear. After they had traveled for many days, they stopped one noon and did *manito kazo*. The old man said, 'Early tomorrow morning we will come upon the Sioux Indians. They are close by, drying meat.' Certain men were sent out spying. They stayed there all afternoon. Some slept, and some made speeches, others did *manito kazo*, among them Cocos. Often she was afraid, even though she knew by her dreams that she was safe; and she was afraid for some of the men. But she would not turn back, as she would get the name of a coward (an appellation charged with male values). Early the next morning they overtook the Sioux. The fog was thick and some of the Sioux were sleeping. There were only eight of them staying there, drying buffalo meat. The young man who had the humming bird for a guardian was the first one to kill a Sioux. They killed seven, and one woman got away from them. They ran all over looking for her, but they could not find her. None of the party were killed, and none were wounded, as there had been forty-two against eight. Cocos cut the scalps off two men, and the genitals of one Sioux. They started for home with seven Sioux Indian scalps. At last the old man's mind was at rest (having avenged his relatives' deaths), and he made his daughter marry this young man (fulfilling the promise with which he had lured the warriors). He was good, and Cocos was willing to do as her father said. When they got home, everybody rejoiced with them. They had their war dance for four days, and she came out while everybody was dancing. She had in her hand the genitals which she had cut off, and she threw them at her mother. 'Here, take this! This is the kind of thing for which you used to fight and quarrel. You used to cut women's faces

and pull their hair over it! Keep it! I brought it for you! I used
to think you were brave when I saw you fighting (with rivals)!'
(This was a public speech, delivered in the midst of the crowd
assembled for the Victory Dance.) Her mother grabbed this thing
and started dancing with it. And all the rest of the women started
dancing with it, and had a great old time with it. Cocos was now
a married woman, and looked upon by the Indians as a brave. Also
her husband had killed two of the Sioux. Neither she nor her husband
ever went to battle with the Sioux again.

"Many many years after, when she was old, and her mother was
very old, the Ojibwa and the Sioux Indians had become friends.
They visited one another now, and smoked their peace pipes together. One time many Sioux came over to have a peace dance with
the Ojibwa. She was there that time, and her mother too. The
Sioux and the Ojibwa used to make long speeches during these
peace dances, and describe how they used to kill one another; and
then they would give lots of things to one another. So this time
Cocos got up and made a speech. She told the people (boasting)
how she cut the scalps off the two Sioux, and also the genitals. She
said, 'I gave it to this old woman here (her mother) because she
was always fighting for it, and that was why I brought it for her.'
This was her speech in that dance, and the Sioux looked at one
another. They were not mad, but they knew she was brave. She
gave a great pile of her things to these Sioux: blankets, goods,
and guns. (This is a masculine gesture, in keeping with her male
status of warrior. Such largesse is considered bravery: it brings
its giver nearer to poverty, and shows that the giver does not fear
to face starvation. It is a peculiarly exhibitionistic act of pride.)
They also shook hands with her. She frightened some of the
Ojibwa when she told that story. They thought she would make
the Sioux mad, but she didn't. The Sioux went back home, and the
Ojibwa went often to visit them, just as they do now.

"She had children, and when she was about fifty years old, she
was not brave any more. The Cree and the Ojibwa used to gather
in one place where they danced and did Grand Medicine and
manito kazo, and played all kinds of Indian gambling games.
She used to sit and watch them playing. The Ojibwa men played
against the Cree. The Ojibwa beat the Cree all the time. (This
statement carries great force, because the Cree are supposed to
be the great magicians of the region and as such practically invin-
cible at games. It is as significant to tell about defeating the Cree
at games, as it is to tell about defeating the Sioux in war.) However
the Cree men would not give up. They bundled up more of their

things, and played for higher stakes. At last they lost all their things and sat watching the Ojibwa dividing the spoils. One of the Ojibwa young men sat there whistling. He had in his hand those little balls which they use when playing the moccasin game, and he was pretending to play. An older Cree man was sitting near him. He was mad because he had lost his shoes, shirt, and hat, and lots of his things. He said to this young man, 'You could not beat anyway!' But the young man kept right on. The Cree was so mad... He took his knife from his belt, and stabbed the young man above his collar bone. The young man jumped up and shouted (the war whoop). Then he grabbed his knife and stabbed the Cree man on the chest. The Cree began to moan, and the Ojibwa said, 'Hey! You start moaning, and it's you who stabbed me first!' The men all jumped up and grabbed the two wounded men. They were each taken to a different little wigwam where medicine men doctored them. The Cree man lived for only one night, but the young man lived for many days before he died. Cocos had watched these men kill each other, and she said that she was frightened at seeing them kill each other. But when she had gone to the Sioux country, she had not been afraid to see the men killing the Sioux. This was the first time she had been frightened. She lived to be very old, and her children and husband too."

The following incident epitomizes as pointedly as a caricature the vagrant impulse of a woman warrior. The story describes the Sioux's sudden descent upon a camp of buffalo-hunting Cree. The Cree men threw up breastworks, the Cree women dug pits for secreting themselves and their children. The fighting commenced, and a man was injured. Thereupon "his wife got so mad that she went straight out (of one of the female pits) and fought with all her might," fighting as she would in any alley brawl. But since this fray was categorized as formal war and not as alley brawl, the woman's sudden personal fury had to be transposed into other conventional terms. It was interpreted as an expression of power which had suddenly been given to her. The story-teller assures us that "she had a guardian spirit. It was a humming bird (the most powerful guardian spirit for purposes of war), and while she was fighting all you could see was a humming bird flying around fighting the Sioux. The man who got his leg broken (the Amazon's husband) had a buffalo for a guardian (an undesirable spirit for purposes of war because it is large and conspicuous and therefore an easy target). That was why his leg was broken." This was the only fighting incident in the woman's life, and did not initiate a war career. It was impulsive and personal, not rooted in any formal sanctions, but pitted against all the restrictions that limit a woman's sphere of action.

For the most part, women show weak untutored orientations in nearly all the male activities in which they engage. This attitude has arisen from girls' early training: girls have not been schooled to view themselves objectively, as individuals being groomed for a proud destiny. In large part their adult lives are passive. They receive visions, but without planning for them; they yield to courtship which is pressed by men; they utilize materials which are provided in large part by men. In the same unaggressive fashion they hunt or make war when the occasion arises. The present is of great consequence to a woman, and the masculine techniques of war, hunting, or vision, are merely tools to use at a particular moment, tools which are laid aside when the emergency has passed. This is of course in great contrast to a man's attitude; for him the moment is a block that has significance for the masonry of his life, and he seeks and adds new blocks as he works continuously upon his career.

However, some women engage in masculine work as consistently as the most conventional men. These are women who in youth have been trained by their parents as though they were boys. They devote themselves for years to one interest, and awake to a realization that their self-respect and way of life are bound up with it. Such women were Iron Woman and Half Sky. Iron Woman practised as a shaman and, like a man, was the victim of her own profession. (Continued sorcery acts like a boomerang upon the practitioner: after it has been sent out and has accomplished its mission, it returns to the home of its owner, and lying there as idle mischief, it causes the death of near relatives, usually young children). "She never cried in front of people when her children died, but she used to go back in the bush and cry. One time an old woman heard her crying and talking. 'Oh, *manito*, what can I do to undo all the bad things I did when I was young, so that my children will be able to live?' When she came back she gave her father a slap and said, 'Yes, it is all your fault that I am in misery. You made me use all this medicine, you old devil!' Her father did not answer her. But later he said, 'Yes, my daughter, it is true that you will always suffer for that. That is why I always advised you never to marry. I will give you some medicine so that you will never have children again.' And she said, 'No, I'm going to have another child soon.' They did everything in their power so that the child would live. She even went through the Grand Medicine ceremony for her unborn child. When her baby was born, they put it through the

11

ceremony also, but it lived just a short time, and then it too died. Iron Woman had almost died when she was giving birth to the child, and her parents gave her medicine so that she would never have a child again. But she did not know this. After her baby died, she said that she did not want any more medicine (shamanistic ability), and she let go even her sucking doctor practise and her gambling. About three years later, when she did not have another child, she was angry. She knew that her father must have given her medicine to drink, and she gave him a good scolding. But after she let everything (shamanistic) go, she became a coward. She never went anywhere alone in the dark, or even in the daytime. Her husband always had to go with her, for she was so afraid. One night when her husband was out walking and she was alone, a woman came in and started to wrestle with her. She did not know who it was, and she was very frightened. The woman said, 'You made a darn fool of me, and I'm here to square up with you.' She could not get hold of this woman for it was the ghost of a woman from whose bones her father had scraped medicine. Of course she did not know it was a ghost. When her husband came in, the ghost disappeared. And she was afraid to stay alone. Some time after that when her husband was out, a man came in and started to wrestle with her as the woman had done. After that she used to faint as soon as they came in." The deliberate abandonment of her established special lifeways, and the obsessive fears and remorse that preyed upon her resulted in a temporary breakdown during which she sent her husband away and wandered about in the woods waiting for death.

Half Sky had developed as special a male personality as Iron Woman's but she did not collapse under its attendant penalties. She was famed for her "supernatural" success at games, particularly at foot-races. Her success aroused the envy of others to such an extent that she was caused to fall ill through the sorcery of a rival. She interpreted this attack as a man would, as a shameful effort to crush her pride, and she reacted in a masculine manner, with the arrogant determination to injure those whom she considered to be her persecutors. She was distinguished also as a hunter and trapper, having been trained by her father. She had her own trapping grounds before her marriage, and after her father's death, she became the man of the family . . .

It is notable that certain women who never engage in men's pursuits, yet bring men's motivations into women's work. That is, they become self-conscious in terms of their work, they develop a self-respect which finds satisfaction in the recognition accorded it, and they pursue their special feminine occupations as a masculine careerist would. For example, Maggie is proud of her beadwork because it is acknowledged that she is more skilled than others. She devotes herself incessantly to this form of embroidery, and receives visions in connection with it just as a man would receive visions in connection with hunting, divining, or war. If another person gained a reputation for excellent work, Maggie would feel shamed. She has a similar attitude toward her tanning, and her tailoring of moccasins. For ten years she devoted herself to the dance organization described elsewhere, and vested her pride in it. But after a time she suspected that other envious ones were endeavoring to undermine her prestige, and she was therefore shamed. She retaliated in the one effective way that would shame her enemies and save her own face: as the owner of a unique resource, she refused to hold the dance any longer... Maggie's mother was a renowned midwife whose work was to her a vital career. She was scornful of others who were competent and who thereby seemed to threaten her view of herself as preeminent. She devoted all her energies to her work, and secured visions that were helpful. She gave the impression, as a male shaman does, of possessing mighty secret reserves, reserves that are awe-inspiring and that cause constraint in others... These women were not trained to these attitudes while they were learning the female skills, but they seem rather to have carried them over from the training that they received in playing games. It will be remembered that the emphases of game playing are the same for boys and girls, for men and women. Men and women alike feel that their self-respect hangs upon the outcome of a game; both play for high stakes of material wealth and personal prestige; both secure visions which give powers. Defeat means personal humiliation, and a man or woman is ready to retaliate for humiliation with fatal thrusts of the knife and with sorcery. It is these values, somewhat muted, which are echoed in the ambitions of Maggie and her mother.

There are women who follow men's work consistently, as they do women's work, but without the drive of the careerist. In this deficient drive they resemble those women who adopt masculine work only sporadically, and like the latter they are women who have not received a boy's training in childhood. Their pursuit of a man's vocations is instead a consequence of training received in maturity from their husbands. For example, Deceased's second husband taught her shamanistic skills and assured her following them by requesting her services continually as assistant. So she practised shamanism for years, even through her widowhood,

11*

until she married a shiftless drunkard, and was demoralized by him. Deceased had natural ability for men's tasks, as was shown occasionally and spontaneously in her early life. Thus, during her marriage to her first husband ... "it happened that they did not have anything to eat. They nearly starved. Her husband could not kill anything. The children cried and slept all day because she did not have anything to feed them. They had a big dog, so she killed and scraped it and cooked it, and fed it to her children, and she ate some herself. Her husband was not home at the time; he was away trying to kill something to eat. He came home that night with nothing, so she gave him the dog to eat. He ate it, and after he finished he said he was going to journey all night to see his uncle, his father's brother. He said he would be gone two days, and that they should eat the dog while he was away. So he went away that night, and after he had gone, she went to sleep. She dreamed of a nice-looking girl dressed in red. In her dream this girl told Deceased that if she would find her the next day before noon their bad fortune would stop and that she was to look for her early the next day. When morning came Deceased was anxious to get out of her sleep. She did her *manito kazo* and thought of dreams that she had had before. She combed her hair and painted her cheeks red (as prescribed in the vision) and got ready. She took the club that she had dreamed about before. She went out and walked around the wigwam, and at once she knew which way to go. She walked about half a mile and came to a place where two cedar trees were lying ... they had been blown down by the wind, and had torn up the roots and earth with them when they fell. It seemed as though there was something there. She poked her club in the ground and a she-bear stuck her head out. She hit this bear on the head and killed it. She could not drag it home because she could not lift it, it was so fat... She went home and got her boy and girl (a male hunter would have done this also). They took a toboggan and carried the bear to their wigwam. She skinned it and saved the head, hands and feet (these human terms for "paws" are in literal translation from the Ojibwa, because the bear is regarded as "almost like a human being"), and heart grease and tongue, and kept them (for the ritual thanksgiving feast which is held by hunters who have killed a bear). Her husband had been gone one night, and he was to be away another. She had lots of grease now because the bear's fat was five inches thick, and she had all kinds of meat for them to eat. She knew (when she saw the red-clad woman in her dream) that she was this bear, because she had dreamed of her before. So she won back her husband's hunting luck (not her own luck, for as a woman she is conventionally disregarded, especially when there is a male hunter available in the family). Her husband returned, and when he approached their wigwam he saw blood all over outside. He shouted, 'Who came here and destroyed my children ?' Deceased answered him, 'Don't say that! I got your children something to eat!' When he went in he saw meat and everything. She cooked a regular feast for their guardian spirits. There was not anyone near there, they were all alone. (Their winter camp was isolated, and so there were no neighbors to invite to the ritual feast, therefore they alone conducted the ceremony.) Her husband brought out some maple sugar and rice and dried blueberries that they had stored away that fall for use in spring. After this he was in luck and killed everything. They got seven bears that spring, and a thousand muskrats (because of the woman's vision)." That spring the husband was killed in a feud with another man. Deceased believed that the wife of the other man had sent starvation by sorcery to them, and the other woman believed the same of Deceased. "Darkening Day died brave, with a shout on his lips. So both men killed each other. Deceased sat there with her children and watched her husband killed. The sun was way up, and the two bodies lay together covered with brush ... and men came and put clothes on them and buried them near the island side by side... She used to say she never cried once so that anyone could see her, but she had it in her heart to kill this woman. After the two men were buried, she started off with her children and went to Fort Frances and took the fur (which her deceased husband had trapped) to the Hudson's Bay post, and sold it. (This is ordinarily a man's work.) She stayed around Fort Frances quite a while (aimlessly) in several Indian villages. In the fall she went back to the bush and camped alone with her children (to hunt and trap, since there was no man to provide for her). After a while she had a baby by some man (which violates the widowhood regulations). It was born back there in the bush (without the assistance of a midwife)." For about five or six years she continued to winter alone in the bush and return with her children to the Indian villages in summer. She bore four illegitimate children during her widowhood, all of whom died. "Later on she met a man from Hungry Hall named Red Sky. He was the chief of the Hungry Hall reserve. She married him, and moved down to Hungry Hall with all her children. So she was the chief's wife, and she became a great *manito kazo* and sucking doctor, and her husband was a great diviner. Oh, they got along fine for about fifteen years. I would just like to have a picture of her right now. She dressed in red, green, blue, yellow, black, and wore beads of all colors and different kinds of ribbon in her hair, and a feather sticking on her head, and earrings, and beaded moccasins, and her face was painted. She dressed like that every day and whenever anyone wanted her to help as a sucking doctor, she took a girl assistant to drum for her while she was doctoring. Twice she asked me to go and drum for her, and she gave me a shawl and six yards of print (in payment for services). When she cured people and they were getting better, she gave them a name (to impart additional strength) and name tokens of a snake game and the Indian dice game, and the medicine rattler that she used when she cured by sucking. She did that for a long time. Then the chief died. She did not have any children by him. She was a widow for two years, and then she married again, her brother-in-law this time. He was a useless man, a drunkard, and she started to drink too, and she just degenerated. When she was sober, people still asked her to doctor them, but even then she was not as good as before. Then her older son got sick and died, and the younger one also, and then her daughter. Her other daughter was married eight times, but never had children. She never had grandchildren. After all her children died, she died too, and left her useless old husband."

The history of White Goose is an instructive instance of a woman who practised shamanism consistently as a result of training received from her husband, but who had no interest in the work on her own account. Indeed, in its degree her case was exceptional, almost like that of Trilby and Svengali in our own literature. For White Goose had been a young lovely girl coerced into marriage by her greatly feared shaman husband. She lived many years with him until his death, always timid and resentful, but hypnotized into obedience to him. "He used her as assistant at all his *manito kazo*. After some time he taught her how to put people through the Grand Medicine ceremony and to doctor by sucking. He taught her all the medicine (which is purchasable in formula form), and also bad medicine. He even had medicine which made a person unable to move when he came near, and she knew this was the medicine he had used on her when he married her." She never ceased to hate her husband and his sorcery. A year after his death she married a Christian half-breed, was baptised, and with relief "threw all her Grand Medicine away, and also all the bad medicine the old man had taught her. She lived a very quiet Christian life and was happy with her young husband."

Eternal Man had received the visionary powers of a *wabeno* (juggler with fire, who divines, etc) but did not think of employing them until she was urged by her husband. "When her twin girls were about three years old, she was very sick and nearly died. Her husband cured her by sucking and said to her, 'You will get better if you do the things which you were taught the time you wandered around the woods without any food. If you promise to do them, you will get better.' She said she would, for she remembered that she had dreamed of these things when she was lost; she had heard someone singing these *wabeno* songs. So she dreamed of them and sang them, and she got better. The songs sounded very nice. Her husband was also a *wabeno*. People from other places used to come to their *wabeno* dances, for she kept on learning more songs" (i. e., her husband had stimulated her so that she received new dreams). The joint perfomances they gave were, however, always on the husband's initiative.

Two Skies was also instructed by her husbands. "She parted with her (first) husband (who was a shaman) and started to practise as a sucking doctor. She got along well, and got all kinds of nice things for it. She was also a great woman to tan hides." She married a young and incompetent man, whom her first husband later frightened away, and she had to return to the latter. Eventually he died. "A year after that she married an older man at Whitefish Bay. He was widowed like herself. His name was Ka'an wi. He was all kinds of *manito kazo*: *tcisaki* (diviner), *mide* leader, and a kind of Indian fortune teller (clairvoyant).... he knew what was going on ahead of time, and usually his dreams came true.... and he had lots of bad medicine (formula sorcery). People said that he wished to keep other people from having luck, and that he made people crazy. He used to be the only one to kill game and fish, when other people could not kill anything. That was the reason they thought him bad. Everybody was afraid to make him angry. So they (Two Skies and her shaman husband) kept on like that for many years, and he cured lots of people. He was a great old gambler too. She lived there with him all this time as his wife, and her first husband's relatives were all made sick: some blind, some crazy and crippled, and some just got sick and died (the implication is that the deaths were caused by her sorcery). Finally they were all dead. He (the shaman) put his wife through the *midewiwin* several times. Then he got smallpox and died, so she was left a widow again. She practised as a sucking doctor, hunted and trapped for fur (like a man), and fished and made rice (like a woman), and made a good living. She was a real Indian woman, dressed like an Indian too. She had dreams of all kinds of games, such as the Indian dice game, the snake game, and the caribou bone game. She gave these to her namesakes, and she gave away songs she dreamed and other games and songs. She did not have any children except the four that died when they were babies. She used to cook a big dinner and pretend she was having a feast with the dead people. She would make a godly speech over it, then she pretended to send it to the dead people; she picked out living people to eat the food, and said that the God of the dead people would send the dishes back filled with Life. She had lots of other kinds of feasts. She made people believe that she had visitors from heaven (as in *tcisaki* divining). Whenever she doctored anyone she told them to go through the *midewiwin* (this advice is generally given by a *tcisaki* diviner, a role which is not undertaken by women), and she herself dressed them up (as she was a *mide* functionary), putting red paint and everything on their faces. Sometimes they lived, but sometimes they did not get better. She tried to do as her old man had done when he was alive. Also she had a rough life that is not fit to tell about (the story teller is a Christian Indian). She is living today. She is very old, but she still does *manito kazo*, and names lots of children and gives out dance songs and games of all kinds. She lives alone now at Whitefish Bay... she has hardly any relatives. She is old and as helpless as a baby."

.....The fact that Two Skies practised shamanism most actively when she lived alone indicates that she personally was interested in such pursuits. It may be that she developed masculine attitudes toward herself and her work. Certain extreme evidences of pride and shame are reported of her in other connections that suggest a native susceptibility to the conventional masculine motivations. In this category, for instance, was her negative reaction to the payment of her sib debt.

The life of Deceased's daughter, Kath, illustrates the aberrant variations which women can introduce into men's work. Kath was renowned for her skill in the technique of curing by sucking, as renowned as any male shaman, but her behavior differed at important points from that of a man. She was cheerful, kindly, and well-liked. The conventional shamans, those who are feared as the most powerful, are sullen, suspicious, quick-tempered, and violent. They demand constant reassurance of their own importance, and everyone must cower before them . Each person's attitude must be impassive and deferential, or the shaman suspects ridicule or arrogance, feels himself humiliated, and punishes the offender through sorcery. Shamans demand too that their services shall be in constant demand, otherwise they consider that people ignore them with the deliberate intent to shame them. And in further token of their megalomaniac view of themselves, they demand exorbitant fees for their services; a small fee is again interpreted as a pointed means of slighting them. Kath showed none of these traits, and had the conventional woman's disregard of violent pride and shame. Here again, the term "conventional woman" describes a culturally fostered ideal which is developed during the early training of boys and girls. A boy is taught that if he attains his personal objective, he may feel proud, and that it is imperative for him to maintain great pride, especially when observers are present as in the village season. The failure to gain an objective arouses great shame in a boy or man, and such shame precipitates some violent overt expression if another individual is involved: the pride of the latter must in turn be humbled.... A girl, however, has been trained to none of these attitudes. Though she may choose her method of life, her individualism is never stressed, nor are the collateral attitudes toward pride and shame.

Kath undertook shamanistic practise when, in native thought, she was quite an old woman. She was about fifty years old, and had been married seven times. According to the storyteller, she became a shaman on her own initiative, though probably she had been influenced by her mother.

"She told her (seventh) husband that she did not want him any more. After she left him she started with her *manito kazo*. She was all kinds. She was a sucking doctor (as her mother had been), and she was given piles of goods, blankets, prints, and other things. And all the people got to like her. When anyone was sick, they ran for her because she was so good at curing. Finally a bachelor went to her. He had never been married. He had a nice home and canoe and a garden. He liked her, so he married her, and then she had a good home. Outside her home she made a wigwam of new bark and mats and green brush. It was nice and clean, and when anyone called for her to doctor him, she took him into this tent and took care of him there, while his relatives camped nearby. She would doctor him through the night. It was a kind of Indian hospital that she had in this tent. She gave sick people medicine to drink, and of course they got better. So she was well off with her new husband. His name was Sky Being. She had no children. She was a great *manito kazo*, and a kind of Indian fortune teller (through clairvoyant visions). She told people what was going to happen later, and lots of things that she told did happen. Everybody in Hungry Hall liked her (never said of a male shaman) and depended on her (said of all shamans). People came from all over with the sick for her to cure. One time I saw her cure by sucking. A boy was dying, and they ran for her, and she came running into the wigwam where the dying boy lay. She pulled off her clothes, and started working on him. She felt his pulse and said that she did not know whether he would live or die. She started (sacred) singing and rattling. At last she asked me to help her. She rubbed him all over his body, and gave him medicine which stopped his convulsions. The boy started to breathe nicely, so she doctored him, and at last he got a little better. The boy lived, and is quite an old man now. His name is Around-the-Earth Bird. She kept on curing like that for over ten years. She was a hard-working woman. She planted corn, potatoes, and everything. She dried fish and meat (the female occupations). She always had lots to eat, and nice clothes, and kept her home clean. She was good to everybody (the exact reverse is said of a male shaman). There was never a time when she did not have someone there for dinner, supper, or breakfast (also not typical, for people do not flock around the conventional shaman). And she took good care of sick people.

"One time late in the fall, before the lakes were frozen, a sick man was brought to her from Rainy Lake, and she took him into her house and doctored him. He was full of cancer. She doctored him for three months; then he got better. His name was Feathered Hide. This was a year before she died; she caught his sickness. It started in her breast, and she told the people that she was going to leave this world, that her time was up. She asked four women to come there a week before she died, and she gave them four of her (sacred) drums, and four of her rattles. The other four were to be hung in the bush. She had eight tom-toms, and eight medicine rattles that she used when she cured by sucking. One morning about four o'clock she nearly died, but she saw (in a vision) that there was no place for an Indian to go, so she sent for the minister, Mr. Johnson, to pray for her and give her the sacrament. So she died as a Christian and was buried like a Christian, and that was the end of **Kath**. All the people were sad, and sorry for her. Before she died, whenever there was a feast, she was the one to make a speech (i. e., conduct the ceremony; a male prerogative). In the speech she made when she cured by sucking she used to say that she dreamed she should have eight tomtoms, and eight rattles, and eight different husbands."

The life histories of most women who assume men's work – regardless of the regularity with which they pursue this work – do not show any unequivocal influences of native inclination or of training. Many women undertake men's work only when the men who should be responsible are not available or have defaulted.

Death or desertion of a husband, or illness, or shiftlessness, necessitates his wife's doing his work for an indefinite period. From the viewpoint of the culture's slight interest in women and in the training of girls, it is interesting that a woman can casually assume such duties, and as casually abandon them when the abnormal situation no longer exists. These masculine tasks demand skill, which presumably the woman has had no opportunity to learn; and a woman can pursue men's work only by violating the menstrual taboo, and therefore causing injury to the men's vulnerable world. Occupationally versatile women must be individuals of great courage and resource, or of great ignorance of the cultural demands. Probably both factors are involved in some measure.

Thunder Cloud was married three times, and during the period that she lived with her husbands she was a perfectly conventional wife, noted only for her competence... "She was never anything.... she just lived." But when she found it necessary to flee her jealous first husband, and to live for some years alone, she had no difficulty in maintaining herself by certain male skills. Apparently she was a courageous woman who lived up to the challenge of the moment in all respects. The story of her flight from her first husband supports this view. She left him precipitately because he threatened to stab her. "This happened right at Manitou where the school now is, and she walked from there to Hungry Hall (about fifty miles west) with nothing to eat. It took her three days to walk that, for there were no white people at that time (about fifty years ago), only the wild bush. She said that it never rained all the time she was traveling. There were big creeks that she had to walk along until she came to a narrow part where she could chop down a tree to lay across. At night she chopped little branches off a tree and lay under them. She had no fire nor anything to eat, and at last her moccasins were worn off her feet. Then she had to walk about twenty miles barefoot along the hardest part of the (Rainy) River. When she got to Hungry Hall the people were afraid of her. They thought she was crazy. But she did not care who was afraid of her so long as she got there. She had a friend there, a woman who liked her, and who gave her clothes to put on, moccasins, food, and an old canoe. Then she went on to Grassy River (where her mother, sisters and brothers lived). It took her another two days to get there. On the way from Hungry Hall to Grassy River, she camped on a little island. Early one morning before sunrise, as it was coming daylight, she peeped out from the bush and looked around to see if there was anyone near, and she saw a canoe with three men in it. She was frightened and did not take

her canoe down, but stayed right there and asked her guardian
spirits to bring fair wind to those in the canoe. She knew that they
were Sioux Indians, and that they would kill her if they saw her
there, so she kept quiet until they were out of sight. Then she took
her canoe to the other side of the island, got in, and paddled toward
the shore against the wind. She came to a portage and saw there
the tracks of the three Sioux. She saw where they had roasted their
food on little sticks. Again she was very frightened. She started
out again, and the lake got calmer just where she would have had
to paddle hard against the wind. As she was paddling she saw
something on the lake again, and she was afraid, but when she went
closer she saw it was only two young moose. When night came, she
just kept on, and it became so dark at midnight that she went to a
place where the grass was high, tied her canoe to this grass, and
slept right in the canoe. It was just daylight when she woke. She
was very tired. She knew that she was near her home, so she started
off again, but when she reached the place where the Indians always
camped, all that she saw was wigwam poles. There was not a soul
there. So she paddled right on, and when she got to the mouth of
the Grassy River, she could see an island called N----, and the Indians were camped there. As she was coming out of the Grassy
River, somebody shot at her but did not hit her. Of course she was
frightened; she thought it was the Sioux Indians that she had seen
passing. But it was not they. . . . it was just men from the camp
that shot at her. . . they thought that *she* was one of the Sioux. You
see, the Ojibwa had moved away from Grassy River because these
three Sioux were after them, trying to kill them. She was so happy
to return to her own people, her sisters and brothers and mother.
Thus she arrived safely after all her hardships, and she told me that
she stayed there at Grassy River for four years hunting, fishing,
and picking berries, and living just like a young girl."

Red Earth Woman was a young girl married to Sheebahyash, a
suspicious man who finally left her in a jealous rage. Grieved
and furiously ashamed, the girl returned to her parents, determined that she was through with men and marriage forever.
This decision made it necessary for her to supply herself with goods
ordinarily supplied by a husband. She lived up to the occasion,
"and killed lots of muskrats, as she was just like a man."

Peewahsheek left her cruel husband at the first opportunity. She
too was no shaman, but guided herself by her dreams; in private
"she was a kind of fortune teller in Indian." During the many
years that she lived alone, she supported herself and her young son
adequately with male and female skills. She trapped muskrat and

traded the fur at the Kenora Hudson's Bay Post (then Rat Portage); she trapped rabbit, and made robes of this fur. She was an expert fisherman, both with the lance and the net; and skilled at the finer female techniques of beadwork, tanning, tailoring, rice-making, and preserving meat and fish.

Hawk Woman was abandoned by her sadistic husband on an unfrequented island. When she realized that she had been deserted, she accepted the situation calmly and undertook such masculine work as was necessary: she caught moose, and cured the meat and hides; she collected birchbark and made a canoe and a wigwam. Later she was rescued by a man, married him, and settled again into the conventional routine of a housekeeper.

The seventh husband of Kath "was a lazy man", too shiftless to do anything but lie in bed with his moccasins off. She stayed with him two or three years, and during that time was very poor because her husband refused to work. Therefore she supported the two of them, and "she lived on her hunting, (fur) trading, and fishing." She had never done such work before. Indeed, her first marriage, which lasted fifteen years, was so comfortable and secure that she deserted because of its very monotony; and in her succeeding marriages she took a conservative female part. She eventually left her seventh husband, and while she was single she continued to maintain herself by hunting, trading, fishing, and shamanism. But when she married for the eighth time, the conventional division of labor was resumed, except for the fact that she continued her curing practise.

The husband of Ice Woman was also so shiftless that Ice Woman had to support the household. She chafed under the obligation but remained with her "useless husband" because she had promised her dying father to do so. It may have been that the husband was lazy because he was actually ill, for he died in his sleep in early youth, but, as no critical symptoms appeared he was simply condemned as incompetent, and so his wife's burden was made doubly onerous. "She was a good worker, but her husband was worthless. She did all the work herself alone, and got along fine. He was so useless that even when he tried to do anything, he never did it right. One day they were fishing for whitefish, and when they put their net out, it broke (because it was not moored properly), and they lost it. At the same time they saw a beaver. He started to shoot it, but the shell blocked so he could not kill it. Then when they reached home, he put his gun near the fire so the shell would blow, but he forgot to watch it and his gun burned also. So they had lots of trouble that one day. When fall came, they moved back (into the backwoods) where the man was going to hunt, but he was so lazy that he never did go out hunting. Ice Woman used to wade out in the deep snow, and carry bundles of wood on her back while her husband lay in the wigwam on his back with no moccasins on. She killed rabbits and brought them home to feed her husband. Finally the man got sick.... at last he died and she was left a widow. She did not care. She remained there for only a little while after that. Then she went away and looked for her widowed mother. A few months later she had a miscarriage. So she was over with everything now and was single again. She and her mother got along fine, as they were both good workers and good hunters."

Two Skies was a shaman, and in all respects a woman of strong character. She deserted one husband because she refused to tolerate his overbearing ways, and she went out on her own and maintained herself ably. "Then she got in with a young man and married him. His name was Evil Place, and they had a little boy. She had to support him (the husband) herself, as he was useless though he was good to her. So she dressed him up in beadwork that he traded for a pony or so." She practised her shamanism desultorily, and this contributed to the support of the family.

Marsh Woman was representative of many wives who devotedly support the household when the husband is too ill to contribute his share. A worthy man who becomes incapacitated by illness is often regarded lovingly by the wife, who remains attached to him and never thinks of deserting for another man. Marsh Woman's husband was paralyzed by sorcery. "After they had been married for two years, she had a baby girl. Then her husband got sick. He became paralyzed in his legs and one arm... he was able to move just one arm. For ten years he suffered like that. Marsh Woman always worked hard trying to make a living for her husband and child. Her parents helped her all they could, but they were old and could not do very much. She did everything" until her daughter matured and married, after which she was assisted by her son-in-law.

Maggie takes care of her invalid husband in the same way. She likes to explain that "John was a hard worker before the asthma got him. There was no one better than he. He made hundreds of dollars trapping fur, and he cleared this brush, and built our house and boat. But now he's hardly a man... just skin and bones, coughing his life away. But he is a good man, and it bothers him that he cannot work. He does not like to see me working so hard." Maggie is a very heavy woman, lame in one leg, and so cannot get about. But she does a variety of sedentary work competently, her tanning and bead embroidery are demanded by white people, and in this way she secures the few dollars that maintain the household. This relationship has lasted about eight years with no prospect of improvement. Maggie complains a little, but not seriously. She never looks ahead; it is important only that the moment be despatched.

Thunder Woman had a comparable protective attitude toward her husband, who had incurred her father's anger by marrying without his consent. "In the fall Thunder Woman and her husband moved to their hunting grounds, but the man could not kill anything. For a long time they did not have anything to eat. He went out every day to try and kill a moose, but everything was afraid of him. One time he stayed out alone on his trails, but that night he could not sleep. He was afraid and so he got up and went home to his wife; but he was no better. The next day they moved to his father's place. His father was able to kill lots of things, and had plenty to eat. After they had stayed there quite a while, his father said to him one evening, 'I killed a moose. Go there and make (tan) the hide, and take the meat for yourselves.' So the next day he and his wife started off, but when they reached the moose nothing was there but bones. Some wild animal had already eaten up the meat. So he said to his wife, 'I want you to go home to your people for your own good, as you will starve to death here with me. I'm going away somewhere to die. Don't you know it is your own father who is doing this to us? He is making us suffer.' But she said, 'No, I will not go back where I will see him (the father). I will stay right here with you, and try to help you. And I want you to fight back, too.' So they made their wigwam there, and she said (divining through her guardian spirits), 'In four days' time he will come to visit you again by his spirits and that is the time I want you to fight back.' Sure enough, when four days were up, the man woke in the morning before daylight, and his body felt peculiar as if he were getting big (like a *windigo*). He spoke to his wife and said, 'Get up! I'm afraid something awful is going to happen to us!' She was going to have a child, and he could see his child right through his wife's stomach; it looked like a beaver to him (symptom of the *windigo* insanity, which is cannibalistic in one form). His wife got up and said, 'No, I do not want anything to happen to us.' She took dried blueberries and Indian rice which she was keeping, and cooked some for her husband, and gave it to him to drink very hot. Then she started to dress up (in preparation for her supernatural ritual). While the man was sitting there, something fell in front of him, and he grabbed it. It looked like a little mouse. He held it hard, and then he spoke to his wife, 'Look what I have in my hand!' She said, 'I told you I did not want anything to happen. Hold it tight until I get through.' She warmed her medicine rattler and started to cure her husband by the sucking method. Also she destroyed the little wolf which the man had caught. This wolf was what his father-in-law had sent to him so that he should become a *windigo*, man-eater. She asked her husband if he did not have any guardian spirits that could help him out in trouble like this, but he said, 'No, I have nothing that I can call upon to help me.' So she did not say anything, but went right on with her own *manito kazo* and cured him. Next day they moved back to his father's camp and stayed there for about ten or fifteen days. This was in March. When the snow began to melt, a man came there and brought the news that her father was dead... he had frozen to death when he was returning home from visiting.... a funny time for anyone to freeze (unless by the intervention of sorcery). She did not appear to be shocked, and she did not care at all. She did not say anything for she herself had destroyed her father. That spring when the lakes broke up, all the Indians moved back (into the woods) to trap bears, and she and her husband also moved back, for now that her father was dead, her husband was able to kill moose, beaver, and all kinds of other things..... (About twenty-five years later) she was left a widow. She never married again. She practised curing by the sucking technique, and that is how she made a living for herself." .....In this story Thunder Woman's resourcefulness stands in marked contrast to her husband's inability to deal with the desperate situation. Thunder Woman displayed the courage and aggressive behavior that are theoretically the man's role, while her husband took an utterly passive part in the proceedings and was unable even to assist his wife. Thunder Woman was never again called upon to save the household in such dramatic fashion, but in other ways she continued to display marked resource and ability. Thus she delivered each of her four children without help, and as competently as though assisted by the best midwife. And later, after her husband's death, she was able to support herself comfortably even though she was at that time quite old.

Widows, and other women, frequently choose to support themselves in preference to marrying; and as a matter of course make casual use of the basic masculine techniques as an auxiliary means of livelihood. A woman can always marry and thus share the work with her husband in conventional fashion. Therefore women who prefer to live alone in all probability enjoy, and even seize upon, this manner of life: they desire solitude, or wish to hunt and trap, or delight in complete self-reliance...'. Ice Woman, Thunder Woman, and Deceased each prolonged her widowhood for obviously personal reasons. It is quite consistent that women so clear-eyed and deliberate as these should employ male techniques when it seems desirable to do so.

"This is a story of a woman named Gaybay. When she was a girl about ten or twelve years old, her father died, and after that she and her mother, Keeshka, stayed all alone in the bush. Keeshka was a great old woman to make things such as mats, rabbitskin robes, and birchbarks (roof-coverings). Gaybay learned how to do all these things, and to set nets. In the summer time they used to cure a lot of rice, berries, and they also made maple sugar and maple syrup. In the fall they killed lots of fish and rabbits, and they dried meat for the winter (which they must have hunted and trapped for themselves). They lived in a wigwam *(mitigo* giwam*,* "lodge made of wood") all winter. Gaybay and her mother used to work together. They never lived among people, they always lived by themselves on islands near the Lake of the Woods where they could get rabbits and fish to kill. By now Gaybay was a young girl (i. e., newly menstruating). They also killed weasels and muskrats in the spring. One spring Keeshka found five little baby foxes. They took these foxes and kept them on an island. They fed them on fish, and when fall came, they killed the foxes and sold the fur: black fox, silver fox, and a cross fox, and they got good money for them." Some years later the girl married, and not long after was widowed. Her mother was still unmarried. So the two widows, mother and daughter, lived together again and returned to the economic ways of earlier years. "She stayed with her mother again for a long time. She was like a man. She could kill a deer any time she wanted to." Then she remarried, but her husband died shortly, and she resumed living with her mother. "After that, she stayed single for nearly eight years. She used to snare (like a man) cross fox, and silver and black fox, also rabbits. Foxes meant good money in those days, and so she lived very well." Unlike her mother, who never remarried, Gaybay had five husbands, and during the married intervals functioned like a conventional woman inasmuch as she never hunted, trapped, or fished, but confined herself to the sedentary activities connected with the wigwam and to assisting her husband on the hunt when so requested. But during the periods of widowhood, which were far longer than those of marriage, she found no difficulty in adjusting to the occupational life of a man.

12

"This is a story of an Indian woman named Blanketed, about her own life. She did not remember how small she was when her father died. She used to say that from the time she was a little girl about six years old, she used to walk around to pick berries with her mother, Companionable Woman, and her mother used to gather some long grass, and twist it fine, like twine, and make a net out of it. Then she would set the net across the creek and so they caught fish. Fish, berries, and Indian rice was all they had to eat. (Companionable Woman was not a hunter, though she proved to be a warrior, and as a warrior could move stealthily and handle a gun.) She had never seen bread. They were all alone, just herself and her mother and her older brother. She often wondered why her mother was always busy in the summer, drying blueberries, fish, moose-meat, and sturgeon, and putting away sturgeon oil. Companionable Woman even used to skin the sturgeon, and make sturgeon oil bottles, and she dried the very sturgeon eggs and put them in a birch container. Then when fall came she made lots of rice and stored it away in a hole in the wild bush. She also caught fish and put a lot away for the winter. She was smart. They never had any lard or tea, but they had plenty of maple sugar, and they had *màskeg* (swamp) leaves for tea. Companionable Woman never drank tea or whiskey, and she never used tobacco. All she had (as a tobacco substitute) was the Indian stuff. (This is the outer bark of the red willow. It is used today, mixed with commercial tobacco in the proportions of about two to one, and is called *kinnakinnik.)* Blanketed said that she never saw a store in those days... only there were traders (at Hudson's Bay posts), and the Indians went to Winnipeg (to trade with them). It took about fifteen days to reach there, and sometimes they brought back hard tack. Blanketed wore only some black cloth (secured from the Hudson's Bay Company) with shoulder straps for a dress, and she wore moccasins, but no stockings. Her mother was never sick, not one of her teeth was out, for they were all good, and her hair was just grey. Blanketed herself was never sick when she was a girl, not until after she started to live close to towns and eat groceries. Late in the fall she used to see her mother gather the high grass that grows near the river, carry it on her back, and make a big wigwam and cover it with this grass. She took all her dried stuff there, and they lived in this wigwam all winter. They never lived in a house in those days. They were just as happy in this tent as any other place. It was kind of dark, but there was an opening in the roof. They had no calendars then, but they went by the moon and the stars. When winter came, her mother often went out in the morning, and when evening came she returned with a load of meat. Someone would come there and tell her to go get some meat (a neighborly gift, later repaid in services). So they were never hard up for anything to eat. But they had no lamp, or modern conveniences. The only thing they were afraid of was the Sioux Indians.

"One time when she was quite a big girl they were living at Northwest Angle River. There were four other families living there in wigwams. One night Companionable Woman became awfully frightened (a premonition which is considered to be of supernatural origin). She sat up all night watching to see if anyone was at the door. She knew that something was to happen sooner or later. While it was still night she put on her daughter's shoes, and woke her son up and told him not to sleep. There were two other young girls and an old woman staying there with them. When it was just about daylight, she heard people yelling at the other end of the camp that the Sioux were overtaking them. She jumped out of her wigwam and saw five Sioux Indians, all with guns. So she grabbed her daughter by the hand, and her son, and the other women followed. It happened that she had left her canoe out in the bay the day before. They all ran through the bush, and finally got into her canoe. (Under her leadership) they went up the river and around the Point, and they saw a canoe on the shore with a loaded gun in it. They knew it was the Sioux canoe. Companionable Woman took the gun and shot holes in the canoe and shoved it out and it sank. All you could see of it was the points. Then they went further up the river and hid in some tall grass. Blanketed and her brother and the two girls and the old woman hid in the water.... just Companionable Woman was in the canoe. As they stood there, they saw three men on the shore near this Sioux canoe. All at once one man dived into the water and swam towards them, so Companionable Woman shot him in the head and killed him. The other two men started shooting in their direction, but did not hit any of them; then the two men ran away. The Sioux Indians pushed all the Ojibwa canoes out on the lake so that the other Ojibwa would not be able to escape. That night Companionable Woman and the rest of them sneaked away. They went out of the river onto the lake, and they went (back) where they had been camping. Companionable Woman was so brave that she put ashore there and went up to their wigwam and took some things from it. She saw one woman lying dead at the door of the wigwam; it was the daughter-in-law of the old woman who was with them. As they were going (back) along the Point, they heard someone splashing water, so they were frightened. They thought it was the Sioux. Then they

12*

saw it was a woman swimming toward one of the (drifting) canoes. She had left her baby on the rocks and when she got the canoe ashore she put her baby in, but as she was pulling out, she saw a girl running toward her... it was her daughter. This woman went along with Companionable Woman. The two girls and the old woman also took another empty canoe, so there were three canoes. They shoved one other canoe into the grass so the Sioux would not be able to follow them. They did not know how many had been killed, nor how many were alive, for they were afraid to speak, or ask one another, for fear the Sioux were there. The three parties went to an island and they stayed there all day. Then Companionable Woman and the old woman and one of the girls left. They were brave. Companionable Woman would not let her son go along. She had the gun, but the other two woman took axes. Blanketed cried when she saw her mother going. So the three women went back where they had been camping. They could not hear a sound... it was still and quiet. Companionable Woman put ashore and went up to the wigwam, and in back of the two wigwams she saw two Sioux lying dead and also two Ojibwa women, and two young men, and three old men. One of the old men was her brother. These two Sioux and the one she had killed made three Sioux that were killed. There were seven Ojibwa dead there, and sixteen missing. She could not find them there anywhere. There were only nine (in the heroine's party of women and children). She hurried and took all the food she could find, for they were all hungry. And she took all the guns, axes, and knives, and carried them to the canoe. So they returned to the island. They ate and then went back and got the scalps of the Sioux and then they left for C----. While they were going along the shore, someone spoke to them. It was the ones who were missing. They brought all the canoes along, and the other Indians got into them. The children that lost their parents were there, and you would think they were singing, the way the children were crying, and also the grown-ups. So they got to C--- and brought the news that seven of them had been killed. Some men went back and took the bodies to an island, and buried them there. After that they brought all the dead people's things and they had a war dance. After they fixed and dressed the mourners, they had this war dance; they danced for two days because they had two Sioux scalps. Even the children were anxious to dance with these scalps in their hands." .... Companionable Woman had acted so bravely that she received the male honorific title of *ogitcida* ("brave", literally "great heart") and "used to have a feather on her head to show how brave she was."

Buhgokway had fine command of the male skills in hunting, trapping, and canoe and wigwam building. During her life several emergencies occurred, and she showed herself resourceful in handling them. "This is a story of an Indian woman named Buhgokway. She was married to an Indian from Denorwick Lake and they stayed there in the bay of this lake. She had two children by her husband. Then he died and she was left a widow. There was a (white lumber) camp near there. When her husband died, she moved to this camp and got stuff to eat from it and about a year after her husband died, she had another child by the cook there. He gave her lots of things to eat, and told her to stay in one of the (bunk) houses there at the camp. She was not short of anything... she had everything that she needed. She was a good hunter too, and got everything she wanted to hunt. She had a gun and killed ducks and other birds and animals. She did not have to go far when she wanted to pick berries, for there were lots of blueberries near by. And when she wanted to make rice, she just made it right there on the lake. When her children were born, she used to be all alone. No one ever kept her (to aid her in childbirth). She kept herself, with just her oldest little girl to help her. She was never sick for long when her children were born... she was so strong.

"She had another baby by the cook, and then the camp went away from there. Later her two children died, the ones she had by her dead husband, so she had only the boy and girl. Her girl was the older. One day when the boy was about four years old, and they were all outside cooking, the little boy said, 'Mama, look! Who is that coming ?' She looked, and it was a bear walking on its hind legs. She jumped up and grabbed her little boy and ran into the house and locked the door. The bear came right there and started scratching on the door. When it could not get the door open, it went to the window and broke the glass. She knew now that the bear would get in and tear them to pieces, so she opened the door and told her children to run out and jump into her canoe, so they did. Then she ran out with the bear right behind her, and ran into the water, and as she jumped into the canoe she upset it, and her children fell out. She grabbed her children, and the canoe too. It was full of water, and while she was bailing out the water she said to the bear, 'Just for what reason are you doing this to me ?' Then the bear left them, and went back up into the bush, so they went ashore and emptied the canoe. She took some things and they went to an island and slept there. The next day they saw the same bear walking along the shore, and that night she dreamed (a supernatural visitation from the Bear Spirit) that the bear wanted her to feed him on maple sugar. The next day she went back to her house and got maple sugar, put it in a dish, and put it on clean ground. She watched the bear go there and eat this sugar, and it never bothered them again. So she moved back.

"While they were living there alone, the father of her two (illegitimate) children came and asked her for her son, for the boy was now twelve years old, 'and if you will not let the boy go, I will take the girl.' He promised to give her money and lots of things. She did not answer anything. He went away and said he would return at a certain time. Every day a boat came with a load—flour, pork, tea, sugar and everything else—but she made up her mind not to let her boy go. She started breaking up her house and took the lumber and everything else across the lake, and made a shack for them over there where it could not be seen from the lake. She had two canoes and one boat. When the time came for the man to come and get her son, they went to a high rock and watched from there. He went away after he could not find anyone, and went to England. So the old woman stayed there with her children. Her son got sick and died, and she took it very hard. She nearly cried her eyes out. People used to come and get her, and she would go with them but she always returned soon, for she liked it there very much. Long after, her daughter died, and she was all alone. Not long after that, she also was found dead, lying on the floor beside the bed. So that was the end of Buhgokway."

Little Bear Woman was interesting as a woman upon whom widowhood thrust male responsibilities, but who was strikingly incompetent at shouldering them, and who sought to escape them as soon as possible through a re-marriage. "This is a story of Great Buffalo Woman. When she was a small girl, her father died. Her mother, Little Bear Woman, lived at the Lake of the Woods at Red Painted Rock. They lived there all alone. They were poor. Her mother fished and made rice, also dried blueberries and hunted and they lived this way for many years. Then her mother got married again to an old man who had a wife and some children." Polygynous marriage is never the most desirable form of marriage, as has been described in the previous chapter. Little Bear Woman got a certain enjoyment out of it however, for she was relieved of the never-ending responsibilities of providing meat and fur. She fell easily into the subordinate role of the conventional woman, and where she had once had to hunt on her own initiative, now she needed only to accompany her husband as his assistant. In time she yielded even this obligation, claiming to be too ill for it, and so her daughter was impressed into the step-father's service. Great

Buffalo Woman had always been unhappy in the new household, and eventually she and her mother left because of the step-father's desire for the girl. Mother and daughter resumed their old way of life, and their old poverty. It was now the daughter, as a young vigorous adult, who was expected to assume the initiative in economic matters, and it is striking that she proved as incompetent as her mother. Yet, unlike her mother, she desired to be economically independent. She attempted marriage once, but threw her husband out of the wigwam after two months of joint life, and never remarried. Since she had the drive to live alone, and adopted masculine techniques at least in hunting, a good portion of her incompetence must be attributed to her mother's example and to the inadequate instruction the girl had received. She was ignorant of even the most elementary and fundamental hunting taboos, which she violated flagrantly and innocently. A terrible injury was attributed to such blundering. "She was always alone in her own wigwam. No one ever helped her out with anything. She just made a living for herself alone (her mother was dead by this time). She never had much. One time the Indians were having a feast of bear (in thanks giving because they had slain this bear), with rice and sugar. She too went and was given some rice and sugar, and a piece of the bear's tongue. She ate the rice and sugar, but the bear tongue she did not eat. She pulled a piece off and threw the rest away, and the dogs ate it up (thus violating the sacred majesty of the bear). Nobody saw her do this. She did not think she was doing anything wrong. Many days after that, she went out to the lake, paddled around, and pulled ashore, and went up the bush to get birchbark to make roofing and some baskets and pans. As she was climbing up and down a birch tree, she saw a bear coming towards her. He was coming from the lake where she had left her canoe. He came right up to her and started scratching. She tried to run away but he caught up to her, threw her down, clawed her, and left her there. When she got up, he ran after her again. She climbed a tree, and he came up and threw her down. Then she jumped up and ran as fast as she could, the bear right at her heels. When she reached her canoe, it had been torn to pieces by the bear. She ran right into the water, with only her head sticking out. Her flesh was torn open, and the water made her suffer. The bear gave three shouts, and went back into the bush. After he had been gone quite a while, she walked ashore and ran along as fast as she could go, although she was in pain. She crossed the water, swam a little way, and got to the mainland where she could reach home. She lay down for a while to rest. She saw a canoe and yelled. It was

an old woman whom she called grandma, and she told her to come
and get her. The old woman took her home, and the Indian doctors
cured her by sucking. They asked her if she knew of any time when
she had said or done anything wrong to the bear, and she told of
the time when she had fed the bear tongue to the dogs. She was told
that was the time she had made the bear mad, because the tongue
is the most important part of him. She was sick for a long time, but
she finally got better. The bear never attacked her again. She died
soon though. No one knew what happened to her because she was
always alone."

Despite the many cases of widows or other lone women who take
up masculine techniques in addition to the feminine ones, and in
spite of the apparent necessity that such women undertake men's
work, there are some who never attempt it in any way. It is difficult
to say how numerous these cases are. Woman Covered All Over was
such a widow, but certain extreme circumstances seem to explain
her conservative, or perhaps timid, attitude. The story of her first
marriage to a shaman and her subsequent paralysis has been told.
When she recovered, she married again. Her first husband (the
shaman) then threatened to kill her. After nearly five years, the
second husband died. Woman Covered All Over was then thrown
on her own resources for self-support. She relied exclusively on
women's work, chiefly fancy work and berry and plum picking.
Even if she had known masculine techniques in hunting or shamanism, it is understandable why she would not have practised
them: the long years of paralysis would have put her out of practise;
and also men's work would have been identified with her hated first
husband who was preeminent in all such techniques. She was also
shaken by the rumors of the shaman's threats. However, the
following incident indicates a coolness of mind perfectly adequate
for handling male problems. "One time when she was picking
plums, she heard a noise as if someone were eating bones. She put
the plums in a sack, and as she was getting up to put the bundle on
her back, a big bear stood on its hind legs right in front of her.
She just stood there and looked at the bear. She said to him,
'Please do not have any hard feelings against me. I am poor,
that's why I pick these plums. And if you let me go, I will give
you some sugar and whiskey.' The bear just put down its fore
legs and walked away, so she went home all right. She got some
whiskey and put it in a little dish with some sugar, and went back
to the place where she had seen the bear. She put the birch pan
with sugar and whiskey there on the ground and went home. The
next day she went again to make sure that the bear had come. Sure

enough, the bear had been there and had eaten the sugar and drunk the whiskey. After he had finished everything, he had carefully turned the birch dish over (as the Indians do when they have emptied a dish or vessel). He never even broke the dish. So when she saw this, she went home, but she did not take the birch pan home. After that, when she wanted to pick berries, she used to get a birch pan ready with some sugar, candies, and whiskey. The bear never frightened her again because he was ,so pleased to get the sugar and candies... he was crazy for the things that she fed him, and he liked the whiskey an awful lot. He never bothered about tobacco. She made her living by picking berries and making fancy work. At last she married another man.''

Curiously enough, the shamanistic technique of *tcisaki* divining is never attempted by women. Maggie said that years ago there was one woman foolish enough to attempt it, but she soon realized her error and abandoned it. This consistent observance of this one taboo emphasizes the fact that all other masculine techniques—though formally as taboo to women as is the *tcisaki*—are adopted by numerous individual women. There is no exception, however, to the generalization that no man ever tries women's work.

The fact that certain women do not try any masculine pursuits, throws into stronger relief the fact that other women do make these techniques their own in greater or smaller part. The same culture that has laid down a glamorous course for men has provided no distinct line of conduct for women. Women therefore attempt nearly everything available in the culture—and by so doing, alter the formulated nature of much that they engage in, heedless of the occupational demarcation so painstakingly taught to the men. Individual variations among women show up conspicuously as differences in objectives, technical accomplishments, and perseverance; whereas among men such variations are only in degree of accomplishment. If men are thought of as the specialized instruments of Ojibwa culture, women are the unspecialized; if men are considered inheritors of the culture's wealth, women are the dispossessed and underprivileged; if men are the material selected arbitrarily to be the finest medium for the expression of Ojibwa ideals, women are second-rate, or perhaps reserve, material.

PART 4.

ABNORMALITIES

The ideals of the Ojibwa, the ends toward which every person should strive, are of several different orders to an objective eye, but to the Ojibwa they are knit into an internally consistent system. The keystone to their culture, the bias which molds all personal actions and reshapes the cultural details that have been borrowed from neighboring tribes, is individualism. Many of the manifestations of this concept have been noted in the previous pages, as well as the associated reactionsof pride and shame. Success in every undertaking — the hunt, courtship, warfare, communication with the supernatural — is of paramount importance.

All the preoccupations of the Ojibwa can find expression only within the limits set by the individualistic attitude. Thus the general interest in physical well-being is a concern of the individual alone; the group, the tribe are not considered. The concern with sickness appears obsessive to an outsider. Every Ojibwa is ridden with anxiety about his health. From birth, a child is provided with curing rites by his parents. An adult continually hires doctors for himself, seeks visions that promise well-being, participates in the curative Sun Dance and Medicine Dance. This concern with illness finds a complement in the cultural provision for curers of several different sorts. The attention given to one's own illnesses, which is based on a rather hypochondriacal self-preoccupation, matures into a relationship between patient and curer in which the patient is interested only in improving his condition, and the curer typically is interested only in demonstrating his power to cure. The attitude of the shaman is extremely exhibitionistic—he wants to show off power, miraculous tricks which have been given to him in a vision by a supernatural who singled him out for this personal attention. Here again, the curer's success is important to him largely because it ministers to his self-respect, not because he has any serious stakes in alleviating the patients' suffering.

These individualistic values are of more importance to men than to women. It is men who have, and who have been trained deliberately to have, the greatest degree of pride and shame, while in women the manifestations are muted and uneven. The cultural distinctions in the training of men and women, and the separate norms of behavior, are epitomized in their varied reactions to an extreme shame situation. A very powerful shame situation in a woman's life is the bearing of an illegitimate child; yet, as has been mentioned, the girl in such a case is usually able to adjust quietly and adequately to the situation. It is the man (in this case the brother) who is overwhelmed by the girl's delinquency and who must leave the locality to forget it. But people, especially men, are not conditioned simply to evince pride or shame as responses to distinct, isolated phenomena. Rather, pride-shame is a continuous theme in a person's life. A man is constantly alive to the need of guarding himself, to the need of keeping his pride intact, and as a consequence vague persecutory trends are manifest in everyone's reactions.

Bravery, or more accurately, bravado, is greatly valued by the Ojibwa, as it is by surrounding peoples. Bravery does not refer to conduct in the fundamental activities of hunting, fishing, shamanism, or love-making. It is ideally a masculine feature, and is defined as the gallantry involved in risking life for something that is not vital to existence. This usually means going on the war-path to kill Sioux or to secure scalps "for the honorific feathers". Bravery also includes a number of other acts which are synonymously described as foolish, and which are not practised with the regularity of the war-party. These include lavish gifts of goods, furs, silver, or horses which are made at the give-away dances taken over from the Dakota Sioux. Gestures such as were made by Young Man when he gave away his wife at a divorce-dance, and risked his life to rescue a stolen pony, are also included in this category. Acts of bravery are initiated by each person at his own discretion, and his self-esteem is dependent upon his success in them. No influence external to a person's own conscience, or vagaries, or his view of himself as proud or shamed, can move him to bravery. A brave does not strive in competition with other warriors, but is interested only in ascertaining the fact that he can achieve distinction, regardless of whether or not others do. Always, the culture's primary emphasis is upon achievement of those ends in which a person is privately interested. But the emphasis upon warlike bravery for men was so insistent in the training of boys that nearly all adults were motivated spontaneously in this direction.

Women who do the deeds of brave men on the war-path and at the give-away dance are called brave, as though they were men; although since women are not trained to these attitudes they have no deliberate incentive comparable to men's. Men sometimes project bravery motives into the conduct of women, as in the case of the girl who was considered brave by the men of the village because she had yielded her illegitimate baby to its father. Informally, women sometimes voice the verdict that certain other women are brave but with women this is not a title, and implies no bravado; it connotes, rather, a favorable judgment upon performance in vital feminine activities such as childbirth, and upon adjustment to the economic demands of widowhood. As in so many other respects, women have taken over the devices of men when the situation seemed to call for it, but have changed the character of the devices in accordance with their ignorance; so women apparently took over the idea of bravery, though they altered the idiomatic masculine character of the idea and the masculine motivations associated with it.

It is still felt that indifference to war and its braveries is as contemptible, as unsexing, in a male as is uselessness on the hunt. Exceedingly few men seem to have exhibited conspicuous cowardice. But one man was so unconquerably timorous, yet so goaded by the cultural requirements, that he resorted to scalping his own crown. Among the neighboring Dakota Sioux, he could have fled to the respected camp of the *berdache* and found there a place for devotion to the arts of peace. Among his fellow Ojibwa he was scorned, and considered immeasurably inferior to his own wife who had sneered at him, armed with a scalp she herself had taken from a Sioux head. The term cowardice is also applied to a kind of agoraphobia that attacks some people, especially demoralized shamans. Of such people it is said, "He got crazy. He was a coward. He would never go outside alone."

The last principle giving form to Ojibwa life is the distinction made ideally between the personalities of men and of women. All of a man's life and training emphasize his innate superiority; women are not only inferior, but their lack of distinct training leads them to ape, and often to distort, men's characteristic motivations.

Ojibwa concepts of what constitutes normal behavior are designed primarily for men. Standards of normal conduct apply chiefly to adults, that is, to those who are of marriageable age. Adumbrations, however, do reach out to childhood, though chiefly to boys. Thus a boy's increasing maturity, responsibility, and ability to fulfill the normal requirements are partly gauged by the feasts which mark his achievements in securing game and by the frequency of his fasting for a vision. But generally children are outside the possibility of abnormal conduct. Only physical aberrations such as harelip are recognized in children.

Since environmental influences are nearly uniform for boys, deviations among men are rather easily reduced to being a function of individual variations in temperament, imagination and intelligence. On the other hand, the influences brought to bear on individual girls and women are in effect left to the discretion of the households in which they live. This uncertain environment, together with the general atmosphere of cultural indifference which surrounds them, cause women to be incomparably more irregular respecting the sketchy and negatively phrased ideals with which tradition makes a pretense of providing them than men with respect to their traditional ideals.

The Ojibwa recognize two classes of deviants from the standard of normal conduct. One class consists of those whose conduct expresses the converse of the normal goals, whose behavior is black where the prescriptive behavior is white. For the sake of convenience, these may be called negativists. The other class of recognized deviants comprises those who pursue too zealously the cultural values, those who are the supererogates.

Negativists are frequently deficient in their quotients of pride and of shame, and in self-assertive, or better, exhibitionistic drives. They are complacent and amenable, rather than acutely alive to the majesty contained within them. Such a man as Shahgo is included in this category. He quietly accepted his wife's flagrant desertion; he continued to reside with the family of his deserting wife, and to rear their child; he married the younger sister of his former wife when this arrangement was proposed to him; he tolerated quietly but unresponsively the advances of his former wife; when these aroused the furious jealousy of his second wife and prompted her to leave him, he made a mild effort to win her back, and when this failed he left the locality. Some years later, when his first wife besieged him with renewed proposals, he spiritlessly acceded. He did not enjoy fighting, did not understand challenges to the ego he should have possessed, cared only for the sedate pleasures of domesticity and economic routine. There are women, too, as deficient as men in this regard, but they are not considered to belong to the same anomalous order. Of men like Shahgo, people will remark wonderingly, or with amusement, or with scorn: "he is hardly a man." But of women, like Hawk Woman, who tolerate desertions and other abuse, it is said simply and pityingly, "she went through a hard life." No judgment is passed upon these women; they are accepted almost as casually as the more usual women who fight against or fly from abuse, and of whom it may be said "she is a brave woman." It is difficult to categorize aberrant women definitely, because there is no absolute standard for women. The sketchy formal advice irregularly given to girls, but chiefly at the ceremonial observance of nubility, prescribe deference to men. The strongly impressed standards of behavior, those which are actually dynamic in a woman's life, are the masculine ones, insensibly assimilated from male housemates. By the mid-Victorian-like standards of the theoretically ideal woman, Hawk Woman's behavior was "text-book normal;" by the actually functioning blood-and-thunder standards borrowed from the men, her conduct was abnormal, though so inoffensively that it was hardly more than pitiable. As in present-day America, a woman's gratuitous long-suffering is accorded a glazed-eyed and sanctimonious respect . . . . . . but, as in present-day America, the vulgar attitude is, who cares to be long-suffering.

Others who are considered aberrant because of their unresisting attitudes include the rare women who tolerate polygyny and even like their co-wives. These instances seem to be few in number, though precise figures are unobtainable. No inferences regarding behavior in other spheres can be drawn from this particular deviation. A daring female warrior may be a very tractable co-wife. A woman undistinguished in other respects may yet have a highly vulnerable ego when it comes to polygyny; indeed, most women, no matter how unaccomplished, are intolerant of polygyny. A similar resistence to plural marriage, in the form of polyandry, occurs among men. This attitude is certainly not remarkable among men since tremendous institutional pressure is exerted against polyandry. Yet at least one man not only tolerated polyandry, but actually esteemed his co-husband. This man, Small Ice, seems to have been temperamentally much like Shahgo: a conscientious worker, devoted only to the joys of an unassuming life. He was regarded as distinctly queer, and some of his own children ridiculed him. It was not until fifteen years had passed that Small Ice was stirred to some feeble shame; but the only retaliation that occurred to him was to leave the domicile, although he returned to it for long visits.

Others who are aberrant through tractability and lack of pride allow themselves to be deprived of their inheritance. Harry Skies was such a man, and he behaved so midlly that people came to view him with the questionable pity usually accorded to long-suffering women. His deceased wife had owned a good deal of real property— house, tent, furniture, canoe, clothes—and had bequeathed it to him upon her deathbed. Her mother, Mrs. Greatbear, who is still an old Tartar, simply ignored the will and seized her daughter's house and furniture. This was a sacrilegious act, but that made no difference to Mrs. Greatbear since observance of the taboo would have stood in the way of her desires. When the son-in-law protested that at least some of the things should go to him, Mrs. Greatbear loudly overruled him, and quiet Skies stepped aside. The old lady had preempted the male rights that should have belonged to Skies.

Shamans are usually supererogates in their abnormalities, but a few are negativists in certain respects. These are the men who know how to practise sorcery, that is, they have the means of increasing their prestige by spreading fear and by displaying supernatural tricks, but they deliberately refrain from doing so. There is a belief that the practise of sorcery has a boomerang effect upon the family of the sorcerer, and causes the death of young people in particular. So it is explained that a "good" medicine man is motivated to goodness by fear of this consequence. They say, "Namepok (Sturgeon) does not want his grandchildren to die, that is why he does not do bad medicine." Namepok himself may be motivated by this fear; he has always been quite mild for a shaman. In his youth he did not lead war parties, and was never conspicuous as a warrior; he did not gain renown as a hunter; he was a shaman, but not an outstanding one; he married only once and was never divorced or temporarily separated from his wife; he paid his sib debt. That is, by natural disposition he seemed aberrantly mild-tempered. Certainly neither he nor any other good shaman receives the esteem accorded bad ones. They do not impress themselves upon the people by their extremes of pride and shame; and since they possess shamanistic knowledge with its armory of evil, the people wonder at them for their deviant behavior.

Some shamans become good after an orgiastic period of badness. They throw away their paraphernalia in despair over the fact that relatives are dying and that their powers of curing and of divining are no longer effectual. They become uncertain of themselves, even timid and fearful. "They become cowards." Such people are aberrant, but apparently not because of any original qualities of character. Rather, they suffer some disintegration of personality which leads to an extreme and rapidly apparent lack of self-confidence. They feel ashamed, but they are too uncertain of themselves, too melancholic to think of striking out at some other person. They simply withdraw, become anxious and sometimes stuporous, have persecutory hallucinations, and may even think of suicide.

But they are considered "good", for they refrain from using the sorcery that they know; and they are considered extraordinarily aberrant just because they have stopped short in their bad medicine career. These aberrants are usually men, a function of the fact that most shamans are men, but there are some women who behave in the same way. One such woman was Iron Woman who possessed masculine techniques and motivations. She was judged just as a male deviant would have been.

Another expression of a pathological lack of pride is indifference to a career, especially when the opportunities are actually presented. John Wilson is the son, nephew, grandson, and cousin of shamans, and has been urged by these repeatedly to take instruction under them, and has been offered all inducements to follow in their footsteps. But he refuses. He does not enjoy the work nor the publicity of a shaman. He wants sociability and peace, just as Small Ice, Shahgo, and Skies did. His wife, who herself has the native qualities appropriate to shamanism, says of him: "He is such a quiet man... always about his business... you would never know he is alive... he even cooks for himself sometimes... he never throws lip to anyone... in all these (twenty) years (of marriage), he has never once laid a finger on me... you can't say that about most men... when he gets mad he just goes off by himself, and does not answer me." Such a quiet, unassuming, cheerful personality is uncommon, both among men and women. The most common feminine analogue of Wilson's indifference to a career occurs among those few women who tolerate desertion, polygyny, and physical cruelty, and who do not see in these situations opportunities for egotistic and individualistic display. Also in this category, but less frequent, are those women who cooperate in some task, who for the time submerge their individuality in the interests of the work. Mrs. Trap and her sisters are as a rule haughtily individualistic towards others, but among themselves their behavior is of a different sort. They share their trapping trails, fishing places, and maple-sugar groves. That is, each sister owns her landed property individually, and owns the end products individually, but takes turns at inviting the other sisters to work on her land. In sugar-making, the three sisters often pool their raw products, cooperate in the labor, and divide the finished products equally. However this friendly, trustful, pride-less grouping is rare; it is the only one of its kind to occur regularly, and is recognized by everyone to be very unusual. The women of this group are unmarried — one is widowed, one was deserted, one never married, and perhaps they come together for this reason.

People may be in general full of pride, and exhibitionistic, but yet respond negativistically to some aspect of the culture. Hole-in-the-Sky, for example, does not indulge in self-pity because of illness. He never has called a curer for himself, and has never gone through the *mide* curing ceremony. Indeed, he bends over backward in his negative reaction to the cultural obsession with illness, and proclaims that he is invulnerable because he is a reincarnated supernatural and can himself arbitrate the term of his life and health on earth. (He has gone through two desperate illnesses where he was so completely disoriented that he was cared for by others without his knowledge. But as soon as he had gained some strength, he grew impatient and tried to dispense with the atmosphere of illness and to resume normal activities.) However he is very much interested in the curing of illness, and has an unrivaled reputation as a curer. It has been indicated that the curer's primary concern is not the welfare of the patient, but the demonstration of his own power of which the patient's recovery is proof. A noted curer, like any other noted shaman, is not a man with a reputation for goodness. He is a man whose great power is used without regard to ethical direction, and who is feared for his very readiness to take action in a good cr bad direction. Hole-in-the-Sky is such a man, and a perfect creature of his culture in that respect. But he is atypical for his lack of interest in the passive exhibitionism of being a patient.

Some shamans are aberrant because they have an altruistic interest in the patient, one which completely obliterates the customary egotistic display of power. But these shamans never become great, that is, feared, and are chiefly women. One of these was Sky Woman who seemed to evolve and practise her power just for the sake of aiding her grandmother, and who repudiated her claims to the power after her grandmother's death. Another such practitioner was Kota, who was deficient in the normal display drives, but tremendously interested in people, and particularly in her patients. No male curer's career was ever characterized by such a pronounced personal interest in patients. Leonard Wilson performed as curer for the first time upon the occasion of his baby daughter's grave illness, and he was then chiefly concerned with effecting a cure, not with displaying power. But he did not continue this relationship with subsequent patients. Many male shamans have fleeting experiences like Leonard's, but do not prolong them. It is quite in keeping with the distinctions in the training of men and women, that the abnormal attitudes should be characteristic of women shamans, while irregularities should be only fugitive with men. A

13

man becomes a shaman as a consequence of training for a career which is of fundamental importance to him; most women simply adopt shamanistic *techniques* which they employ in the service of their momentary interests. For several years, **Dave Daylight** cured like a woman, that is, he placed his hopes in the cure of his patients (his wife, children, and brother), and when they died, his morale as a shaman collapsed. He threw his paraphernalia into the bush, and said that since his relatives had died, he had no further interest in a shamanistic career. Had he behaved in typical masculine fashion, with every effort bent on displaying his power, it is not likely that he would have been moved to abandon his supernatural claims. He would have sought further visions and increased his power, he would have discovered that another shaman was plotting against him, and used his powers in retaliation for having been shamed. He would have justified himself by future cures. But **Dave's** doom was that he was overwhelmingly concerned with his patients instead of with his ambitions. His abnormality held its own penalty.

Another serious deviation, which is found chiefly among men, is lack of concern with the economic needs of the future. This means that the hunt is neglected, as in the case of Ice Woman's husband. It is remarkable that many husbands are judged "useless" as hunters. Men and women alike scorn them, but the guilty ones themselves remain indifferent. Indeed, these men are apathetic. It was impossible to find a single man who was a poor hunter but who was competent or in earnest in some other sphere. A man's inadequate skill or interest in the hunt stamps him as a generally inferior person. There are women, too, who are similarly incompetent. Little Bear Woman was such a woman. Her daughter, Great Buffalo Woman, also seems to have had little ability, but she was ambitious for economic independence and therefore taxed her powers. She grew into a decidedly unhappy and seclusive person.

Since marriage is a romantic and not an economic arrangement, "useless" men marry just as other men do. The wife soon learns that she alone must be responsible for the economic success of the household. Most wives accept this burden for a longer or shorter period of time. But as the husband's apathy becomes confirmed, the woman becomes impatient. This type of man in addition seems to be very querulous and susceptible to groundless and violent jealousies. Finally the wife deserts, and the husband is left to his own resources. Conventionally he tries to recover his wife, but fruitlessly. Then he becomes an outcast until another woman will risk supporting him. Many of these inadequate men died young apparently of obscure constitutional defects.

Incompetent men are scorned, since every man must be a Titan. Incompetent women provoke only pity or impatience. Women are not expected to act with decision; if they do, they are rewarded for their supererogatory zeal; if they do not, they are tolerated. Inadequacies among women are described rarely as such, and only through inference. Women are not thought of as being tested, therefore their deficiencies do not come into prominence as men's do. Furthermore, there is no lack of skill among women so great that it prevents marriage; and through marriage these women are insured maintenance and security.

The one type of negativistic deviation that is richly rewarded is the assumption of masculine techniques by women. The occupationally deviant woman is acknowledged because she has been invested by the supernatural with the attributes of a man. It is possible that some men tend to deviate from the normal in a way which is comparable to that described for women. Thus it may be that those men who are "useless" hunters, "cowardly" warriors, or "good" shamans, have tendencies toward feminism which are not allowed expression and which therefore are exhibited as incomplete regressions from the normal masculine behavior.

Some people are aberrant inasmuch as they are indifferent to love and marriage. It has been seen already that abstinent girls are considered reprehensible. They are made to feel culpable by the remarks of relatives and by the generally censuring attitude of others. People make obscene remarks about their sexual deficiencies. Even the traditional body of myth has a brief prepared against them, though it is difficult to estimate the extent of any individual girl's acquaintance with the pertinent mythology. Sexual relationships are the one sphere in which a clear, directive standard for a woman exists, especially as it forbids celibacy. A woman must give herself to love and marriage when a man so wishes, for he will be offended by refusal. No such traditional rule exists for men, though because of the variety of behavior patterns open to women, an individual woman may choose to respond shamedly to a man's rejection of her. Because voluntary abstinence is a gross violation of traditional requirements, not merely a slighting of an ideal, a bachelor girl is more criminal than she is abnormal to the Ojibwa. She is anti-social and committed to her individualistic whims even beyond the gaping limits allowed in Ojibwa. For its hostile implications, her act can be compared with a hunter's criminal trespass upon another's private trapping grounds. But to the native view, the latter's act has at least certain economic warrants, while a girl's

13*

abstinence has nothing to justify it and is rooted in offensive irregularities of character.

A bachelor man is not criminal, and no thought is paid to the abnormality of his state; he is accepted. There seem to be, and to have been, a greater number of women than of men who have not wished to marry. This may be linked to the fact that occupational irregularities are open to women but not to men. That is, a woman who chooses to live alone can usually learn to support herself adequately. However a man cannot practise feminine techniques, therefore voluntary bachelorhood means that he is deprived of a woman's valuable economic contributions.

Thus, all the native arrangements conspire to make women deviate from the ideal. Their deviation is abnormal and even criminal; yet women are rewarded for whatever success they achieve. On the other hand, men are urged to approximate the cultural ideal. A bachelor's failure to do so brings no conventional censure; still, punishments, in the form of poverty, come to a bachelor automatically, swiftly, and most uncomfortably.

It is interesting that the social effects of negativism are completely opposite for individuals of opposite sexes. In general, negativistic women are given approval, whereas the men are dishonored or ignored. This is a consequence of the fact that the masculine norms are the only ones of real concern, so that all approximations to them are rewarded. The preceding pages are filled with testimony to this view.

Those people who exaggerate the cultural values can be called "supererogatory". Many individuals in this category foster personal pride and shame to a degree that is abnormal even to the Ojibwa. There are several graduated degrees of this aberration. A mild departure from the normal attitude is shown in the following story: Two households — those of a sister and of a brother — were on very friendly terms and for twenty years had been neighbors. The daughter of one house, English Woman, grew up with her cross-cousin who was a son of the other household. The children played together constantly, and in time became lovers, but without the knowledge of the older people. Finally they decided to marry, a natural result of their life-long friendship and of the conventional sexual joking that had gone on all through their childhood. They announced this to the older people. The two fathers objected furiously, for in this locality the marriage of cross-cousins was regarded as incestuous. When the two married nevertheless, each of the fathers felt tremendously humiliated. Offended pride demanded some outlet, and each man disowned his child and forever maintained the repudiation. But the men went even further. To each man, the other became an intolerable reminder of his shame. The outcome was that the men moved from the vicinity, ceased being neighbors, and without regret disrupted a tie that had survived a generation. They never altered their decision, for they never ceased to brood over the shame. They avoided each other forever. And when their children suffered, each man in his heart rejoiced over this vindication of his shame. The two mothers, however, did not react in the same way. They saw no offense in the course their children had taken, and they did not repudiate them. They always maintained relations with them, and with each other. In the public opinion, the men were over-righteous, while the women were quite justified in subordinating the problem of incest to the ties of affection.

A more extreme attitude toward pride and shame resulted in a boy's almost complete alienation from the world. "This is a story of a boy named Earth Bird. He had one brother and three sisters. He was the youngest of them all. His parents were living also at the time. One day his brother asked him to go out paddling, but he refused to go. This made the older brother mad. He took him by the shoulder and beat him and threw him into the canoe and paddled away. Earth Bird did not sit up, but lay face down in the canoe expecting that his brother would punch him on the back every once in a while. He did not move or do anything, and so his brother kept paddling along. They went ashore and the brother got out and killed a moose, but Earth Bird stayed right in the canoe. All at once he made up his mind that he would go away. He got up and out of the canoe. He took some matches from his brother's coat pocket, and also some other things. He was very sad because his brother had been mean to him. He took off his old coat and cap and threw them on the water, and then ran away towards the north side. He did not care where he was going, just so that he could get away from his brother (to remove himself from the reminder of his humiliation). When the man came back to the canoe, Earth Bird was gone. He looked out on the water and saw something floating around, so he jumped into his canoe and paddled to it. Just as he was nearing it, it sank, and he thought that it might be his brother. He started to cry. He left his moose and everything there and started for home. As soon as he got close, he yelled to his parents and sisters that his brother had drowned. His parents did not believe him. They all accused him of drowning his brother. They went to the spot where he had seen something floating, but they never found anything. They all moved where the moose was, and camped there drying the meat. Sometimes the mother missed a piece of her dried meat. One time she lost a pail, and again an axe. She never said anything, but she used to wonder who it (the thief) could be. She thought it might be some of the other people who were living nearby. The old man was very sad. He missed his son. He took it very hard also because his son's body was never found... for he always thought that his son was dead. That same fall the old man died on account of all this. People always thought Earth Bird was dead. But he was not; he was seen many times, only no one ever knew it was he. One time he was seen by his sister-in-law, the wife of the brother who had beaten him. As they were returning from Kenora one time, her husband was drunk, and they stopped to make tea and he fell asleep. She went across to a place where there were some blueberries. She was picking them when she looked over where her husband was sleeping. She saw a man walking around and she wondered who it was. She got in the canoe and went back. When she got there, she found that all their groceries were gone, and also her husband's moccasins. They did not know who had stolen them. Another time a gun was lost. Another time an axe, and many other things. Once an old woman saw Earth Bird, but she did not know who he was. About three years later while his mother and little sister were in the bush somewhere, smoking a moose-hide, he made up his mind to let his mother see him (a tender gesture). So he went up close to her, and he spoke to her, 'Mother, do you want to see me?' She turned around, and said, 'My son! Is it you? Are you alive?' He said, 'Yes, I'm alive, just as you are. I'm not crazy either, and I did not die, but I'm still mad, mad at my brother because he made me ashamed when he beat me. I was very proud of myself at that time, and when he did that to me, the bird that was in my body flew away (the supernatural *alter ego*, token of the power granted by the guardian spirit, and basis for the young man's original state of pride). That is why I am wandering around because I am no good any more... I don't want anybody to see me... and so do not tell anybody that you have seen me. If you do, you will never see me again.' The old woman was afraid of her son because he was an awful sight with his old ragged pants, and dirty and filthy, and his hair was very long, and it was all tangled up. But she soon calmed down, and she was glad to know he was still alive. She said, 'Now, my son, wait for me here, and I will go and get something for you to eat.' She ran home and got all she could, and also a pair of moccasins. She gave these things to him, and he told her, 'If you want to see me again, come to the bay over there, and that is where you will see me.' And he went away. She told her little girl not to tell. The child was about eleven years old at that time. Then the mother started to make and keep moccasins and other things for her son, and several times she paddled around the bay. She did not see him again for a while, but she saw where he had camped, and she put moccasins and food there. When she returned later, she found that the things had been taken. Again, about three years later, she went out to pick berries with only her daughter, and soon her son came close again, and asked her if they were finding any berries. She said no, and he told her where to go the next day; and when they went there, they found lots of blue-berries. She did not see Earth Bird again, but when they reached home, they found a birch basket full of blueberries. She knew that her son had left them there. Soon they had enough blueberries to last all winter. That night while walking around outside, she told her daughter they would go home the next day. Her son must have heard her, and he said, 'Are you going home tomorrow ?' And she said yes. She asked him to go along with them, but he refused, so they left him there. She never told of seeing her son, but she used to worry because he went around the bush like a wild animal. He told her once that he was not afraid... but at first he had been... there were so many wolves around. He had a gun, axe, knife, and other things. She also gave him traps. Then he disappeared. Though she went many times to the place where he had been, she never saw any sign of him. She left moccasins and food for him, but when she returned, they would still be there. Then she gave up trying to find him. She thought that at last he must have been killed by wolves. She often walked around there and found caves where he used to sleep, but she never found any trace of his having been killed. He disappeared for about five years. One time while she was camping with some Indians, she overheard some Indian men telling one another that they had seen a man working in a logging camp somewhere, and that when they had sopken to him, he had never lifted his head to answer, so they could not make out who he was. She thought to herself that it might be her son. So she got ready and went to all the logging camps she knew of, and finally she did find her son. She would not have known him, only he asked her what she was looking for, and she recognized his voice. He was changed; he had shaved, his hair was cut, and he was dressed like a man..... so different from the way she had seen him last. She asked him to go home with her. She told him that his brother was sick, and might not live long, and that it was time to forgive his brother (this is a woman's reasoning, not a man's). But he refused again. He said that he was all right wandering around, and that he did not want anybody to know that he was alive. He gave her five dollars, and told her to go. So she went home and she never saw him again. Her older son died. He was worried and also sad because it was his fault that Earth Bird had been lost. The mother died too... also the other two sisters, and then just the youngest sister was alive. She went from place to place. Finally one time she returned to the bay where she used to see her brother, and just as she was going around the bay, she saw someone coming down the bank for water. She knew that it was her brother. After he was gone, she came closer, and she could see places where he had camped. Then she went ashore and yelled to him. No answer came. So she yelled again, 'My brother, answer me! I am coming here to stay with you! Don't you know, my brother, that only we two are living? Our sisters and brother, also our mother are gone! Oh, can't you find a place in your heart for me? You are the only one I have now, and that is why I have come here to find you!' Then she saw her brother coming towards her. He was different now. His hair was short, and he had on clothes. He was living in some kind of a cave. He was very sorry to hear of his mother's death. He took it very hard and cried, saying, 'I was cruel to my poor mother! Why didn't I listen to her! She pleaded with me many times to go home with her. For her sake, why didn't I go home? Only now I realize the heartache I caused my poor mother! Maybe it was because of worry over me that she died...' and then he said to his sister, 'We will live right here. I will make a shack for you. We will hunt wolves this winter, for there are a lot of them here.' So they lived there all summer in a wigwam. He made two shacks, one for his sister and one for himself, and that winter they lived in their shacks. He hunted and brought home moose and deer meat... Also he killed lots of wolves. He was very good to his sister. He went with her when they took their furs into town. Only then people realized that he was alive, and had lived alone in the wilderness for nearly twenty years. They lived there for a couple of years. Then he got sick. He was not sick for very long (that is, he soon died). And as he was dying, he told his sister that at the time he had disappeared for five years, he had gone to Eagle River (where nobody knew him), and had had a wife over there, and also a child (but had left them after five years). He told his sister to go and see his child, and to tell the woman that he was dead. So he died. There was no one at all there at the bay. She was alone. So when she got through crying she set to work and made a hole. She dressed her brother, and fixed him up nice. Then she buried him."

Earth Bird's prideful shame apparently lost some of its original force through the later years. Its drive became transmuted into mere habits of seclusiveness. Secure in the knowledge of his brother's death, he was able to lavish affection upon his sister. He commenced to expand in sociableness. He was not averse to having his identity known. He enjoyed the companionship of his sister, and taught her to hunt. After his death she continued to hunt alone, having profited so from his instruction that "she was like a man. She killed many wolves. In the spring she took her furs to town in Kenora, and she got lots of money." She married a Negro who was ignorant of the way of Indian hunting, so she taught him what her brother had taught her.

Shamans, particularly "bad" shamans, emphasize pride and shame inordinately, and the common people, to whom these sanctions are by no means foreign, regard the shamans' extreme valuation as abnormal. We would class their over-emphasis as fundamentally megalomaniacal or as paranoid. Most shamans, however, suffer from a persecutory paranoia that is also aggravated by grandiose delusions. When the megalomania is not complicated by paranoia it is thought merely humorous, and in the native myth cycle such behavior is broadly satirized and is epitomized by the buffoon culture-hero. Behavior that would be called paranoid, on the other hand, is feared because of the violence and vindictiveness associated with it; in legend it is personified as the villain, and is regarded as dreadful.

The profession of shamanism itself is defined in terms of paranoid deviation. A sorcerer is expected to be "evil... greedy.... jealous ... living just to kill... it is like a game to them." The shaman is the earthly representative of the supernaturals. The shaman who is patronized by the greatest number of supernaturals is the most powerful, and therefore the most evil. All shamans strive continually to secure more guardian spirits so that through sheer numbers they will gain sufficient power to realize their most arbitrary wish. They feel that they control the fate of ordinary people, and demand from them a deference which concedes the shamans' powerful association with the supernaturals. However they have no official means of coercing respect, and on that account they are extremely sensitive to any real or fancied slight. Behavior that is more poised or relaxed or indifferent than outright fear and cowering is interpreted by them as insulting, and they retaliate with suffering and death for the shame they have suffered.

Bad shamans tend to come from certain family groups and good shamans from others. Thus three of the sons of Resting Ash, all trained alike to be shamans, are evil; one of them, Hungry Ash, is unrivalled for his practise of sorcery and is one of the most feared men of the region; another, Crashing Ash, has a son Dan who is trying to emulate his uncle Hungry Ash in sorcery. Their cross-cousin, Chief Arnold, was more evil than any of them, and shared this reputation with his father, who in turn was the most feared of four evil brothers. But even in cases where the environment has been constant there are variations in kind as well as in degree. Thus one son of Resting Ash, Red Sand, is not at all malevolent; he is a good shaman, and his goodness in contrast with his brothers' evil is probably due to a difference in temperament. Among good, or less daring, shamans, the emphasis of the environment is similarly reflected by all, or most, of the related group. The Horton brothers have come out of such surroundings, and all are "good"; their cousin Bunyan is also a good shaman.

The following story gives a typical account of the way in which evil shamans are expected to behave. Sioux Woman had been taken captive from the Dakota Sioux by a young Cree warrior, and had lived happily with him as his wife for about ten years. "She was there over ten years and her mother was also there with her. They went out walking one time, and one old Cree man ("old man" in this connection means sorcerer) was sleeping. She and her mother passed him, and they were talking. She used to laugh very loud. This old man woke up suddenly (startled by her laugh, annoyed that he had been awakened), and heard her laughing. He jumped up for he thought that she was making fun of him. He got mad and said, 'This winter you will eat many Indians (i. e. become insane, *windigo*)'. But of course she did not hear him. Sure enough that winter before Christmas she got sick and crazy. She used to sit in one place for a long time. . . . not a word out of her, and she did not sleep or eat or do anything at all. The people were frightened: they knew she was going to be a *windigo*. For twenty days she did not eat anything. Then her mother started giving her medicine; she smoked medicine on her, and used the sucking cure. She made a long speech when she started to cure by sucking, and made signs with her hands. All the children were taken away, and some of the grown people went away too. Only a few stayed there to watch her. One day the old woman told her son-in-law to get a frog or a snake. The man asked some old people for a snake, and he got a little snake meat. The old woman made medicine out of it, and gave it to her daughter to drink. She also gave her dried blueberries and Indian rice to eat. This was to stop her from being a *windigo*. Sioux Woman was like that for a long time. The old woman kept on with her *manito kazo*. She fought for her daughter (against the shaman who must have been persecuting Sioux Woman) and finally she got the best of him. After he was beaten, he got sick and died in four days. Then Sioux Woman got better. She never was out of her mind. When this old man died, everybody was glad, for he was a very bad old man. He had destroyed lots of people by his bad medicine. This Sioux old woman was the first one to outdo him by her dreams and put an end to him. After her daughter got better, her grandchildren all came home, and they lived happily after that."

To the Ojibwa such an affliction as Sioux Woman's must be occasioned by some outside agency, a human agency with a personal, vindictive objective. It is not insanity, for insanity is active, responsible behavior which is a function of traits of personality. Her disorder was a foreign thing inflicted upon her, like club-foot, harelip, or a humped back.

In case this crippled state persists and is seen to effect fundamental changes in personality, the individual is considered abnormal. Feathers had been a noted sorcerer, who had won his miserably fearful wife, White Goose, through love medicine. He had been extremely devoted to her and considerate of her, and had taught her to be as competent as himself in many shamanistic techniques. But she never ceased to fear him, for to her as well as to others he was still the dread shaman. She did not trust him, for he was too well acquainted with the means of doing evil. Then when he was quite an old man, approximately in his seventies, "one time he got sick and was crazy, and nearly killed her. He stabbed her on the chest, but it happened that it was on kind of a thick place. And then she used to cry an awful lot because she did not have any relatives or friends to go to, and her children were all married. He got awfully mean to her. He used to beat her with the long stem of his pipe. He was jealous of another old man, but it was not true (that his wife was guilty with the other man). Then this old man (the accused) heard that Feathers was jealous of him, and it made him mad. And through his bad spirits and bad medicines he made Feathers a *windigo*. So that fall Feathers became a *windigo*, but it took a long time. He sat in one place and he did not eat anything that the old woman gave him. Then he ran away. This was at Willow Creek, and he ran away to Cass Lake to a logging camp. The white men took him in and tied him up, and wrapped him in blankets, and gave him a good drink of alcohol and made him drunk. They kept him there, and later a dog team brought him to Little Forks, where his son was. So the old woman went there. Feathers was like that for four years. He died crazy."

This account gives a rather elliptical statement of a complex situation. Elliptical, that is, to the outsider, for to the native each word is idiomatic in its rich associations. Thus, it is understood that the rival shaman did not render Shandioo insane merely because he resented the accusation of coveting White Goose. Rather, the rival seized upon the accusation as providing a good opportunity for resuming an ancient duel. The two men were professional rivals, that is, each thought of the other as a threat to himself. Any success of the other was viewed as an insulting triumph, and any calamity as the other's victory. Shandioo's mental illness was proof enough that his rival had triumphed. He fled from the scene and died a miserable death.

A typical account of imagined attack is the story of Bombay, the shaman. Bombay had been under a great strain, caused partly by starvation and partly by a feeling of unrest resulting from the fact that his daughter had slighted her husband, son of another shaman. In true paranoid fashion he sought for some explanation of his inability to command food and weather, and found it in the sorcery of the rival shaman, who was in this way avenging the insult to his son. Finally Bombay's anxiety reached a crisis, and he experienced the hallucination of combat with his imagined tormentor, and lost consciousness for a time. His belief in his interpretation of events was strengthened when he was able to find game after he had thus in fantasy defeated his enemy, and when he found later that the other man had actually died at about the time of their shamanistic combat.

One shaman does not except other shamans from the general group of "others" who owe him deference. There is no professional etiquette which brings shamans together as a group against the group of laymen. The intense egocentricity and self-preoccupation which characterize shamans prevent any such truce from operating. Indeed, the relations between shamans themselves are more conventionally paranoid than those between a shaman and an ordinary person. In the latter situation, the struggle is soon over because it is unequal, in theory and in reality, because of the shaman's greater power and stronger motivation. But in the case of two shamans, especially if both are evil, the combatants are evenly matched and the struggle generally continues until one or the other is defeated. A bitter and vindictive relationship such as this existed for years between the shamans Pahwah and Frenchman, and their deaths, in old age, were supposed to have resulted from it. Frenchman resented the fact that the other was more in demand than himself, that "he was making too much from the people." Pahwah's superior skill was a direct reflection upon him; Frenchman's habit of self-reference saw it as a maliciously deliberate effort to discredit him. "So Frenchman used his guardian spirits to kill Pahwah. But Pahwah was such a *manito* that nobody could kill him....... In the fall Pahwah used all his bad medicine on Frenchman so that he could not kill anything (this is inference, of course, based on the fact that Frenchman suffered misfortune while Pahwah did not). He could not even kill a rabbit or a porcupine. He was about to starve to death. He could see the (evil omens of) night owls and fire (will-o'-the-wisp) all over his place. And then Frenchman started to fight. He made divining tents, two of them, and they had their big fight in there (shamans generally fight through the supernaturals that they invoke in the divining tent). At last Pahwah gave up, and Frenchman was badly hurt. They never saw each other, but by their spirits they killed each other. So Pahwah died that very day, and Frenchman died soon after."

Half-Sky was one of the few women to become affected like a man. She defeated all other women in races, and as a result she inspired great enmity. One time she fell ill, and interpreted her illness as an act of sorcery arranged by jealous rivals. After she was cured, she retained a fixed idea that she was being harrassed by rivals and that she would have to "show" them. All of her subsequent behavior was ruled by this motivation, and since her natural ability was fortified by her fanaticism, she continued supreme in her field and continued to arouse enmity and to feel persecuted. Finally people refused to compete with her. It is intelligible that the male-like paranoid delusion should have developed in a woman who was a runner, for, as we have mentioned in Part 1, in the sphere of games boys and girls are treated alike.

Although exceedingly few women have the systematized and persevering paranoid ideas that are found among many men, women often do have slight and irregular tendencies in this direction. The shaman Thunder Woman displayed the reaction importantly only once. On this occasion she directed evil magic against her father, and deliberately tried to kill him supernaturally since she considered that her misfortunes were directly attributable to him. However, this feeling was not generalized by her into a readiness to feel ill-treated by others. It was an affect which belonged to that one period, a consequence of her father's repeated actual persecutory efforts...... Apparently it was only once in her life that Sandy Skies showed pronounced paranoid ideas. She was a relatively wealthy person and liked to feel that her ample means aroused envy. At one time she suffered from "twisted mouth" (partial facial paralysis). This is always thought to be a shamanistic device to humiliate a person. Sandy believed that someone was jealous of her wealth, and used this means of tormenting her. "The right eye and left side of Sandy Skies' mouth were twisted for about a month, and she was out of her mind for about two weeks. She had influenza. When she was out of her mind she would say that people were trying to do something to her because they were jealous of her nice clothes. And she was always talking about money....... 'Where's that money I put here? They are jealous of me because they want my money.' Maybe a woman was jealous and got a doctor to do that to Sandy"...... A certain Cree woman of the White Dog Reserve had similar ideas about her misfortunes, and attributed them to some personal vindictive agency. At one time, a certain turn of the wind carried her astray in her canoe. This was charged to the evil temper of some shaman. Shortly after, her brother was drowned. This too was attributed by her to some shaman, although people believed that the young man was simply careless. She finally identified her alleged persecutor when "she saw fire coming towards them from where this bad old man lived. It was coming just above the water. And when they wanted to shoot it, it hid, and they could not see it any more. That was the reason why she blamed this old man. They did not find the body of her (drowned) brother until the next spring. When the body was found in the spring, this old man was sitting there, smoking. She got so mad that she said to him, 'Now that the body is found, why don't you eat him now? You killed him!' (Cannibalism is abnormal, as is sorcery, and the two practises are often associated). The old man thought that (her accusation) was dreadful. After the body was buried they moved away from there. The only reason that they had stayed there all winter was that the body had not been found. That fall, after they had moved away, her mouth got twisted. She blamed it on the same old man again, for she knew that he was bad. It was not only to her that he did these things.... other people also blamed him for their troubles, for he had bad medicines and bad dreams." .... Marsh Woman was a wholesome, demure person. But when her lover became ill and remained paralyzed for ten years until his death, she attributed this to the vindictiveness of her former husband. This belief remained fixed in her mind, and her neighbors agreed with her. After her lover's death, she seized the first opportunity to kill her suspected persecutor.

Bluesky, was persistently, though mildly, paranoid. She detested her son-in-law for she felt that he was her rival for her daughter's affections. She complained incessantly, though unjustly, about the young man, and vilified him in every way. Her husband and daughters tried to maintain some peace by ignoring her. This she took as offensive, and felt that all her family was against her. One breakfast, she seized a large wooden spoon, "and hit her old man across the mouth and said, 'It's a wonder you don't help me and say something to your son-in-law. You know that he is mean and good-for-nothing..' The old man said nothing, but a while after he said, 'Well, I will tell you now just what I think of you.' The old woman said, 'All right, go ahead, and tell him right away.' She thought he meant his son-in-law. But the old man said, 'No, I don't mean him, I'm talking to you. And first of all, I'm asking you... do you love your daughters?' She answered, 'Yes, of course I love my daughters. What makes you ask me such a question?' The old man replied, 'Well, the reason I ask you this is that I have been thinking of you all this time. I have heard you abusing your son-in-law. He is good to your daughter. If you knew how to love your daughter, you would not be mean to her husband; you would try to be good to him for her sake. That is why I never say anything (in rebuke) to my son-in-law... because I have love for my daughter and for her sake I am good to her husband, because I know she cares for him. If I did not love you, I would not have married you.... and they too are the same way. He is a good hunter. Who do you think is bringing all this meat and ducks and other good things to eat? It is he that is bringing it all. What more *could* he do to please you? You are just mean and selfish and jealous of your own daughter because you really want your son-in-law to be coaxing you (sexually) all the time. So I am telling you that you might as well stop this nonsense, or you will make trouble soon.' She said, 'Huh! Jealous of my own daughter! You see that dog out there? I'd rather sleep with that dog than sleep with him!' Her son-in-law was sitting right there.... he never said anything. (Conventional avoidance relations between parents-in-law and children-in-law forbid conversations under any circumstances. The story-teller's remark indicates that **Bluesky**'s statement was so malicious that it would have sanctioned the son-in-law's breaking the taboo had he cared to retort). She sat a long time staring at one place. Then she said, 'Huh! I never knew that *he* was on his side. That was why he never spoke when he (the son-in-law) did things.'" **Bluesky** gradually estranged her daughters and son-in-law. Her elder daughter commenced "talking to a young man" and **Bluesky** tried to break up the intimacy. "She tried to stop her daughter, but the latter would not listen to her mother. Then one time the old woman was going out to look at her net, and she noticed this young man fixing his canoe on the shore. She said to him, 'Don't ever come to our tent again to try to see my daughter! I respect her a lot, so I don't want you to come around her any more because you are good for nothing, not good enough for us. It is enough we have one man there that is useless, and I don't want another.'" The young people continued their relationship, however, and the mother imagined that her daughter was hostile to her and was deliberately trying to torment her. When the young man brought bridal wealth to his prospective mother-in-law, **Bluesky** "got up and threw everything out, and gave her daughter a good beating, and threw her out too. The girl said to her mother, 'I'm very glad that you are throwing me out. I have his child anyway, and I care for him a great deal.' Her mother said she would choke the child as soon as it was born if she was there. So the girl left without letting her mother know; she did not want anybody to choke her baby. She took an axe and a knife (from her mother's house) and stole away from there. She went back in the bush and she stayed near a creek. She made a little wigwam out of birchbark, and snared some rabbits with native hemp. She got ready for her baby's coming. She cut wood, and gathered moss. After she had been gone for four days, the people there missed her. Her mother was the very first one to cry. They made divining tents and got diviners to find out if she was alive or dead. Three of them tried to find out but no one told the truth. The girl's brother-in-law was the next one to divine, and right away he started to laugh and said, 'She is not dead.. she is alive and is some place around here. If anyone wants to go and look for her in the morning, he can go straight west, to a creek. Walk along that creek, and soon he will find her there.' The old woman said she could hardly wait until morning to go and get her daughter. The girl's lover went out right after the divining was over, and went to his canoe. He got in and paddled, for he knew just where this creek was. He went along the creek a little way until it got too shallow. Then he walked along the shore. He came around a little point and saw a light. It was a camp-fire. He knew he had found the girl. He crept along so as not to make any noise. There she was, sitting near the fireplace and roasting a rabbit. He made a little noise. The girl jumped up and looked. She could not see who it was because it was so dark that night. The young man spoke to her and said, 'Don't be afraid, it's me. I have come to look for you because I'm so worried and lonely for you.' He went up to her, and she asked him, 'Well then, how did you know I was here?' And he said, 'Your brother-in-law

divined and found out where you were. So I came here to find you
first before anybody else. I'm going to take you right home to my
parents for if you don't come with me, your mother will come for
you in the morning. I want you to come with me tonight, so your
mother will never bother or hurt you again.' At last she went with
this young man. It was nearly morning when they got home to his
parents. The next morning one of his relatives went around yelling
his name and saying that he had come home with a wife the night
before. Later her mother went there. She had a stick in her hand.
She lifted up the rug on the door of the wigwam, and looked at her
daughter, 'Oh, my daughter is back now.' That was all she said.
About ten days later, the baby was born. It was a boy. She did
not want her mother to know when she became sick, for she was
afraid that her mother would do something to her baby. After the
baby was born, someone took some tobacco to her mother and
asked her to come and see her little grandson, and to name him.
But she would not even go and kiss her grandson, and they did not
bother her again. She did not go there even once, for she hated her
son-in-law very much. The daughter did not mind about her mother
for she was happy. Finally one morning someone came over and
told her that her mother was missing. Everybody hunted all day
for the old woman, and in the evening someone found her hanging
on a tree, dead. She had hanged herself that night because she was
worried and ashamed of having been so mean to her sons-in-law.
Also she had the reputation of being the meanest old woman there.
When they found her, she was dressed in all her best clothes
(suicides do this, perhaps as an analogy to dressing the deceased
for burial, or perhaps as a defiant proud gesture). She used a leather
strap with which to hang herself. Her tongue and eyes were bulging
out. She looked terrible........ Everybody (in the family) was
happy after the old woman was dead. They were never in fear of
anything now......."

Under favoring circumstances, a whole village can become affected with paranoid hysteria. On the (Cree) White Dog Reserve each
person felt that he suffered from misfortune visited upon him by a
certain sorcerer. The people talked continually about this shaman,
Kingfisher, and they became so excited that their moods shifted
crazily from challenge to abject fear. Finally they grew so desperate
that they decided to kill Kingfisher. "One spring they went back
to the White Dog reservation, for all the people gathered there to
have the *wabeno* dance. There were many guests at the dance,
and lots of offerings. This same old man was there too. Everybody
feared him. The people were so frightened of him that they were

14

afraid even to laugh for fear they would make him mad. They gave him lots of things, trying to be good to him (so that he would not injure them through sorcery). Besides being a *wabeno* (shaman who juggles with fire), he was a sucking doctor, a diviner, a shaman of the *mide* order, a bear visionary, and all kinds of *manito kazo* (shamanistic ability). All the people at this *wabeno* dance planned to destroy him. They fixed up nice dishes of good things to eat, and put bad medicine in them to poison him, and gave them to him to eat. He ate the things, and he gave some to people near him..... perhaps he knew there was medicine in there. One dish that he ate had Indian rice and blueberries and maple sugar. Of course the people were dancing and when they passed where he was sitting, they kicked his legs for he was dying now (a rare thrill of horror, and even of bloodthirsty ecstacy, for ordinarily no shaman could be approached with impunity). He was having convulsions. But they did not admit that he was like that, because some of his relatives were there. When the *wabeno* dance was over, and they went to him, he was already stiff and cold. They took his body and looked through his things. In one of his bags he had over three hundred human tongues of Crees that he had killed. They were all dried up and tied together. (These are alleged trophy strings of evil shamans. The victim, supposedly killed by the sorcerer, was taken from his grave by the same sorcerer, and his tongue extracted. A few Indians claim to have seen shamans in this act, during which the shaman assumed the shape of a bear.) They took all these tongues and all his birchbarks (sacred mnemonics of *mide* shamanism) and *mide* furs (*mide* shamanistic instruments) and his bad medicines, and they burned them all with his body; the Cree said that he was not fit to be buried. His daughter also said he should be burned for she knew that he was bad. After they had burned his body and everything else, all kinds of worms and little snakes and frogs (his evil, supernatural spirits) crawled out of his body. They threw them all into the fire. At last he was burned to ashes. So that was the end of him. That was one bad Cree old man (all of the adjectives are idiomatically synonymous). The people were happy then, after he was dead."

At Little Forks too the people were cowed by one dominant medicine man, Chief Arnold. They never rose against him, but remained paralyzed by their fear and suspicion, or hypnotized by him into acquiescence. He died about 1927, but his memory is fresh in the minds of all and symbolizes misfortune and evil even though sorcery can no longer be attributed to Arnold himself. He seems to have been a markedly capable person, and possessed all the twenty-odd abilities allotted to men by the culture. This meant that he was pre-eminently "powerful" and freely practiced and threatened bad medicine. He lusted for material wealth and for ascendancy over others. He obtained both. He did all the curing and divining for the people of his village. Lesser shamans with the same ambitions had to content themselves with a poor second place, or leave for another village. He was so feared that few shamans, even, dared to enter into shamanistic combat with him when he insulted them with slighting remarks. Arnold was a perfect instance of a culture's creating its own Frankenstein monster. When a patient thought his illness was mild enough to be cured by the sucking technique, he called Chief Arnold. If this treatment failed, divination would have to be attempted. Arnold would be called to do the divining, since any alternate course bore its obvious consequences. Through Arnold, the supernaturals would diagnose that the ailment could be cured only by the *mide* ceremony. Arnold had to be called to conduct the ceremony. If the first ceremony failed, another was attempted, for the *mide* is the ultimate therapeutic measure. Unlike medical treatments in our society, the cost of successive treatments in Ojibwa increases almost in geometric ratio to the frequency of treatment. Arnold would conduct several ceremony-treatments for a patient. If the patient died before he was cured, a ghost *Midewiwin* had to be held, a ceremony that cured the soul of the deceased on its journey to the next world. And Arnold conducted that. If he were not engaged for the ceremony, members of the patient's family knew that they would soon feel the effects of sorcery. Arnold divined, too, for war-parties and for hunting. As his power over the people increased, he fell into the improper habit of dictating the nature and quantity of the fees he desired. When a patient sent for him, he would fall into a trance before the messenger and murmur, "The *manito* (supernatural) requests a raincoat and a dozen boxes of snuff, and a gun......" He taught some shamanism and sorcery to his wife and daughters, so that they could act as his assistants. In Arnold's village, therefore, all the wealth came to be concentrated in his domicile.. The village did not find any relief until after the great man's death. Since then it has ignored the shamanistic claims of his widow and daughters.

Sometimes a whole community takes its impotent revenge upon the shaman who has persecuted it by destroying his possessions after his death. "Coming Cloud (a dreaded shaman) and his wife got ready and took their youngest son with them. The lakes were already freezing up. The ice was going back and forth, and it was

14*

in the night and stormy. They got into their canoe and started out
on the lake. As they were going along, two big pieces of ice crashed
against them. They could not do anything. The canoe froze to the
ice, and they froze to death right there. They were not found until
the lake was frozen hard enough for a man to walk on. Their canoe
was filled with ice, and they were covered with it. The oldest little
boy was not with them and he lived a long time after their bodies
were found. The men opened the shaman's shack and found a great
many sacks where he kept his bad medicine. There were lots of
human tongues tied to a string, which showed that he must have
destroyed many people. They also found night owl skins (evil
omens) all painted up. The men took only some nice things, blankets
and other things they wished for, and then they burned the rest,
the shack and all. It was this boy that told (i. e. allowed) them to do
this. So then that was the end of Coming Cloud. He caused much
death, and he himself died a terrible death."

Megalomania, or grandiose ideas about the self, is found among
all shamans of supererogatory personality. It is expected to occur
among them, though its specific expression differs from one person
to another. To the Ojibwa it makes the paranoid attitude plausible;
for a person who believes himself to be the embodiment of certain
world forces is bound to resent being ignored or directly challenged,
and is alert to insult or disloyalty. A shaman's arrogant attitudes
naturally increase the fear in which he is held. When Chief George
reached the self-confident point of referring to himself in the third
person as "the *manito*," or "the supernatural," people were at
first bewildered because his move was sacrilegious, but soon they
were awed since George suffered from none of the traditional
consequences of sacrilege.

Hole-in-the-Sky's reputation for evil has become very much
greater since the news has leaked out that Hole is own brother to
the Eagle Spirit, and is himself a temporarily incarnate Eagle.
Hole's family ties with the supernaturals are the more impressive
because he makes a great show of reticence about them. Nevertheless, interested persons know that he communes with his
"brother" regularly. He goes into an unfrequented place, in the
house or in the bush, offers some tobacco to his brother, smokes,
feels the presence of his brother approaching, and commences to
talk. There can be no doubt of the fact that his brother is real to
Hole. Hole sometimes sees him — "he looks like a man, just like
me, about my figure" — and always hears him — "he talks like
me.. you couldn't tell our voices apart... he always talks good....
he's a gentleman.." He talks about everything imaginable to his

brother, and the latter questions him. Hole says that he cannot anticipate what his brother will ask. At one time Hole was exercised about the writer: he felt that a man (83 years old) and a woman (24 years old) should not work together unless they were married, and that marriage in general was a good thing between a smart man and a smart woman because they could practise together shamanistically. During this time he talked with his brother, while the writer stood about twenty feet away trying to grasp the import of the murmuring. After the conversation was over, Hole said, "Ain't it funny? *He* asked me about you. 'Who's the woman?,' *He* said, 'What are you going to do with her (respecting marriage)? Are you going to leave the old woman (his wife)?' I wonder what made *Him* think of that?" The brother advises Hole about all his problems, and Hole never undertakes an important step before consulting him. The reassuring effect of this belief upon Hole must often be considerable. He believes, for example, that he holds his own fate in his hands, and that he cannot die until he himself sets the time. He feels that he is "in" with the gods, for his brother gives him reports upon the conferences that the spirits hold in all parts of the world. Hole has revelatory information about the *mide*, theology that is known to him alone, imparted to him by his brother. He feels more powerful in sorcery because of the aid he can secure through *Him* and *His* friends. Other people are fully aware of this relationship, too, and are therefore greatly intimidated. Hole's grandiose ideas are being elaborated continually, having started originally with the simple statement that the Eagle guardian spirit addressed him, the beneficiary, by the title of "brother," instead of by the stereotyped title "grandchild." Though Hole is coming to live more and more with his brother, he preserves perfect contact with reality in every other respect. This form of megalomania, of identifying the self with the greatest powers in the Ojibwa world, is unknown among women. This may be related to the fact that all supernaturals are thought of as being masculine — either completely male, or neutral with an inclination to masculinity.

Another expression of megalomania occurs in displays of technique, of supernatural power. Tokan considered himself a very great shaman, and surrounded himself with a splendid atmosphere. He used to attempt quite difficult feats in the effort to impress people with his greatness. Among other things, he used to have four divining tents displaying polter-geist phenomena while he sat outside smoking. Another man had four tents, all connected only by a silk thread which ran over their roofs. This shaman had himself intricately bound, and then secreted in one tent, whereupon all four tents simultaneously displayed identical poltergeist phenomena; and during this technical display, the shaman would have loosed himself from his bonds and crept out of the tent. Other men stunted elaborately with red-hot coals, and one man used to finish with the flourish of going to sleep with live coals in his mouth. Visiting shamans vied with one another in tense displays of their greatness. These exhibitions always ended unfortunately, however, for the superior ability of another shaman, and especially outright defeat, were taken as personal insults and gave rise to serious feuds. Women rarely engage in this type of display. There are relatively few female shamans; they are not as versatile as men and so have fewer occasions for exhibitionism; and they do not have men's intense egocentric view of themselves and of shamanism. Women's chief opportunities for expression of megalomania occur in competitive games; in this sphere Half Sky and Iron Woman are excellent examples. The following "true" story in Ojibwa folklore recounts the adventure of some boys with shamans of this class. "This is a story of two Ojibwa brothers who lived somewhere on Rainy Lake. Every winter they went up north to trap and hunt. They did this all winter long, and they came home only in the spring. One spring the boys had a lot of fur to take home to the Hudson's Bay store. They started out by canoe, and they passed two lakes. But when they came to another lake, the ice was still floating around and they could not get by. They were afraid to stay there long because the Crees there were great shamans and were always trying to outdo one another. The older boy said that he was afraid to stay there because they would surely meet the Crees, but the younger boy started to *manito kazo* before he went to sleep, and the next morning when they got up and looked out on the lake, they did not see any ice (as a consequence of the boy's successful practise of weather-shamanism). So they started out, and paddled as fast as they could, but they could not reach a place where they would not meet Crees. The older boy told his brother not to do anything to hurt the feelings of these Cree men. The younger boy said to his brother that he was not to take anything offered him if these Cree men were doing any shamanistic performance... but that he should wait for his younger brother.

"Then they went ashore and ate, and started off again. In the middle of the afternoon, they saw a canoe coming with three men. They knew that they were Crees. The Cree men met them, and asked them to go ashore and eat. The older boy told them that they had already eaten but the Crees would not listen, and asked them to go anyway. They could not refuse the Crees for fear of hurting their feelings. They went ashore and gave each of the Crees a duck. The Cree men cleaned the ducks, and the boys also cleaned two ducks, and the Cree men took some sticks and put the ducks on the sticks and, stuck them near the fireplace.... stuck the sticks right into the rock, as they were camping on a rock. The boys' ducks were stuck in the same way. After their lunch, the older boy gave one of the Cree men his coat (as a bribe-gift, so that the shaman would not choose to become offended and injure them) and said that he and his brother would have to start on their way again. But the Cree men would not hear of it. They asked the two boys to spend the night with them. They could not refuse, as they were in fear of the Crees, so they stayed there. One of the Cree men took a pipe with a long stem, and put in some tobacco, and lit it. He handed the pipe to the older boy, but he would not take it as his brother had told him not to take anything first. Then the Cree man handed the pipe to the younger boy, and he took the pipe, but before he put it to his mouth, he pulled a little snake (supposedly evidence of sorcery on the part of the Cree) out of the pipe stem and handed it back to the man and said, 'I guess you will have to take this little snake back because we are not good enough to know such things' (this humble phrase expresses the complacence of one who knows his supernatural power). Then he began to smoke, and after he finished, the Cree men said again, 'Let's have a little fun before we go to bed.' So they cut poles and made three divining tents (specially made structures whose outstanding characteristic is the depth to which the supporting poles are sunk in the ground). They stuck the sticks right into the rock, just as if it were soft ground. The three Cree men went into the wigwams (each went into one divining tent), and the divining tents commenced to go back and forth (a polter-geist phenomenon appearing in this form of divining). Sometimes the tents went around. At last the tents just floated around on the rock. The two boys sat there watching the three tents. Finally the Crees stopped and came out and one of them said, 'Now, it is your turn.' The older one did not move because he did not know what to do, and he said, 'We can't do it, so you might as well not ask us.' But the Cree men said, 'Oh, try anyway. There is nothing to it!' So the younger boy got up and went into the divining tent, and it went around as it had with the Crees. But he did more: he made the tent go down to the lake, right into the water, and it floated around on top of the water while he was in it. After he had gone around like that on the water, the tent went right back again where it had started from. Then he came out. The Cree men did not say anything, and they did not do anything more, and they went to bed. The older boy could not sleep for he was afraid, but the younger one slept. He knew that he had made the Cree men mad (because he had made them feel frustated and inferior) when he had handed back the little snake to them.

"When morning came, the boys started off. They had a long way to go before they could reach the place where they would sleep. The younger boy said to his brother, 'We won't stop anywhere until we come to that place where we will sleep,' for he was quite sure that the Cree would send some of their bad dreams to them that night. As it was getting dark, they paddled faster, and came to this place. They kept looking back in the direction they had come, and sure enough! while they were looking, they saw a big ball of fire coming towards them (will-o'-the-wisp; an omen of sorcery which is being practised upon the observer). It was coming along just the same route that they had come. The younger boy told his brother to have patience and to look at this ball of fire, not to look anywhere else for a while (sometimes one who is able to stare a ball of fire out of countenance, as it were, defeats the evil sorcery). The older boy said that he would try to do as his brother said. The younger boy started to *manito kazo*, and then he got up (charged with the power that he had just invoked) and walked into the water, and disappeared under the water. While the older boy sat there looking at the ball of fire coming closer, all at once he saw it go out. He just sat there for quite a while and looked at the place it had been. Suddenly he heard sticks crackling behind him. He turned around and saw his young brother coming from the bush instead of from the water. The younger boy said, 'Well, I guess it is all right for us now. I guess I won over the Crees.' The next morning they started off again, and they did not see anything more. They took their furs to the Hudson's Bay Company. That is all."

This story shows clearly with what ease sacred institutions — such as divining, and the sacred pipe of friendship — are turned to the altogether mundane ends of boasting, or testifying to one's own abilities. These two mentioned techniques are favorite means of display, and as such are closed to woman.

One shaman showed an aberration so mild that in an ordinary man it would have been considered only absurd. This took the form of professing unusual knowledge of the earliest hours and years of life, a knowledge which he had because he had been *manito*, supernatural, from the very beginning. "This is a story of an old man named Tomorrow-Woman. It starts from the day he was born. He used to tell how he knew things when he was an infant. First, before he was born, he knew that his mother had the insides of a moose. And he knew that she had prepared the head, nose and tongue of a moose, and also other things to use for his birth feast. He thought he was in a tight wigwam (the womb), and he never moved. Sometimes he was rocked hard. And then one time it got very tight for him there. He started wiggling and turning and then he pushed himself out into the light. He saw a lot of old women. They were all excited and y.elling. Then someone slapped him, and he cried for the first time. He was wrapped up in warm clothes and put to bed. He slept for a long time as he was very cosy. When he was two days old, he saw some old women cooking (this implies that they were preparing for his birth feast). Later he heard an old man talking about something (giving him a name at the feast). He knew then that this was his first feast. He listened closely and took in every word this old man was saying. His mother was holding him. He saw all the things his mother had kept for his feast. He was very pleased to know that his parents were doing everything for him. (All these sentiments and observations are of course those of a conventional Ojibwa adult. Sometimes, however, an observation is made that has the appearance of an individual memory, as in the following remarks about the baby's hands and feet.) Then for a while he did not know anything. It was not until he was a little older that he remembered again. One time someone was singing, and he was rocked. He was tied onto a cradle and he was crying. He stopped crying and looked... it was his mother rocking him, and she was singing. Then she put him down and untied him. He looked at his hands (which had been fastened by his sides in the cradle-board before) and wondered what they were. Then at his feet—again he did not know what they were. He was afraid of them too because sometimes they scratched his face. His mother took him again, and tied him up (in the cradle-board), and put him against the wall. Then he looked around. Soon he got tired and fell asleep. When he got older, his mother used to make him sit up, and soon he was able to sit up alone. Later on again, he began to wish for things, but they were beyond his reach. He wondered how he could move around. He used to lie down on his stomach and then he began to creep around a little. He began to wish he could walk around too. He got up and stood on his feet and took a step; then he would fall. Oh! it used to hurt him to fall, but he kept trying and at last he was able to run around. All this he knew. He remembered it all as though it happened yesterday. Then when he got to be quite a big boy, he used to dream of a pigeon coming toward him, and the pigeon would say, 'I want to be your guardian spirit. I will take care of you. I will bring you things, and you will see how I look. You too will look like that.' Often he dreamed that.''

Not only shamans but some ordinary people have tendencies toward megalomania. When these are mild, such as an incompetent sterile woman's claims to ability as a midwife, they are viewed with a certain sneering lightness as fit only for women's merciless gossip. When the tendencies are more serious, they are considered highly reprehensible. One relatively common form is a false claim to supernatural power. This sin is common to both men and women; it probably arises from the fact that a person has the conventional ambitions for ability and glory but has not the natural talents for realizing his desires. The culture presses hard on constitutional inferiors. Furthermore it is believed that in these cases a fitting punishment is given by the supernatural whose power has been invoked falsely. "When Tokan was a young man, he used to hunt ducks and cranes on the prairie. He went on horseback, out to the little lakes. One time he went with another young man, Standing Person, to hunt. As they rode along, Standing Person said all kinds of taunting things to the crane for having such long legs. (Only a person with great powers should risk offending the supernatural prototypes of any animal, as this young man was doing.) Tokan told him not to say such things to the bird, because they did not know what might happen. But the young man said he would kill the bird anyway if it got mad at them (another offensive challenge to the crane supernatural, for an animal is killed only because of its own voluntary surrender, dictated by its prototype if it is friendly to the hunter). As they were going along the shore of a little lake, two cranes overtook them, and ran after Standing Person. Tokan and Standing Person were on horseback, and the horses were racing, but the cranes caught up with them, and they stabbed the horse with their long bills until the poor animal was laid open to its stomach. Of course, the men were shooting at the cranes, but they could not kill them. At last Standing Person fell off and the cranes stabbed him to death. Before he died, he said to Tokan, 'Go home to my people and tell them that it is my own fault, that I made these cranes mad.' So Tokan reced home, and told the others that this young man had been killed by the cranes. If Standing Person had dreamed that he could kill the crane, then it would have been all right. Long ago Indians had to have dreams before they could say things to wild animals, and if anyone did not have a guardian spirit to overcome the animals, then it would be too dangerous for him.''

A boasting girl met with a similar fate. "There was a lake called N——. Three girls were in a canoe paddling, and they were having a very hard time because the water was too shallow. The girl that was sitting in the middle of the canoe said (sacrilegious) things that she should not have said (about water supernaturals). The other girls that were with her tried to stop her because they were afraid (of supernatural retribution). Shortly after this, the water started to run, and there was foam all over it. Suddenly they saw a tail come out of the water and raise itself over their canoe. This tail was all copper, and it had a lump on the end of it (this is a phenomenon believed in by Ojibwa over a region of several miles). It was pulling their canoe down into the water. The girl that was steering the canoe knew they would all drown, so she started to commune with her guardian spirits, and she sang to the Thunders. (The Thunderbirds are hostile to the under-water supernaturals, and since they were the guardian spirits of this girl, they were expected to fight the creatures who were injuring her.) Then she took her paddle and hit this tail, and she said that the Thunder gave her the power to hit anything (an analogy to lightning). She broke off a piece of the tail with her paddle, and the piece feel into the canoe. Then the (guilty) girl was drawn down into the water (in punishment for her sacrilegious boasting) by the end of the tail that was still sticking up. She came up again and stretched out her arms. This happened eight times, and then she went down for good. That was the last they saw of her. The other two girls who were in the canoe paddled away fast, because the water was still running (angrily)." In the following story the boasting man was not killed, but he suffered a punishment which he never forgot. "This is another story of two men who were cross-cousins. They were both good hunters, and they used to go hunting together. One time one of them said to the other, 'What is it that you are not afraid of (i. e. what is your guardian spirit)?' He answered, 'I'm not afraid of a lynx;' and the first one said that he was not afraid of a ghost. That was all they said. For a long time they never slept alone anywhere (that is, each returned at night from his private hunting grounds to the shack which the two shared together; there they smoked, ate, and slept together). One time when they had gone out to different places, they had to sleep apart for it was too dark to return to the wigwam. The one who had said he was not afraid of a lynx got ready; he made a fire and lay down to sleep. All at once he saw a lynx standing there. He could not move (paralyzed by fright). He just became numb. The lynx came up to him and started to lick his feet, hands, and his whole body, until he was raw and bleeding.

Then the lynx left him there like that. He could not move; he was sore all over... but he lived... the lynx did not kill him. The other man, who was not afraid of ghosts, cut lots of wood, and lay down near his fire. He heard someone whistling, and he opened his eyes and saw Someone standing there. The Visitor was all dressed in white. They started to fight. They fought all night. The ghost did not overcome him and he could not do anything to the ghost either. As it grew light, the ghost said to him, 'Let me go!' But he answered, 'I won't let you go!' And the ghost kept on saying, 'Let me go, please! If you don't let me go before daylight, they won't take me in again at the place where I'm from!' But he would not let him go. At last the ghost did not move at all. When it was broad daylight, he saw that it was an old rotten birch tree with the bark on that he had been holding; this was what he had been fighting all night. So he let it go and he got ready and went home and when he reached home he found that his cousin was not there. He went on looking for him. When he found his cousin, he was lying there all raw from head to foot. He said, 'Ah, my cousin, whatever made you say such a thing when you knew that you were not telling the truth? Didn't you have any kind of a dream at all? What made you say that?' Then he took his cousin home. After that, the (guilty) man used to tell young people that they should never say that they are not frightened of something unless they know that they can defeat it. The other one knew that he could control a ghost, that was why he had said he could."

Expressions of paranoia and of megalomania vary not only among individuals, but also in the same person at different periods. Chief George, for example, showed persecutory reactions in his youth, at a time when they served his lust for power and importance. When his position was assured, he entered the phase in which he identified himself with cosmic forces. He became not simple *manito* (supernatural power, spirit) in the limited plural, but *manito* in the inclusive collective. His self-esteem amplified itself undisturbed, bulwarked by the reputation he had established in earlier days...

Hole-in-the-Sky has a different history. Like George, his earlier life was laid on a persecutory basis; and as his position advanced, grandiose ideas became more pronounced. However they never outweighed the persecutory reactions. He alternates continually and rapidly between suspicions, fears, violent retaliations on the one hand; and impressive assertions of his *manito* character on the other. Environmental differences may account in part for the differences between the two men—for the fact that George developed a self-congratulatory system of ideas while Hole has continued uneasy, for George lived in a conservative Indian community that had no intensive contacts with white people, while Hole has lived lately in regions that are in close contact with white culture and which therefore have abandoned in great part the traditional Indian ways..... **Dave M'Ginnis** was trained as a child by competent relatives and his early career of shamanism had grandiose bases. However, when failure overtook him, his self-confidence was destroyed and he went through a persecutory phase in which he saw himself abandoned by his guardian spirits and at the mercy of the evil forces of his sorcery.......... Iron Woman, the female shaman, was utterly self-confident until the death of her three children was attributed to her practise of sorcery; after this she became utterly frightened of the forces of the universe.... Half Sky in her early life had a wholesome enjoyment of her powers and a delight in displaying them. Later she developed a marked paranoid attitude, and at the same time a compensatory megalomania in connection with athletic games..... **Hawk Hunter** is a former shaman who has renounced Indian life after conversion to the Anglican faith. He has unsystematized persecutory ideas, and delusions of grandeur, also unsystemized, but far more pronounced. It is perhaps better to say that he is in an almost constant state of euphoria about himself. He talks endlessly about his accomplishments in hunting, trapping, fishing, the conduct of funerals, etc. He claims perfect knowledge of all the religious forms he has renounced. This happy state, based upon grandiose ideas about himself, is considered ludicrous by the Ojibwa. If he were still a practising shaman, one who could entrench his megalomania behind barricades of sorcery, he would not be ridiculed, but feared. However, he is now only a Christian.

Another traditional path for supererogatory deviation results in a type of personality that the Ojibwa call *windigo*. The term *windigo* refers primarily to a mythological figure who is the personification of death or insanity from starvation, and who has an insatiable desire to satisfy his hunger by eating human beings. This figure is visualized as a giant skeleton of ice. The ice skeleton symbolizes the fact that starvation occurs in winter. In summer, the mythological *windigo* melts away, or, as it is alternately phrased, he is no longer disturbed by hunger; again in winter he comes to life and feels maddening hunger and a desire for human flesh. There is therefore a periodic death and rebirth of the *windigo*. In the same way, people who are *windigo* are supposed to become harmless or normal in the summer, but are expected to suffer from a recurrence of the insanity in winter.

A person who is *windigo* is one who is tormented by an unceasing hunger that can be satisfied only by human flesh. The insanity is therefore only an exaggeration of the universal worry over starvation—either actual lack of food, or fear of the imminence of starvation. Hunger-anxiety is a fundamental emotion which *windigo* sufferers have seized upon for the path of their deviation. The fact that the mythologic and human *windigo* are both featured as cannibalistic reflects the real circumstance that people in the final stages of starvation do eat their neighbors—usually their own domestic relatives. There is nothing else to eat.

The Ojibwa believe that a person "becomes a *windigo*" through one of three influences. One of these is the visitation of a *windigo* spirit. For the *windigo*, in common with all mythological figures, is capable of becoming a guardian spirit who reveals himself to a protégé in a dream or vision. The prospective protégé may reject the *windigo*, but if he does not, he is molded into the image of his guardian. He acquires a pathological taste for human flesh that can no longer be excused by the fact of starvation. Another cause of *windigo* insanity is starvation. It is understandable to the Ojibwa that a starving person can kill his comrades for food. An enforced fast when there is no food available in winter is very different from one which is undertaken voluntarily, as in the pursuit of visions; the latter does not lead to insanity.

A third occasion of becoming *windigo* is through sorcery practises of an enemy. This is really identical with the preceding—starvation—but an inimical personal element is added. It is a sorcerer who "sends starvation" to the hunter he desires to injure. He influences game so that it does not enter the territories of his enemy; he creates adverse weather—either too little snow or too much, or driving winds. Then famine sets in upon the victim. Another device of a sorcerer is to send the *windigo* spirit to visit his enemy and cause him to become insame.

The human *windigo* shows characteristic and conventional mood disorders. Usually the first manifestation of insanity is a state of melancholia. In this phase the sufferer is very anxious, he becomes progressively inactive, and generally falls into a stupor from which he cannot be roused for weeks or months. He does not sleep, eat, move, talk, or attend to the elementary wants. He simply sits and stares with a profoundly anxious expression. He is worried about poverty, and specifically about lack of food. It is the melancholy and especially the stuporous state that to the Ojibwa presage the climax of the *windigo* attack...... When Sioux Woman became ill, she fell immediately into a melancholia. Her attack was considered mild because the shamans were able to cure her and "she never got out of her mind," or became violent. . . . Shandioo, on the other hand, passed from the melancholy state into one of violence. He fled from his home and had to be put in a strait-jacket. He was violent for four years, until his death. . Melancholics are called *windigo* because the cannibalistic delusions are germinating in them, although many persons persist in this stage and do not progress into the violent final period. The Ojibwa insist that every man-eating aberrant has once been a melancholic, and that every melancholic, if allowed to become ill enough, will manifest cannibalistic tendencies. People suffering from melancholia are simply arrested *windigos*. *Windigos* are simply melancholics whipped out of their apathy.

The melancholy state may sometimes be preceded by one of violence though this first violent phase is not considered an essential part of the *windigo* syndrome. . . . Shandioo's melancholia was preceded by a violent and abusive mood that was associated with paranoid fixations and which was not related to any fear of starvation. The detailed contents of his other moods are not reported; but the Ojibwa lay stress upon his anxiety and melancholy stupor, and therefore call him *windigo*, "actual or prospective man-eater."

The cannibalistic state is the final development of the *windigo* personality. The *windigo* has become a person dominated by a fixed idea, to the realization of which he applies all his energies. All conventional obstacles are swept aside, all interests recede into nothingness... only the one end, of satisfying the desire for human flesh, must be served. According to Ojibwa psychiatry, the developed *windigo* exhibits great violence and surliness. The prototype of this emotional state is the figure of the mythological *windigo*. He is so violent that the earth quakes under his footsteps, the heavens darken, the elements rage, and great noises fill the air; his personal strength is immense, and he lumps humans into his maw; he growls and is uninterruptedly furious. It may be that the Ojibwa project the violence of their fear of starvation onto a predatory *windigo*, and so arises the picture of his rage and passion. Even when a dog is considered *windigo*, (suffering from rabies ?) the same phenomena of violence appear. . . . Yet violence is not necessarily a part of the *windigo* temperament. As will be seen in an instance described later, people who are called *windigo* may behave in a perfectly casual manner, and go about the business of killing men as coolly as they would about killing animals.

According to the native view, therefore, the *windigo* may go through three great distortions of mood: an initial violent period, a succeeding stuporous one, and finally another of violence. But it is noted that the first phase is rare, and that most people go through the second only.

In the stuporous state cannibalistic ideas presumably are developing, for people who emerge cured often say that while they were in the depressed mood, those around them appeared to be beavers (therefore edible). It may be that this is only a conventional view of what a melancholic's thoughts *should* be, and that the sick person suffers from falsification of memory after his recovery. Certainly the alleged psychic content is monotonously the same for all melancholics. The experience of Thunder Woman's husband is typical. At one time he was extremely downcast over his failure at hunting. He became discouraged, developed the persecutory view that his father-in-law was aiming sorcery at him, and finally stayed in bed nursing a variety of imaginary ills. The time came, as he told his pregnant wife later, when he could see the foetus right through her belly, and occasionally it looked to him like a young beaver, and sometimes he wanted to take it but had not the energy, and at other times he realized that his mind was disordered.

From an analytical viewpoint, it appears that the melancholy of the pre-cannibalistic period is at least in part a function of mental conflict. The sufferer is torn between several ideas. One is his realization of starvation, and his dread of it. Furthermore, since there is no food, human food may be substituted. Of course this is not a spontaneous idea but has all the weight of legend behind it. The sufferer realizes that it is horrible to eat human beings, and the conflict between the desire to do so and the repugnance at the idea, gradually resolves itself in the delusion that people "look like beavers," and therefore the eating of them is not cannibalism. But in the melancholy phase the resolution is not complete, as evidenced by long lucid intervals in which the sufferer realizes that he is deluding himself with the beaver belief. Many stories are told of mothers who have cried out to their children, "Go away (lest I eat you)! You look like beavers to me!".... One form of escape from melancholia was taken by Mrs. Gilbert a generation ago when she ordered her brother-in-law to bind her, stun her with a blow on the head, and then burn her. He did this, while her daughter and husband stood around and cried..... In the third stage of the insanity the mental conflict has been resolved. The victim now sees everyone as beavers, he is not disturbed by lucid periods, and he goes to satisfy his hunger with single-minded craftiness.

The pre-cannibalistic phases are considered curable, and a person is always attended by shamans then; but the last stage is not considered curable. The fully developed *windigo* is regarded as the greatest menace, as the most powerful of evil shamans, almost in a class with the supernaturals. People are in terror of him. *Windigos* are often killed, both in fantasy (as in the story of Bombay, page 196) and in reality. In fantasy, they are killed in personal combat; in reality, they are burned to death, as Mrs. Gilbert was. A killing of this type is not regarded as murder, and does not lead to feuds of revenge; for the *windigo* has ceased to rank as human. A person who is considered to have killed a *windigo* is honored as a brave, or as a shaman who has overcome a supernatural.

In each locality there are always some persons reported to be, or to have been, *windigo*, especially arrested *windigo*. Men and women alike have this type of insanity, and it has been mentioned that even dogs are thought to suffer from this anxiety over starvation. Babies and young children also can be considered *windigo*. In mythological tales, young children occasionally appear who are reputed to be *windigos*, or who are supernaturally enabled to kill *windigos*—statements synonymous to the Ojibwa mind. An infant son of the great shaman Great Mallard Duck was viewed by his mother's co-wife and by his half-sisters and brothers as a *windigo*, and was therefore killed. This happened during a period of starvation, when seven out of Duck's family of sixteen persons died of hunger. "The baby that was nursing was just crazy. He was eating his fingers up (this is considered cannibalistic) and biting off the nipples of his (dead) mother's breasts. They knew he was to become a little *windigo*. His eyes were blazing and his teeth rattling (*windigo* symptoms, indicating fever, privation, and neurotic fury), so the old woman killed the baby boy."

There may be some constitutional basis for *windigo* insanity, for few persons suffer from it, especially in the final stage. On the other hand, some people are readily taught to be cannibals. Thus, in one story given below, a mother taught her children to murder and eat one another. In another story, mother and daughter together murdered and ate relatives and neighbors. This utter coolness is reported only of women. Male *windigos* are endowed through gossip with the obvious and thundering qualities of the mythological *windigo*. An exception exists in the case of a boy who was taught to be a cannibal; his aberration, however, was not spontaneous but was taught him by his mother and his actions were even conventional if judged by the standards with which he was surrounded.

The ordinary reactions to starvation and to general discouragement in hunting are considered and realistic. People trudge to a

15

distant neighbor to solicit loans, even though it is painful to borrow from a chary neighbor. Caches are stripped, first one's own emergency stores of rice and berries, and finally any other stores that can be found. Theft is preferable to cannibalism. People try to live as long as possible on the bark of trees. And when all these efforts fail, they simply lie down... and doze... perhaps doze into death. These people cannot face the thought of eating a fellow-human; they can be compared to some Ojibwa individuals who are so tender-minded that even in an extremity they will not eat a deer or bear that has been raised as a household pet. The very delusions, or the alleged delusions, of a *windigo* testify to a general tender-mindedness; for it is believed that the *windigo* does not reach the point of eating men until they appear to him as conventional edibles of some sort.

The following story tells of a woman who became lost and suffered such strain that people fully expected her to become *windigo:* it also illustrates the readiness to impute the *windigo* disorder to anyone who appears disturbed. "This is the story of a woman named Glowing Woman, and of her great adventure when she got lost and wandered around. She had gone out alone to pick berries, and she went far into the bush. She went so far that when she had filled her pail, she knew that she was lost. It was a cloudy day and she did not know which way to go. She walked and walked, and sometimes she ran. She ran around the bush wildly, and she got so that she was even afraid to see anyone for fear someone would find her. At last she got used to being in the bush. At her home village, there were people looking all over for her. They did not know what had happened to her. She was about thirty or forty miles away from her home by this time. At last, after several days, she came to a lake and she heard voices and went down. She saw people eating, and as she went towards them (desiring their food), they saw her and were afraid as she came running, with her hair hanging, and hardly any clothes on. They jumped into their canoes and left all their food there, because they thought she was *windigo*. She took all the things that these people had left—an axe, knife, tea pail, and some food, and she settled in one place. She was all right after she got this food. She used to tell that the mosquitos there were awful. And the beasts she saw! Such funny looking snakes, birds, and all kinds of animals. She was not afraid of these at all, but only of a human person. She snared rabbits with twine. When her food was nearly all gone, she started off again. She had been lost twenty-five days. She came to a place where there was no water. For four days she traveled with no water, only at the swamps she would suck at the damp moss. At last (because she was weak) she threw her blanket and tea pail and everything away, and kept only the axe and knife. As she was walking along she came to a road. She did not know what it was, but in pictures she had seen railroad tracks, and this is what the road was. Then she came to a little house. The door was open, and she went in. She was awfully thirsty and hungry. She took a drink of water, and before she had time to have a bite of anything to eat, she fainted. The man who lived there came in and saw her lying there. He thought she was dead, and he yelled to his partner, who came in. She came to again, and they fed her. Then they took her to the station, and sent her to Kenora. They thought she was crazy. She did nearly lose her mind because of being lost for forty days and being frightened all the time. They took her to the doctor in Kenora. The doctor said there was nothing wrong, only that she was frightened and had gone so long without water or food. If she had gone for two or three days longer, she would have wandered to death, the doctor said. They got her clothes, for she was all in rags, and they kept her there in Kenora, and sent word to locate those who owned her."

In the following story, the sufferings of winter starvation are described, while the shadow of the *windigo* hangs over the household. "This is a story about Ayash. He married when he was a young man. His parents and grandparents lived with them, so there were three families. This man killed a bear, but they did not give any to the Indians who were living close by (i. e., did not hold the ritual bear feast, a failure which is a bad omen for future success in hunting). Later on the three families moved away from there, and as they camped along, his wife set snares. In the mornings before they moved on again, she used to look after her traps, but there were no rabbits... only a stick or some other thing in her snare. She used to wonder what it meant. When they reached their hunting grounds they killed lots of mink and other fur animals, and moose too, and they stayed there. When their food was almost gone, the husband killed a bear, so they had food again. When that was gone, they moved to different places (various hunting territories that they possessed), and when they camped at night, his wife would fix up one of the furs and that was what they would eat. They were just about starving, and the husband started to *manito kazo*. The next morning, as they were traveling, he killed a moose. And when they reached their next camping place, his wife was busy cutting the wigwam poles for the three families, and the rest were cooking and eating moose meat. It did not take long for them to eat all the moose up, and then they had to eat the lynx skins again (the

15*

precious furs which were to have been traded at the Hudson's Bay store) and all the other furs which they were going to sell. They ate even the moose hides. After they had eaten up everything, they just about starved. Ayash could not kill anything. Everything was afraid of him. For two months his wife never ate anything. She was just a living skeleton. They could see right through her skin between her bones. They kept right on moving, but they were weak from starvation. Ayash's grandfather was dying, and he wanted to kill himself. He said he was ashamed to die of starvation. Ayash talked to his grandfather and dissuaded him. So when morning came, his grandfather said to him, 'Get ready and go along. We have lived long already. It is all right for us to perish here. But you are young. Leave us here and go where we left our food (in a cache), and if you get there before you die of starvation, come back and look for us.' These old people were raising a young girl who was their granddaughter. She was not a bit thin. Ayash told this young girl to stay with his grandparents and cut wood for them until the rest returned. It was a four days' walk to the place where they had left their corn, rice, and berries that fall. This was at Warroad before there was a town there. His parents and his wife went along with him. The young girl cried because she wanted to go along, but he would not let her go with them.

"It took them a regular four days' walk to reach this place, and when they did get there, all their cache was gone. Someone had already taken (stolen) their food. Ayash's wife's parents were there. They asked only their daughter to come over and eat, and they would not give the others anything to eat. It was almost spring now, and the men were not able to go back and look for the old people they had left behind (because the frozen lakes were just commencing to break up). When the lakes were opened up, the husband began setting nets, and he killed some jackfish and ducks. He did all kinds of communing with the supernatural (for success in the food pursuit), and he did kill something to eat. It was about a month before he was able to go back and look for his grandparents. When he did go, he found his grandfather lying on the road with a gun in his hand. He was dead. And when the others came to the wigwam, his grandmother was lying beside the fireplace, dead. She had died of starvation. They could not find the young girl anywhere; they lost her for good. There were no bones or anything found that would be left of her (had she been eaten by the old people. Note how casually the remark is made). So they just left them there and they went home."

The next account describes a family of nonchalant cannibals.

"This is a story of a young man named Long Bear and his parents. They went back into the bush to hunt and snare rabbits and they stayed there for quite a while. One day when his father was away looking after these snares, his mother said to him, 'My son, I want to ask you if you would kill your father when he comes back,' and he said, 'All right.' He waited along the road for his father and when his father came, he shot and killed him, and they ate him up. He had a sister older than himself, and brothers and sisters younger. His older sister helped him while he killed his younger brothers and sisters, and ate them up too. His mother was the last one they ate. They did not eat them all up, but they ate all the good parts. When they had nothing more to eat, Long Bear told his sister that they would go away and try to find some Indians (to eat); so they went. When night came they stopped, and he got so hungry that he killed his sister and ate some of her. When morning came, he started off again. He took the rest of his sister's body with him, and ate her as he went along. Then he came to a place where his uncle named Nahko and his family were camping. He went into their wigwam. His uncle asked him why he was coming home alone, and he said, 'Oh, they all died of starvation and I came away and killed a porcupine along the road, and that is what I ate.' He took a chunk of meat out of his sack, and showed it to them. It was the meat of his sister, but they did not know what it was. When night came they all went to bed. He slept with his cousin, who was a young man like himself. The young man became afraid, for Long vayko kept feeling around his body (to see if he was fat enough). The young man got up and said to his father, 'I wonder why my cousin is feeling around my ribs? And he also stinks so bad!' So the old man got up and started to commune with the supernatural, and rattle and sing and while he was singing (a shamanistic process which summons the aid of supernaturals) he had a vision of his nephew's killing his sister and his mother and his father. Then he knew for sure that his nephew had became a *windigo* and had eaten up his own people. He stopped singing, and asked his nephew just what had happened, why it was that he was the only one that had not starved. Then Long Bear answered, 'Well, it was my mother who first said that I should do this, and eat up our father. We had lots of other things to eat, but she wanted to eat father very badly. So I shot him.' After he told that, they were very frightened. The old man said to his family, 'Get ready, we will move from here and go where there are some Indians.' They all got ready that day, and they moved. This old man had two sons, and these two boys went along ahead with their cousin. Long Bear would run on ahead, and then stop and wait for his cousins; he would stop by the side of the road and hide, and the young men were afraid of him.

At last they came to a place where some Indians were camping; the *windigo*'s mother's brother was camping there with some other Indians. It was almost spring now, and nothing happened there. The *windigo* was just like a harmless (i. e., normal, ordinary) man now. But anyway the Indians were afraid of him. They used to fish on the lake with hooks. They made holes in the ice and caught jackfish, and the *windigo* too would roast a jackfish and eat it (having tastes, now, like a normal person). When the lakes were just about opened up, all the Indians decided to move to Warroad (the summer village) to fish, and all the young men went to hook some jackfish to take along with them to eat on the way. Long Bear also went and caught some jackfish and roasted them. They were to move the next day, and they were all busy. Long Bear helped carry the bundles and wooden drum to his toboggan and then he returned to the wigwam for his jackfish. The rest of the people (who were his relatives: uncles, aunts, cousins) had already planned to shoot him, and his closest uncle waited for him to return. And as he came up the hill, he was shot right in the chest. He dropped dead on the road. The rest of the men ran back and set fire to his body. (Evil shamans and *windigos*, who are their brothers in evil, are cremated instead of buried. This is done to destroy the material and spiritual selves of the deceased. In the case of the *windigo*, there is the additional belief that the ice-skeleton nucleus of a *windigo* can be destroyed only by burning, that is, by applying fire to melt the ice.) When his body was almost burned up, they found a chunk of green stuff on his back (this is some evil spirit). They never knew what it was. So they burned him all up. They were afraid that if he lived through the summer he would become worse again in the winter. That was why they killed him while he was harmless (to kill a *windigo* at the time of his winter strength is supposed to be a difficult feat). Then they moved to Warroad for the spring."

In this story the taste for human flesh was not a consequence of starvation, for other food was available. The unmistakably aberrant person was the mother, who initiated murder and cannibalism in her family group. No description of a *mood* disorder is given, nor is any gradual development of her abnormality indicated. She set aberrant standards for her children during the winter period when isolation prevented contact with other people's standards. So Long Bear came to hunt human beings as he would hunt game; the account he gave to his uncle was straighforward and naïve, quite untroubled. Apparently he was a docile person, for he accepted his uncle's manner of living as readily as he had accepted his mother's suggestions. His relatives, however, believed that his insanity would recur and therefore they felt forced to kill him.

The desire for human beings which also appears in the following story is characteristic of the last *windigo* stage. In this case the abnormality was apparently of long standing, and was more elaborated and refined than in the previous history. It was not confined to the period of winter loneliness, but persisted even in the social atmosphere of the village. "I am telling you the story of George. He lived in a little village with his mother and brothers and sisters. His aunt and grandmother and a lot of other Indians lived in this village too. George's grandmother and aunt were made into *windigo*s. They ate all the people in the village and ate George's mother and father, brothers and sisters, except for one little sister and George himself. They even dried the meat of these Indians (as they dried animal meat). Every time they wanted to find out if George was getting fat, they cut him in the forehead. They used to try to make George eat human meat, but he used to go away and hide it. They tried to feed the meat to the little girl too, but he took his little sister away with him when they did. One time he heard his aunt saying that she wanted fresh meat, that she was getting tired of dried meat. One day when he had been out and was just coming home, he heard his little sister scream. He ran into the tent. His aunt and grandmother had just killed the little girl, and were preparing to cook her. They tried to make him eat her, but he would not. It was almost spring, and they moved where there were some people. They camped not very far from them. The little boy made up his mind that he would tell these people about his aunt and grandmother. George ran around and tried to play with other children but every time he did, his aunt and grandmother called him back because they feared that he would tell on them before they had had a chance to kill him.

"A little later, George's grandmother sent him over to a neighbor's wigwam with some human meat. The man was standing outside, and he told George to go inside where his wife was. Then George told this woman about his grandmother and aunts being *windigo*s, and he showed them where they had cut him on the forehead, and he said that they had eaten up a whole village of people, that they had eaten up his mother and father and had killed his little sister not long before. He told them to watch these people that night.

"He went home and a little later this man called George over, saying that he had something to give to these people (in return for

the meat they had sent). He told George not to go to sleep that
night, and to run out when he knew that it was safe, and to hide.
This man and his wife got to work a fast as they could. They made
a snow bank sloping down from the door of the grandmother's
wigwam, and they fixed it up with water so that it froze. Not long
after, the two women came out, the daughter first. She slid down
the bank and they hit her on the head and killed her. Then the old
woman came, and she slid too and they hit her and killed her. Then
they chopped up the *windigos* and burned them. It took four days
to burn them up (they were such mighty *windigos*). These people
took George and adopted him. They left for another Indian village
and lived there."

Other aberrations of over-emphasis according to the Ojibwa
point of view, consist in an undue concern with one limited feature
of the cultural life such as love making. Shebahyash, for example,
devoted too much of his life to philandering: his energies were
steadily drawn from other interests to serve this one. "People
did not have much use for him" for this reason. He ignored the cultural challenges to manhood, and even his lovemaking was not
pursued in a manly way for he seduced wives when their husbands were away, and lived in constant fear of discovery, unable
even to boast of his conquests. Even after his marriage his love
relations were abnormal, in the native judgment, for he developed a monomania on the subject of his wife's fidelity and abandoned
all pretense at other activities in order to spy on her.

Rabbit also had an overwhelming interest in sex, to the ex-
clusion of a normal life. She continually sought new thrills; she
stooped so low as to take another woman's husband; she made no
effort to maintain a home or to raise a family; yet she felt no
hesitation at disrupting another household if the husband pleased
her. She had the brazenness and the leisure to dress herself daintily
every day—certain proof of insouciance and of nymphomania. For
a woman, she was entirely too bold, too intent upon her objectives,
never deterred, never offended, quite unconcerned with popular
disapproval. In the world of women she was a deviant, and ostracized.

Sorcerers who are concerned largely with sexual conquest are
also considered abnormal, though in individual cases this over-
emphasis may be merely a detail in the far greater abnormalities
of paranoia. Thus Michel used his love medicine to intimidate
all the virgins he met; yet seduction was little more than an
incident in his career of shamanistic terrorism. *Mide* shamans
often practise love sorcery to round out the general view of themselves as tyrants, rather than as an end in itself.... Many women

who are not shamans are known to use love medicine, but they do so only sporadically and therefore their practise is regarded as a desperate measure rather than as a symptom of abnormality.

Likewise, unduly stressing ceremonial proofs of bravery or bravado is considered "foolishly" aberrant. For example, it was foolish of Young Man to risk his life in order to rescue a mere pony. Belonging in the same category of bravado, but considered more offensive, because another human being is involved, is the discarding of a wife through the divorce dance. A person who performs the Give-Away dance is also considered foolish because he indulges in an orgy of gift-giving which is for the Ojibwa without meaning.

Mourning for the dead is emphasized among the Ojibwa, as it is among all the surrounding Plains and Woodlands people. But mourning is to be fulfilled in certain ceremonial ways, and any indulgences beyond these are considered gratuitous and abnormal.

Sky Woman's mourning for her deceased son and husband was considered abnormal. Her mourning behavior was the more noticeable because it departed extremely from her usual conduct. During this period she became disoriented, suffered from clouded consciousness and from hallucinations, and experienced melancholy of the profound *windigo* type. "Her son was accused of murder (by the Canadian police) and he was arrested and taken to Winnipeg and kept there for three years. At last he was found guilty; he had murdered a man, a bartender. So a telegram was sent to his parents, John Fiddler and Sky Woman, that their son was to be hanged that day. As they were sitting around crying and mourning over their son, John Fiddler sat in his chair smoking, and Sky Woman lay on the floor crying. And when she got up and spoke to her husband, he was dead.

"After her husband was buried, she was out of her mind. She was crazy for ten days. She sat and never ate or went to sleep either. She was always seeing things; sometimes she saw a bear passing in front of her, or a train, and she would tell people to get out of the way of the train. Sometimes she saw her dead son killing somebody right there in front of her. For ten days she was like that. At last she thought (received a vision) that her beloved dead grandmother came to her and told her to straighten up.... that she had many years more ahead of her.... that it would not be nice for her to die crazy. She thought she waked about noon. She felt like a different woman.... she could not recognize herself. She was very weak, and her mind felt very tender. She wondered if she had slept that long, and if she had dreamed all this. She was glad that she had heard, or dreamed, her grandmother speaking to her once more, and she thought, 'I will live some more as my grandmother wants me to live.' She got up and went out. She looked around but she did not know where she was. She knew that there were men and women watching her, but she did not ask any questions. This was a hospital where she was. She asked them what was the reason for her being there, because she did not feel sick. They told her that she would have been very sick if they had not brought her there.... that it was over ten days since she had eaten anything. And she told them that she was going to get better."

In the cases of supererogatory deviants and also of the negativistic, the personality of the aberrant is generally preserved. When the personality does go to pieces, it is always in the supererogatory type. It is this group who develop their individual biases to the most extreme and destructive lengths. Sufferers from extreme melancholia have insight and usually recover; while sufferers from persecutory psychoses have no insight and become progressively worse. But the supererogate of either kind is characterized by intense interest in his chosen sphere, whether it is anxious worry over economic security, or persecutory shamanism. He dedicates himself entirely to dealing with the situation. He is continually preoccupied with his own doings, and with the world's relation to him. He is tense, and everything matters. Is the preservation of the negativist's personality to be related to the greater casualness with which he meets his world? For the woman who takes up the work of a man, and the man who refuses to take up the challenges of pride and of shame, are alike in the coolness with which they ignore the usual standards.

The cultural mean lies between negativism and supererogation, and is different for the sexes. It is achieved by a number of persons, chiefly by men. These are men who see life as an exceedingly delightful game into which they enter for the sport of it and in which their talents bring them recognition. They are men like Ahtushkish who are successful with women, with marriage, in hunting, trading, fishing, war, games, shamanism, and who are warmly liked by all into the bargain. Not all approved men need be as versatile as Ahtushkish: thus Shaboyez was pre-eminent only as warrior and as shaman. The woman who is a cultural mean is a person who is almost never met with, and almost entirely undescribed in gossip and tale. It is impossible to piece together a life history that depicts such a woman. Rumor credits their existence; but it requires an exceptional combination of circumstances to preserve any woman throughout the course of a whole life from even the conventional irregularities.

PART V.

LIFE HISTORIES.

The preceding pages describe the course of women's life among the Ojibwa. They are analytic accounts of the cultural situations and of the ways in which women are expected to meet them. They make clear the standards which must be lived up to, and the personality traits that are developed within the culture. But on the basis of this material alone, it would be impossible to reconstruct the history of any actual life; the sequence that events, decisions and accidents will take in any particular life are unpredictable.

This section therefore is devoted to the life histories of several Ojibwa women. The histories are chosen at random, for no other moral is intended than that of showing how the typical Ojibwa requirements interweave to interrupt and reinforce one another in the actual existence of individual women.

I.

"This is a story of a woman named Little Owl, of how she gave birth to her children. Her husband was named Mahween. One spring when they were moving... as the Indians long ago used to move from one place to another... this Little Owl was carrying a child, and as they were walking along she got sick (labor pains). So they stopped and shoveled the snow away and made a brush wigwam, and also put some wild hay in this wigwam. And this was where her little girl was born. She stayed there for two days. The other people moved on, only her grandmother stayed with her. Her husband went on ahead to make another wigwam where they were supposed to stop again. This was in March and so the snow was (still) hard. After they had been there for two days, she got ready. She put on little snow-shoes and followed the other people. That night she walked about five miles. That day of course she did not carry anything. When they got to the stopping place, her husband had already made a wigwam. He did not stay in the same wigwam because long ago when a woman had a child, she was looked upon the same as a girl who receives her first sickness (i. e., dangerous to men and to other women's babies because of the lochial blood). Her grandmother cared for her and the baby. The next day, Mahween killed a moose, and so they stayed there for a while. Her mother-in-law cooked (for a woman with lochial or menstrual discharges can cook only for herself). Little Owl was keeping a box of dried blueberries and also some Indian rice, and these her mother-in-law cooked with meat for a big feast to be held over the new-born baby. There were about five other families moving along with them. Everybody ate except Little Owl (whose close proximity was feared). Then they named a day when they would have another feast so that the baby could be named. They continued to move along, and when they came to the Lakes where they used to camp in summer, and when they had moved to the groves where they were going to make maple sugar, they had the other feast over the baby. They got an old woman to name the baby. (Some parents try to secure several "namers" for their child, in order to secure the good-will of several supernaturals. But it is not good to have too many names in case the respective supernaturals should quarrel among themselves, and so leave the child quite abandoned.) The old woman, Little Owl's own grandmother, called her Podo. About four days after that (this is a stereotyped phrase that has no more actual meaning than our "several days after") her father-in-law dreamed (received a communication from the supernatural) that her baby was not supposed to have only that one name, but that it would be better if she were named from above (the attributes of some supernatural being living in the sky-world). So Little Owl told her husband to give her father-in-law some tobacco (the conventional introduction to the making of a request) so that he would name the baby girl. So the baby was named again. It was named Humming Bird. They all stayed there and made maple sugar.

"After they were through, they moved to another place again (the summer village). And also many other Indians moved to this place before blueberry picking time. All the Indians camped there, and were dancing and performing *Midewi* and playing moccasin games, also lacrosse, and squaw hockey, and other Indian games. Little Owl never went to any of these things but just stayed at home working around and caring for her baby. (It is usually men and unattached women who attend these affairs, for they are the ones who have leisure in the summer time.) But her husband was never home at night, and returned only at daylight. He hardly ever spoke to her, and she never asked him where he was spending his nights. (This silence is a conventional expression of pride. Little Owl resented being ignored socially and sexually by her husband, but would not confess to her humiliation by questioning her husband.) For about twenty days the Indians stayed there, and then they began to move away. The next morning, as it was coming daylight,

she got up. Her husband had not come in yet. She untied her baby
(from its cradle board) and nursed it sitting up. She heard somebody coming. It was her husband. He came in and lay down. After
a little while, he got up again, and came over to her. He kissed the
baby, and said to her, 'Take good care of our little girl!' She did
not answer him, but she wondered why he was saying this. She lay
down and put her baby back to sleep on its cradle board. Her
husband threw her two pieces of print, and went out with his
blanket, gun, and sack. Of course she did no say anything. She
knew very well that he was after another girl. That day the other
Indians moved away. Only a few remained. Mahween was missing
(it is understood that he had deserted, without giving notice to his
wife). About three days later, a young man came back with Little
Owl's canoe, and he brought the news that Mahween was married
(again). She was ashamed (because she had been abandoned, and
without notice or consultation) and she made up her mind that she
would not stay there in the village of her husband's parents but
would go elsewhere to join her own parents as they were living
then. She got ready and took her grandmother along. As she was
leaving, her mother-in-law spoke to her and said, 'I do not like it a
bit that you are taking our grandchild away from us!' And she
answered, 'Well, what am I supposed to stay here for? My husband
does not want me, and I am not taking my baby away for good! I'll
bring her here any time you want to see her, and also I am not
taking her far... you can come and see her whenever you like.
Only I am not going to stay here. I am going where my parents are
as I have not seen them for a long time.' So she went where her
parents were, and soon the old people (the parents of her husband)
went there and gave her baby a blanket and some other goods. They
told her that they had gone to see Mahween, and that they had
begged him to come back. But he had refused, as he said that he did
not care for Little Owl any more... he wanted a woman with
earrings on (this is probably symbolic of the fact that he desired a
gayer woman than Little Owl). He had told his parents to visit his
little girl often. Little Owl did not care either, as her parents were
very good to her, and also no one bothered her (sexually). For four
years she never went anywhere. Her parents went to Leech Lake
(Minnesota) every summer, the same place where all the Indians
used to camp to dance and *midewi* (Leech Lake was until recently
a sort of Ojibwa Mecca, and its former reputation is still familiar).
But she never went... she always stayed with her grandmother and
some other old women. Her parents were gone for at least twenty
days, and upon their return they always had a lot of news to tell her.

She heard that Mahween had had two children, but that they had not lived long, and that their third child too was dying. The old people (the parents of Mahween) stopped coming to see Podo, as they blamed Little Owl for the deaths of all these children. (They believed that only Little Owl could be interested in causing the deaths of her rival's children and consequently they accused her of killing them with bad medicine.) But she did not know about this.

"That spring when her little girl was four years old, her grandmother died, so she did not have anyone to stay home with that summer. She went with her parents to the Indian celebration (at Leech Lake) though she did not care much about going. When they reached there, the other Indians were all there already. The people that were her in-laws were there, and her husband and his wife a'so. She did not care (about the presence of her rival and of Mahween). She saw his wife. She was sick... nothing but skin and bones... she had tuberculosis. She was always staring at Little Owl. Little Owl never went about... she did not care what was going on. She never watched the *Midewiwin* as this sick woman was going through it (for a curing). Then one day as she was sitting in her wigwam, she saw someone grab her little girl's hand and lead her away. She jumped up... it was her husband! She ran after him and caught up with him just as he was going into this sick woman's wigwam. She grabbed her little girl and said to Mahween, 'Who told you to take my girl here!' And he said, 'Nobody... I just brought her so my wife could see her, and also I want to see her.' She said, 'What do you want to do with her? You threw her away for somebody else, and I don't want you to bother her now!' So she took her little girl back to her wigwam. And after that Mahween used to come and bother her (sexually) every night. He tried to lie down with her, and he was always trying to steal the little girl away from her. She was very frightened. She told her father about it, but he could not do anything either. She had a widowed aunt, and she said to her aunt, 'Let's go away from here. I do not like to stay here, as Mahween is bothering me and he wants to take my little girl away from me.' Her aunt said she was willing to go. She told her parents, and they told her where to go and wait for them, for they were remaining a while to catch and dry fish. That night she went with her aunt and little girl to this island. Of course nobody knew... just her parents. They stayed at this island for a long time. Then her parents came for them. They said that Mahween's wife was very sick and was not expected to live. And about the middle of the winter some men came and told them that Mahween's wife was dead. Little Owl was very sorry to hear this, as she knew for sure that Mahween would come and bother her now.

"When the time came for them to move to the sugar groves, they moved and started making sugar. One day as she was going for the sugar water, she saw Mahween following her. He came closer. She took a stick and started to fight him. She told him that she did not want him to bother her, as it was enough that he had destroyed one woman already. (The deceased spouse is said, in a conventional phrase, to have been 'destroyed' by the surviving spouse. This is in keeping with the general belief that illness and death are not consequences of natural causes, but are the consequences of deliberate sorcery.) She ran away from him. That night after she had gone to bed, he came again. She fought him and sent him away. He said that he did not want her, but wanted to see his little girl. So Little Owl said, 'Why then do you come here in the night? You should come here in the daytime to see her!' Finally he went out. Next day her father told her, 'If you do not want Mahween, I suppose it is best for you to marry someone else. That will be the only way to keep him from bothering you.' So she did what her father advised. She married a man from somewhere else, and he took her away to his own place. It was not long before he started to be mean to her. He used to beat her and also her little girl. He would take the little girl and throw her out, and he also forbade her to eat anything, and he never allowed his wife to wear anything nice as he was jealous of her (and fine dress would attract lovers).

"That next spring, before sugar-making, she heard that her father was very sick. Of course she was worried about him. One morning her husband went away after he had given her another beating and had thrown the little girl out. He said he would be away seven days. There were some old people living close by her. She made up her mind not to stay there any more as she felt very badly when her husband threw her little girl out. (The step-father's cruelty was probably motivated by jealousy of Mahween, of whom the child was a reminder.) So she went to these old people and asked them to give her a pair of old snow-shoes, also a toboggan, and they did because they knew she was abused, and they would not tell (of her flight) either. That same day she left for Leech Lake. She walked all day, and far into the night. Then she came to the place where the old shacks were, but there was nobody home. She went where the graves were, but there was no new one, so she knew that her father was still alive. She went into her father's shack and slept there. The next morning she started off (after her parents). She followed their trail, and about noon she came to the place where they were making sugar. There were many wigwams there. She peeped into every wigwam, and then she recognized her father's. She went in... nobody was home. Her little girl was very tired, so she told her to stay there while she went to look for her parents. She heard someone chopping wood nearby, and went there. It was her mother, and she spoke to her mother, who came running to meet her daughter... she was very glad to see her! She yelled to her old man, and he came running home. Her mother asked her, saying, 'We heard that you are always getting a beating.' She answered, 'Yes, I'm terribly abused, so I'm coming home here. It was my father that wanted me to marry! (i. e., it was not my wish that brought this misfortune upon me!)'

"So she stayed there, helping her parents make maple sugar. Then she heard that her (second) husband was very sick, that when he was coming home with some other men, they were drunk, and started to fight and someone stabbed him in his ribs with a pocket knife. For a month he was sick, then he died. No one could come for Little Owl as the Lakes were breaking up. She did not go back even after her husband had died. Then she began to realize that she was to have another baby. She never went anywhere. There were only about five families there. At strawberry picking time, she used to go out to pick strawberries with her little girl, as Podo was six years old now (and strong enough to pick by herself). Her parents went away somewhere for a little while. One day as she was picking berries, she had some pains. She knew that it was time now for her baby to be born. She tried to hurry, but she could not get home. So her second little girl was born. She was all alone, only Podo was with her. When everything was all over, she got up and picked up her baby. She wrapped it in her old skirt, and her little girl carried the strawberries. Her parents were not home yet. So she made a small wigwam and sat in there. When her parents returned home, they told her to come into the (regular) wigwam. They were very frightened, but she got better soon. Her second little girl was named Standing Woman, Sheena for short. Little Owl picked blueberries, made rice, and put away other things for winter. She lived with her people.

"About a year later her father died. Then she just stayed with her mother, and she never bothered her mind about men. But when her younger little girl was about three years old, her brother came with some other people to visit them. He had a wife from the Rainy River, and that was where he lived. A man had come along with him; and as soon as Little Owl saw this man she fell in love with him. His name was Bahsheeta. When the visitors were leaving for their home, she just left her little girls and her mother and followed Bahsheeta (to his home on the Rainy River) and married him. For about a month she stayed there. Then she went back with him to get her little girls and her mother. Bahsheeta was a widower and had two children, a boy and a girl. He liked her children, and she liked his children too because she liked him so very much. She liked him because he used love medicine on her... that was why she had followed him (blindly) and left her little girls behind. Then she stayed at Little Forks Reserve. She had six boys by this man, and the other four children made ten in their family. When her children were to be born, she never had a nurse to look after her. She always tended to herself at the birth of her children, and she was never sick for a long time after they were born. She would just get up and start walking around. It was easy for her to have children, as she had a mare for a guardian spirit. Her mother got very old, and became blind. She had to lead her mother when she wanted to go outside (to the bush), and finally the old woman died. Little Owl had a sister too, who came to live with her.

"One day after she had come onto the Little Forks Reserve, she was doing something all alone, and she saw someone coming. He had a moustache, and she yelled and said, 'Hey, women! Look at this *manito* (extraordinary creature) coming!' The women started to laugh at her because it was a white man. That was the very first time she had seen a white man. After that she got used to seeing white men. One time when her oldest girl Podo was a young girl (i. e., nubile) some white men came there. They had asked for Podo, and when her parents refused to let her go, they became mad and wanted to tackle (rape) the young girl, also her mother. They started shooting, and Bahsheeta got shot in the arm. He fell down and pretended he was dead, and the white men ran away. Then he got up.

"Soon after that, Little Owl let her daughter Podo marry an Indian as she was afraid that the white men would do something to her daughter some time when she was alone. Her husband's daughter was also grown up, and also the boy, and the man's daughter married a man from the mouth of the Rainy River. Also the other children grew up and married. So they were very old. The end."

II.

Tupuhsi and her husband Buhnah were members of a Cree group living intimately with the Ojibwa, and sharing their customs. For about five years Tuphusi and her husband lived happily. "He was

16

a good hunter and made a good living. They had only one child, a
boy. When he was about four or five years old, the boy sickened,
and after a long time he died. They had done everything to cure
him, she had even tried her Power, but nothing helped. She used
to wonder where Buhnah went sometimes. He used to stay out
late. And then when the boy died, she was sad. She missed her
little boy... she was so lonely.... but the worst of all was that
her husband would go out in the night, stay out all night, and only
come home in the morning. He never spoke to his wife, but he
would just come in and lie down to sleep. She never asked him
where he went, she simply continued working, and pretended to
pay no attention to him. But she wondered and wondered where
he went at night. Each night he went out, and each day he slept,
and always towards evening he woke up and ate. He would never
say a word to anyone. One time he took his sack and took out an
otter skin and cut it into strips. He took a comb and combed his
hair, and braided it in two long braids. He took the strips of otter
skin and wound them around the braids. He put on his nice clothes,
and nice moccasins, but he did not put any paint on his face. Then
he took a new blanket, and went out again. His wife made up her
mind to follow him. She followed him among the wigwams to the
very end of the village. Her husband went into the very last wigwam.
She peeped in and saw two old people and a young girl. The old
people had already gone to bed. Just the woman was sitting up,
and Buhnah sat down right beside her. Right away she started
caressing his braids. Tupuhsi stood there for a long time and
watched them. Then she went home and went to sleep.

"The next morning her husband returned home and slept all day.
She did not say anything. But she cried an awful lot, and her
mother-in-law spoke to her while she was crying. She told her to
stop crying, that nothing or no one would have pity on her anyway,
and people were beginning to take notice of her husband's being
dressed up all the time; they were beginning to think of the pair
as no good on account of Buhnah's carrying on. Yet he continued.
She made up her mind to do something. After Buhnah went out
again that night, she went to bed and pretended to be asleep. Then
she got up very quietly, washed her face, combed her hair, and
braided her hair into two long braids at the back, tying on bunches
of ribbon. She put on new moccasins, and a good dress and waist.
Then she took a shawl and wrapped it around her. She took the
leather strap she used for carrying wood, and then she went out
very quietly. She went to her little son's grave, and cried very hard.
Then she went along and came to some grey willow trees, and she

tied her leather strap to the trees and said, 'What is there left for me to live for ? No one cares for me, and my boy is gone. So I too will go and join my boy.' Then she put the leather around her neck. But before she was ready to do this (i. e., hang herself), someone grabbed her by the shoulders and said, 'No, you cannot do this to yourself because you are too good and nice-looking. I know what's been on your mind since you learned about your husband, but don't worry yourself about him. I will take you away from here so that you will not know what he is doing. I will take you where your parents are, and you will never leave them again as long as you live. (Troubled wives often return to the parental lodge for security, and even to insure actual protection against a difficult husband, who may pursue them. The parental lodge is the one relatively safe base in the world; so the son-in-law who lives with his wife's people is on enemy territory, living there by a courteous waiver, and must conduct himself with suitable prudence.) I have been watching you for a long time, and so I know what's been on your mind.' He took her by the hand and led her away from there. He said, 'Get ready right away if you want to take anything along with you. And please hurry up.' She never said one word while he was talking. She did not know what to do, but anyway she went along with him, and he took her to her wigwam. 'I will come here with my canoe. Be sure and hurry.' So he went and after he was gone she stood there puzzled.... who was he ? She could not recognize his voice either. Then she went to the wigwam of Buhnah's second wife. She peeped in again and saw her husband sleeping with the woman, and she got very mad. She was wondering what to do when this same man came up to her again, put his hands on her shoulders, and said, 'Come away from there, and go with me. It will not do you any good to stand there and look at him. He's not good enough for you. But I will try and be good and make up to you for all the misery you've been through.' So she returned with him to her own wigwam. He told her to take the things she liked best, and to hurry. She went into her wigwam and took some things. She had a little pup and she took him along too. Then the man took her down to the canoe, and they went away. She did not paddle but just sat in the canoe (a sweetheart, wife, or daughter paddles for a man, but not a stranger).

"They went through a big portage, and after they got on the other side, the man stopped and made a fire (this is ordinarily the job of sweetheart, wife, or daughter) and made some tea. It was still night. She tried to see his face, but he had his head down, and she could not tell yet who he was. He gave her some good things to

16*

eat. He began to play with the little pup. She thought to herself, 'Whoever he is, he must be very silly.' The man said to her without looking at her, 'I know what you are thinking of me. You think I'm silly because I am playing with your pup.' Then she began to fear him (because he manifested the supernatural power of telepathy). After their lunch, they went down again, and started out with the canoe. He said, 'There are rapids near here. We will not go over them until morning.' So they stopped close by. He told her she could sleep in the canoe, and he got out and lay down in the grass (this continence of the man is the ultimate expression of respect), and they slept."

For several days he scrupulously avoided Tupuhsi, although they were alone on deserted islands. After the passage of a few days they became more friendly, though still shy. "He asked her if they could not stay there for a couple of days and dry the moose he had killed (this is a wife's work). She said it was all right. Then they made a little wigwam. He told her that he had cared for her all the time she had lived with Buhnah. He had heard people say that she was blamed for the death of her little son, therefore her husband did not want her any more; and he had found out that Buhnah was flirting with another woman. Then he made up his mind to look after her, and he started spying on her. He loved her all that time, and that was why he never married anyone else. He never bothered her while she was married to Buhnah, but when he knew what Buhnah was doing, he realized that he had not waited in vain for her. And he told her that he wanted to marry her no matter what she had done. Tupuhsi only now understood why her husband did not care for her; but it was not true that she had caused her son's death, for she had tried her best to save him.

"So they slept there that night. They stayed there for three or four days drying meat. Once they saw two men coming in a canoe, and she ran and hid. She did not want them to see her. The men came right up to the wigwam and said, 'Oh, this is where you are making meat.' He said, 'Yes,' and they said again, 'We have been sent here by the people back there to look for you. Your grandmother is worried about you because she thinks you are lost, and also one woman is lost.' He said, 'We are not lost. We know where we are. And also we know what we are doing.' Then he gave them some meat (to buy their good-will) and they went away. Tupuhsi returned to the wigwam, and he told her what the men had said. She was very frightened, but he said, 'Please don't be like that, scared.... I will take care of you so that no harm will come to you. Don't you know that I love you an awful lot ? and it hurts me to know that you don't trust me and are afraid.' He took her in his arms then. Right there she said she would care for him. So he told her to get ready, that they would go to her parents (an announcement of marriage).

"So they went, and her mother saw them coming. She went in and told her old man, 'Our daughter is coming, but with another man.' And her father said, 'I suppose she is doing something to make us ashamed.' The old woman went down and met her daughter, and kissed her. She also cried for her little grandson. But the old man did not come out at all; he was worried, and ashamed of his daughter. She told her mother everything that Buhnah had done to her, and how she had been blamed for the death of her little boy. Her mother went in to see the old man and told him all about it, but he did not say anything. The man (second husband) made a wigwam close by, and this is where they lived. Tupuhsi had a young brother, and he was very proud of his new brother-in-law because he knew he was good to his sister. She never lacked anything. Her new husband was very good to her, and also he was a good hunter. The old man got over his shame soon for he saw that he had a far better son-in-law this time.

"All the Indians came together for a celebration before rice-making time. Buhnah came too with his wife. The men played the moccasin game, and the women played squaw hockey and other kinds of Indian games, and danced. Tupuhsi's husband told her to join in the women's games. One time she was asked to play squaw hockey because she had nice clothes and wore nice shoes, and people wished for her clothes (in the gambling stakes). So she played. This other woman was playing too — the one who took Buhnah away from her. She was poorly dressed and her old moccasins were no good. As they were playing, she was in Tupuhsi's way. Tupuhsi pushed her over and as she fell, her feet went up. And Tupuhsi said laughing (in insulting ridicule), 'Look at her old moccasins! They look like lynx paws!' Tupuhsi's side won the game. After she went home, her husband said, 'Don't do that to tease anyone, especially that woman.' So she never said anything again because she always did what her husband told her.

"Then the next day, the man played the moccasin game. Her husband went, and took a gun and blanket, and his brother-in-law went with him. Buhnah was to play against him; he also brought a gun. Before they started to play Buhnah was working on his gun, and the shell fell out. This young man (the second husband) took the shell, and Buhnah did not know that it had fallen out. While they were playing, Buhnah knew that his side was getting beat. He took his gun again and started to play with it. Of course the young man was watching him, and he knew what was going to happen. Sure enough, Buhnah pulled the trigger when the gun was pointed towards him (in the course of the game). Buhnah started to shout (the murderous war-whoop), but there was nothing but gun powder in the gun. The man that was supposed to be shot laughed and said, 'Here man, here is your shell. You forgot to put it back in', and he said also, 'I have a knife in my pocket.' He drew his knife out, but as he was going to stab Buhnah, his brother-in-law grabbed his hand and took the knife away from him, and took him home. Buhnah went home also, and soon they saw him paddling away with his wife. All the men yelled after him, saying he was a coward. Tupuhsi's husband told her that they would stay there only four days more. So after four days, they went to a different place to make rice, and Buhnah happened to be there also. Tupuhsi's husband told her not to go back in the bush to cut wigwam poles, that his brother-in-law and he would cut them, for he knew that Buhnah intended to kill her with the axe she would use. Sure enough, Buhnah shouted that the women should cut the wigwam poles. Tupuhsi did not go, as her husband had told her not to, so Buhnah failed to kill her. Again he moved away.

"After ricemaking time they moved back to their own place. The railroad was under construction now, and her husband worked on it. The white men thought a lot of him because he was a good worker. One summer, about three years later, she was washing at a kind of dock. Her brother, now a grown man, was inside the wigwam with a sore foot. While she was washing, someone spoke to her, 'You make me mad when you are so happily married, and also because you did not care that our boy died, and the man you are married to now is very proud.' She answered, "You did not care either when our boy died. You were the first to marry.' Then he pushed her into the water. She could not swim, and each time she came to the surface and grabbed the dock, he stepped on her hand and kicked it off. Each time she yelled. Her brother heard her, and he came out, though he could hardly walk. He saw this man standing there. He had a stick and came up behind Buhnah, hit him with the stick, and knocked him into the water. Then his sister had time to get out of the water, and they both went away from there. Buhnah came ashore too, and he ran away as fast as he could. Her husband came home from work as she was putting on dry clothes, and her brother told him all about it, how he saved his sister from getting drowned. Her husband was very mad, but he did not follow Buhnah.

"The following summer, while they were again living there, Buhnah came there with two men in a canoe. He told Tupuhsi's husband that he had come for her, that she was his wife, and that he was going to take her away whether or not he (the husband) would let her go. And the husband said, 'No, you will not take her, away from me as long as I'm alive. You cast her aside for another woman, and I saved her when she was going to take her life on account of you, and I care for her an awful lot, and I'm going to fight to hold her.' Buhnah went right up to him and started to fight. Buhnah was thrown down and he cried. 'All right, men, come and help me!' But the men did not move. The two men kept right on fighting, and Buhnah was getting beaten very badly because he was older. He said he was going to take Tupuhsi anyway, and her husband said, 'No, Buhnah, you're not going to take her away because I'm going to kill you, because you are always bothering us. We never bother you, and you've done enough to us now, and I cannot stand any more from you. Twice you nearly killed my wife. You did not care for her. You're just jealous because I'm proud of her. So I'm going to kill you now with my own hands so you will never bother us any more.' He started to hit Buhnah harder, and one of his blows knocked him dead. The men just stood there, looking on. After he knew he was dead, he told the men to take the body home, and they did. Some people tried to get him into trouble by telling the white men, but they couldn't because the white men believed his story, and they also liked him. So he was free.... nobody ever bothered them any more.".....

III.

"This is a story of an Ojibwa woman. She was named Josie. Before she grew up, her parents got in with some old people who had a son. These two families were very friendly (a fact which is decidedly conspicuous among the Ojibwa), and they planned that when their children grew up, they were to marry each other. Josie grew up, and she found that she did not care for this man. His name was Feather. Also the young man was not so crazy for her, though she was a nice-looking young girl, and she was handy at doing all kinds of Indian fancy-work, and all the other work that an Indian woman does. Her parents were afraid of the parents of this man (for the latter were sorcerers); they could not refuse these other old people who wished for Josie very much because she was a good worker and was very quiet. There was another young man who cared for her a great deal, and she cared for him a little, too. For three years she refused to go to the man whom her parents wanted her to marry, and went secretly with her lover, who was named Lynx Cub. Often he begged her to marry him, but she had to refuse him because she really belonged to Feather. She was afraid that she would cause trouble to her parents (through the revengeful sorcery of the boy's parents who would be shamed and infuriated if she rejected him). For three years Feather waited, and one time while all the Indians were camping in one place (summer village), the parents made Josie and Feather a wigwam and told them to live in there. Josie had to do it because that meant that she had to get married now. Their parents gave them blankets and a canoe and other things to use. She was very unhappy. She hardly ever spoke to her husband, and he never tried to make love to her, either. They were both shy of each other because they had never really been acquainted with each other (during a courting period before marriage). Sometimes the man's parents sent them away on trips, thinking that they might get acquainted (sexually) that way. But they were more shy than ever of each other on these trips. When they went off anywhere to eat, her husband would take his plate of food and go off and eat alone. She too ate by herself. And then they would go back. But after a while, they got acquainted (sexually). Feather never said a wrong word to her. In fact, he was good to her, and she also never tried to hurt his feelings. Lynx Cub felt very badly when she got married, but he never tried to see her again. The summer after that, he also got married, but he never ceased to care for Josie. Of course she did not know (of his steadfast love), and she tried to be a good wife to the husband who had been chosen for her by the old people. She lived with him for five years. He was a great man for traveling, and she never paid any attention to what he was doing. He used to bring her a lot of things. In fact, she was always well-dressed, and had lots to eat. And her mother-in-law and her father-in-law were good to her, also her sisters-in-law. One time after she had been there five years, her husband went away. He said he was going trapping, and that if he found work anywhere, he would send her money. For several months she waited for some word from him, but she never heard. One whole winter went by and she had not heard from him since he had left at blueberry-picking time. She heard that her mother-in-law and sister-in-law were saying that the reason Feather had gone away was that she did not have any children, and that he wanted children. She did not care what they said. She noticed too that her in-laws were no longer the same to her; they hardly ever spoke to her now. She had already gone back to live with her parents.

"When blueberry-picking time came again, all the Indians moved again to the same place to pick blueberries. Her family moved too, and she used to pick berries every day. She sold them, and bought herself goods for dresses. One day while she was sitting all by herself picking berries, she saw a man coming toward her. She recognized Lynx Cub. He did not come very close, and he said, 'So you are alone again! I wish I were still alone too... I wanted to marry you very badly. I would have been very proud of you!' She smiled at him and said, 'Well, it was not my fault. It was our parents that wanted me and my husband to get married.' The man said again, 'Do you know what is keeping your husband away?' She said, 'No, I don't know.' He said, 'To tell you the truth, he is married to another woman. I am not fooling you. Do you believe it?' She said, 'Yes, I would not deny it, and I do not care either. I knew he did not care either. I knew he did not care for me.' The man said, 'Yes... and the people with whom he is staying (the parents of his second wife) are coming here soon to pick blueberries, and he is coming with his in-laws. You will see him here soon.' She did not say anything more, and Lynx Cub walked away. In the evening she went home. She was very quiet (downcast), but she said nothing to anybody. She wished she could go away somewhere, for she hated to be there when her husband arrived with another woman. She was ashamed to face her husband with another woman. Her mother asked her what was wrong, and she told her mother that her husband was getting married to another woman. She said, 'It is your fault that I have to face such shame. If it were not for you two, I would be happily married to another man who cares for me!' Her parents said, 'Yes, it was our fault because we cared for you. We were afraid that those old people would ruin you by some of their bad medicine, and that was why we could not refuse though we longed to keep you single.' Then Josie said again, 'I can't stay here to face such shame! I might as well be dead!' Her parents said, 'Do not take it like that. Try and live for our sakes. You are still young, and it would be cowardly for you to destroy yourself.' She did not answer them, and they never mentioned it again.

"Three or four days after, when they were returning home from picking blueberries, they saw a lot of Indians coming. She knew right away it was the people that Lynx Cub had told her about. She went home and sat down. All the Indians were busy putting up wigwams. And as she was sitting there, she noticed a man standing near her in-laws' wigwam. He had on a white shirt, red arm bands, and a red silk handkerchief around his neck (gala attire). He was standing with a woman who showed she was going to have a child soon. Josie knew right away it was Feather and his new wife. She tried not to care, but she was ashamed. She went into the wigwam. She did not want anyone to see her.

"A couple of days after, she picked up her dirty clothes and went down to the lake to wash them. As she was sitting there wa hing, she saw a man coming in a canoe. She paid no attention to him. She knew that the man was coming ashore close by her. He dropped the paddle in the canoe, but she did not look. He dropped the paddle again, and finally she looked. It was her husband. When he saw her looking, he called her by name, 'Josie, so this is where you are!' And she too spoke right away, 'Yes, this is where I am! And where have you been keeping yourself all this time? You said you were just going out working and trapping!' He said to her again, 'Why don't you get married, you too? Because I don't want you any more. I have a wife now, and she has my child. And don't ever try to see me alone anywhere.' She said, 'I don't care whether you are married or not.' Then she asked him, 'What is your wife's name?' He said, 'Josie is my real wife's name.' She jumped up (at this slighting of her question) and ran where he was standing and grabbed his paddle, but as she was going to hit him, she saw that there were a lot of ducks in the canoe. She let the paddle go and said to him, 'I came pretty near breaking this paddle on your old head. But I won't. Instead, I am going to take some of these ducks,' and she picked out the biggest ones there. (This is a great breach of form, for only a man's wife is supposed to appropriate the game that he has caught. Feather understood that Josie wanted to offend the new wife.) She took them to the place where she was washing. And Feather took the rest of the ducks home. They were small ones (that remained from Josie's raid), but of course his new wife did not know anything about it. But there were some children playing around near there and they had seen the ducks lying beside Josie while she was washing. They ran and told their mother, and she came down out of curiosity and saw the ducks. She said, 'Oh, I did not know you were washing here. I am coming for water.' Josie said, 'Yes, this is where everybody washes, but everybody gets water from over there,' and she pointed to the place. So the woman went away, and went to Feather's wigwam, and told his new wife about the ducks that she had seen in Josie's possession. Of course this woman (the second wife) started quarreling with her husband.

"When Josie finished washing, she started to clean the ducks. When she was through she saw an old woman coming. It was her old mother-in-law. She knew she was coming for the ducks, so she hid them. The old woman said, 'I am coming for those ducks because my daughter-in-law is fighting my son. She claims that he gave them to you (which would be the equivalent of courting overtures). That woman that came here and saw you went and told her.' And Josie said, 'No, I will not give you the ducks. She can come for them herself. If she comes (and humiliates herself, thus gratifying Josie's wounded pride to some extent), I will give them to her.' So the old woman went back without the ducks. Josie stayed around there waiting for this woman (her rival), but when she did not come, she took the ducks and went along holding them so everybody could see them. She was not afraid of anybody; she was just teasing this woman that had taken her husband away from her. Although she did not care for her husband, she had been shamed. When she got to her wigwam, she cooked the ducks, and she and her parents had a nice meal. Her parents never asked her where she had gotten them because they knew; the woman who had seen the ducks had told them.

"Every day Josie picked blueberries, and made good money, and was dressed well; she was a nice-looking woman. When blueberry picking time was over, all the people moved away again, and she also moved away with her parents. They paddled all day, and slept, and again all day they travelled along with some others, and that night they camped, and after everybody was asleep, Josie also went to sleep. All at once somebody shook her, and she wakened. It was dark and she could not see who it was, but he spoke to her saying, 'Josie, will you let me sleep with you?' She recognized his voice, it was Feather, but she pretended she did not know him, and she said, 'No, I will not let you sleep here. You must have some other place to sleep, and you do not have to sleep here.' He said, 'Don't say that to me, because it is enough that I have been following you for a long time.' Then she said, 'Why are you following me? I have nothing of yours. Why don't you follow the one that has your child, not me? I have nothing for which you need to come to me. I have nothing that you can be proud of. Go back to the woman who has your child. I am just as pleased to be alone, and it was not our plan to get married: it was your own parents that wanted us to marry. So you might as well go back home and leave me alone. I did not take those ducks because I was jealous, I just wanted to tease a little. That was all. I knew long ago that your parents did not care for me any longer because I did not have a child.' Feather said, 'No, I'm not going back. I'm going to stay here because my wife is always scolding me. She is jealous because you took those ducks .... that is why she is always fighting me.' She said, 'I do not want you. I want you to go back to your wife and (unborn) child and do what is right.' But Feather sat there for a long time, and he said, 'You've been like that always. You never cared for me, and that is why I went away to another woman, to get what every man wants from his wife—love. But my (second) wife is too cranky. Remember this, I will always have you in my mind and I will always be your husband.' But she said, 'No, you've got another wife. You thought more of her than you did of me, so go now, and forget that I ever married you.' And he said, 'All right, I will go, but please give me food first, and then I will go home.' She got up and gave him something to eat, and then he went away. Her parents said to her that she did right to send him away.

"They reached Kenora and sold their berries, and when they had been there for a few days, some other people came there and brought the news that Feather had nearly been killed... that all day they watched for him to draw his last breath. She felt very badly for him, and she was always quiet. Her parents watched her, but they did not say anything to her. One time a woman came and asked Josie to go and stay with her and help her. Josie went to work for this woman, and while she was there, she saw Lynx Cub again. He passed there often, and one time he stopped and spoke to her, saying, 'Did you hear that your husband was brought to town two days ago? He nearly died because his wife tried to kill him.' She said, 'No, where is he staying?' and he told her. 'He was brought there to a doctor. His head was nearly broken.. the doctor had to cut him bald-headed because his hair was too thick.' She did not say anything further, and the man walked away.

"That same evening, after she finished her work, she took a walk to the place where Feather was staying. When she came close, she saw him sitting up on pillows, and his wife was sitting close by. She was going to pass right by, but he spoke to her, saying, 'Josie, come her.' He said to her, 'Isn't it true that you sent me away when I followed you the time you moved away after blueberry-picking time!' And she said, 'Yes, it is true.' He said again, pointing to his (second) wife, 'She would not believe me when I tried to tell her that. She said that you were glad to see me (and therefore received him sexually), and that is why she split my head and nearly killed me.' Then Josie said (maliciously), 'Well, who would not be glad to see her husband coming back? I never did you any wrong. It is all your fault. You went away and left me for this woman, and now look what you get.... she nearly killed you.... but I never did that to you,' and she left. The woman never said one word, but just turned her back to Josie (showing that she was ashamed, but at the same time furiously resentful).

"Josie did not see them again, but late in the fall she heard that Feather was better, and that, instead of him, their baby had died. After the baby died, Feather's wife left him. After she had been gone for many days, his parents told him to follow her. He went because his parents were afraid of her parents... they were bad people (shamans). His parents told their son that if his wife wanted to fight him again, he was to run away and leave her. When he got to his wife's home, she had already gone away with another man from the Ocean Shore (Lake Superior). So he went back to Kenora without her.

"In the meantime Josie had met a man named Glowing Man. He was from Sahging. She married him, and he took her away to Sahging. She left her parents in Kenora. As soon as she got over there (to Sahging), she learned that her husband was already married, and she did not like it (to be a co-wife), so she made up her mind not to stay there because this woman (her co-wife) already had three or four children. Josie went with another woman to the little log store, and there they saw her husband's other wife. The woman she was with told her that Glowing Man was not any good, and was very mean to his wife. Josie told this woman that she was not going to stay there, and that they should take her as far as the horses could go, and that from there she could walk the rest of the way. The next morning, after her husband had gone, they took her as far as the road — they called it the Dawson road. White men were already beginning to work on the railroad, and this was the road she started walking on. Every time she came to white men working, she went off the road and went around them. She walked for many days, and soon she was out of moccasins, and her feet hurt very much. She tied old sacks on her feet. She was very tired, for she used to walk every night..... Once she overslept by the road, and was wakened by white drunkards. She fled in fright. Fortunately she met a kindly white trader, not far from Kenora. He gave her good employment, and later helped her return to her parents in Kenora.....

"After Josie had been there in Kenora quite a while, Feather heard late in the fall that she was back again, so he went there to look for her. Josie felt badly about Feather, and when he came there, she said that she would marry him. 'It was not my fault that we left each other, and it was not I that ruined your looks either,' so she married him and for a couple of years they lived together. They learned to care for each other a great deal. He was very good to her then, and he got a lot of nice things for her. Their parents were pleased to see them happily married to each other now. Josie never had any children, but his parents were just as glad because his other wife was mean to him, and anyway his child did not live.

"Several years after, all the people went to Kenora in the spring to take their muskrats and other furs to the Hudson's Bay Company. Josie and her husband went to camp there too. They had brought a lot of muskrats and other kinds of fur. On the other side of town some other people were camping.... they were from Eagle Lake, the place where Feather got his second wife... the one that nearly killed him. But Josie did not know that this woman and her parents were there too. This other woman had come back from the Ocean Shore as her husband had sent her away when she had become too mean to him. When she got to Eagle Lake, she heard that Feather had gone back to his wife Josie. She was very mad, for she was a bad woman. Some women heard her sharpening her knife one night, and she said that she was going over to Feather's wigwam and kill him and Josie. Feather did not know that his other wife was there, so that night they went to bed as usual. He was lying on his stomach, and Josie had her arm around him while they were sleeping. They did not know when this other woman came in and stabbed him on the back, and at the same time she stabbed Josie, too, on the arm where it was around Feather's back. Josie jumped up right away, but as she started to run out of the wigwam, the woman grabbed a stick of wood and hit her across the nose right on her eyes, and she fell back for she was knocked unconscious. Feather jumped up with the knife still in his back and shouted the shout every brave Indian shouts when being killed. He said, 'Someone come here and pull this knife out of my back. Someone stabbed me. Also my wife is killed.' Of course, all the men that were sleeping close by in wigwams jumped up and came into the wigwam, and they saw the woman lying there as if she were dead. The men pulled the knife out of Feather's back and great quantities of blood poured out. Feather and Josie were covered with a white blanket, and it became soaked with blood. The women came in too, and started to work on Josie. After a long time she came to. Feather was dying from loss of blood. The woman that stabbed him ran home. Some men ran over to tell the people on that side (of town) that Feather was dying, and the woman (who had stabbed him) got very frightened, for she was afraid of the Hudson's Bay man, and her parents took her away that night. Her mother was crying all the time. Feather's father tried to doctor him, but before daylight he died from loss of blood. But Josie was a little better the next day. She was very sorry about her husband's dying, as she loved him by now, and she missed him very much. He was buried, and her in-laws and her parents were very good to her. They were together most of the time.

"For two years, she gathered a man's whole outfit (to pay the sib debt), and she gave these clothes to her in-laws. This was what you call *gi wenige* — 'paying for her husband's death so that her in-laws would let her go' (free of surveillance). Her in-laws were very proud of her (because she observed all the respect-conventions): they fixed her up with fine clothes and face paint and combed her hair and tied it up (instead of permitting it to hang loose and unattractive, as it must during the mourning period); also they washed her face (removing the soot and other filth of mourning), and they talked to her, and told her that they were glad because she had always been good to her husband, and that he would still be alive if it had not been for this other woman who had killed him. They never saw this other woman either, because from then on she never came to gatherings where there were people. She was always in the woods hiding (fearful of Feather's relatives' revenge).

"For another year Josie stayed single. About the time Feather died, the wife of that other man with whom Josie used to go, died too. And she got in with him. After they had both been widowed for three years, they married each other. She lived with him the rest of her life. He had two children, a boy and a girl. She took care of these children as if they were her own. He was a Cree man (all the other characters in this story were Ojibwa). He was a shaman who cured by sucking, also other kinds of *manito kazo*. He was very good to her, and she also was good to him and to his children, who both grew up to be big people. Her parents both died soon after that. So her bad luck never ended. But in spite of it all, she was happy. She and her husband grew very old, and the boy and girl got married. That is all."